FRESHLY BREWED

TWELVE SHORT PLAYS FROM BEWLEY'S CAFÉ THEATRE

FRESHLY BREWED

TWELVE SHORT PLAYS FROM BEWLEY'S CAFÉ THEATRE

EDITED BY DECLAN MEADE AND EMILY FIRETOG

WITH AN INTRODUCTION BY CHRISTOPHER FITZ-SIMON
AND A FOREWORD BY MARK O'HALLORAN

The Stinging Fly

A Stinging Fly Press Book

2 4 6 8 10 9 7 5 3 1

Freshly Brewed: Twelve Short Plays from Bewley's Café Theatre is first published in November 2008
© Individual Authors

Fred and Jane first published in *Fred and Jane and Whistling Psyche* (Faber and Faber, 2004)
Reprinted here courtesy of Faber and Faber

Set in Palatino
Printed by Betaprint, Dublin

The Stinging Fly Press
PO Box 6016
Dublin 8
w w w . s t i n g i n g f l y . o r g

ISBN: 978-1-906539-04-7

The Stinging Fly gratefully acknowledges funding support from
The Arts Council/ An Chomhairle Ealaíon and Dublin City Council.

Contents

Introduction by Christopher Fitz-Simon

IN IRELAND WE ARE WONT TO MAKE outlandish claims for international pre-eminence in regard to certain qualities (such as hospitality) or achievements (like the invention of the submarine or the discovery of the Orion Nebula). There may, however, be some reasonably plausible grounds for asserting that in the early part of the twentieth century we did hold a special position in that concentrated form of literature, the short story. The same may be said, with a very real degree of assurance, for that equally concentrated literary form, the one-act play. We only have to look at the yield of such dramatists as Colum, Gregory, Fitzmaurice or Robinson to bear out the contention. In what other country can this be found?

Certainly, in its early years, the National Theatre Society produced an unusually high number of short plays that were published immediately after their first performance and classified by librarians as 'literature'. In fact, more than a third of the plays presented on the Abbey stage in the first decade of its existence were 'one-acters'. It could be argued that the reason for this was due to the inability of many of the early (and inexperienced) dramatists of the movement to sustain a stage piece for more than forty or fifty minutes. It was common for an evening at the Abbey to consist entirely of three or four short plays, and there does not seem to have been public resistance to such programmes.

Even when the main draw was a play of conventional duration, the tradition persisted well into the 1950s of producing a curtain-raiser or an afterpiece – and sometimes both – rendering the evening something of an endurance test for both actors and audience. Certainly it was management policy – as it had been during the eighteenth and nineteenth centuries in commercial theatres throughout Europe – that the audience must be given value for money in terms of duration as well as artistry. It would be wrong to suggest that the 'main' play at the Abbey, perhaps a three- or four-act drama, was the more substantial part of the bill – often the one-act piece(s) said more, and certainly said it more succinctly, than the principal attraction.

In spite of this rather late survival of the one-act play at the Abbey, the genre had virtually ceased as a dramatic form elsewhere on account of the arrival in the 1930s of radio drama. Here was a new and wonderfully flexible medium, ideally suited to a brief examination of the topic in hand, and one that paid the author more liberally than did the theatre. Yet, in a curious way, the stage continued to hold its magnetic impulse for dedicated writers of short plays, even if the venues ceased to be the major houses and performances moved into lofts and basements.

Bewley's Café Theatre is neither a loft nor a basement, but the term café is somewhat misleading, especially for tourists. Its Parisian resonance suggests something louche, something not quite serious. If it has been anything at all over the past ten years, Bewley's Café Theatre has been an assiduously serious and professional enterprise, as the writing in the twelve plays selected here amply demonstrates. These plays should certainly be seen (and heard) again, and this volume should pave the way for future performances for all of them.

The energy in S.R. Plant's *Buridan's Ass* springs from its verbal precocity as much as from its surreally comic situation in a laboratory in which various dead animal species calmly observe the mental turmoil of the taxidermist Mahone – *mo thóin*, one supposes – whose family has been stuffing animals for several generations and whose business has now apparently reached its final spasm of disintegration. The final commission, the preservation of a customer's adored badger, is clearly en route for failure. Mahone is, not surprisingly, suffering panic attacks as he attempts to resolve the practical problems of his dwindling practice and the serious 'psychic crises' of his private life, which are occasioned by a state of terminal indecision. His assistant, the resourceful Ernest Blades, helps him on his way to 'kiss Buridan's Ass goodbye'. The reference is to the syndrome identified by the fourteenth century philosopher Jean Buridan who developed the concept of *impetus* – the first step towards the modern notion of inertia – illustrated by the donkey that starves to death while pondering which bundle of hay it should eat.

This is the Skit Articulate. 'Torpor beckons,' remarks Mahone in a convulsion of Beckettian déséspoir.

The conversations between Christy and Dominic in Mark O'Halloran and David Wilmot's duet of comedies, *Too Much of Nothing* and *One Too Many Mornings*, put one in mind of the outpourings of Flaubert's pretentious pair of provincials, Bouvard and Pécuchet, who are interested in arcane branches of philosophy and literature but do not possess the mental capacity to understand them. The contemporary Dublin couple sit in Bewley's Café – the plays are site-specific – arguing the toss of their current creative and scholarly preoccupations. Christy, a poet, announces that he's writing again. Dominic dilates on the origin and nature of words: for him, 'a word does not begin as a word. It's an end product'. For Christy, words are 'birds from the soul'.

The conversation moves on to matters social and demographic, Dominic observing that the coffee that has Christy so nervy is an evil drug produced by the poorest countries and consumed by the richest. On such profundities the wide-ranging dialogue proceeds. Christy reveals how he was suddenly released from his writer's block at a party for his much disliked father at which he felt the urge to 'bury the hatchet', and a poem, 'Homage à Mon Père', quickly made itself manifest on a beer mat. The recitation of this oeuvre leads to the revelation that his father is not his father. The topics of denial and rejection are then discussed in the café. Dominic discloses that after twelve years he's been taken off the live register for telling lies: 'The people of Ireland have turned their backs on me.' Christy, who has been scribbling all the while, finally reads out a frightful piece of doggerel that sums up the subjects of their conversation and leaves both of them deeply moved.

In the second play, which takes place a year later, Christy has bid farewell to poesie after 'a titanic struggle with my muse', because it's either that or be thrown out by his girlfriend. This abandonment of the act of creation comes as a shock to the intellectually enthused Dominic, at present engaged in a crusade against the dehumanisation of language. Christy has recently sustained the trauma of the loss of his recently discovered natural father, a victualler, who died shortly after a nasty accident with the mincer. He admits, under pressure, that since his promise never to write another poem, he has actually composed a sonnet 'To Mickey the Butcher,' which he then covertly recites. The temporarily mollified Dominic opines that this (dire) work is 'up there with your best'.

Julian Barnes has referred to the novel *Bouvard et Pécuchet* as 'a vomitorium of pre-digested book-learning' and that is what these two modern Dublin comedies disclose with such squirming accuracy. There is no physical action, except for that recounted as having happened offstage; this, and the trenchant exchanges of the protagonists, is sufficient to keep the plays moving at a fair trot.

If Dominic in *Too Much of Nothing* exhibits his scientific understanding of words, Red in Mark O'Halloran's hilarious and macabre *The Head of Red O'Brien* is crazily obsessed by them. Repeating words (his ailments) in his hospital bed – 'Anablepsy, Aphrenia/ Ophthalmoplegia, Orexia/ Blephorospasm, Micrographia' – he pauses to ponder on several, such as Echolalia, 'the forced repetition of someone's words over and over again'. This is a monologue play, a genre that has recently and inexplicably come in for much denigration (rather too late) from the critics. We think fleetingly of Frank in *Faith Healer* who compulsively recites the names of Scottish and Welsh towns, and equally fleetingly of Michael in *Dancing at Lughnasa* who, in his final monologue, likens memory to dancing, 'as if language no longer existed because words were no longer necessary'. At the outset, Red O'Brien has an intense need for words. In his demented state he volubly describes his disastrous relationship with his wife, Mary Motorhead, who resorts to chuckling endlessly over *Ulysses* in order not to hear his nightly iteration of the plot of *The Hunt for Red October*, with copious quotations from the dialogue. Unable to bear the tension any longer, Mary plunges a knife into his head where it enters that part of the brain that controls words. As Red explains, 'I was wiped free of words'. When the words slowly return he realises that Mary's knife had set him free: 'Without words the world is beautiful and with them there is fear and misunderstanding and hatred and fights and cruelty and loneliness... because words can never say enough of what we mean.' That is, love.

The late comedian Cecil Sheehan had a fictitious character called Sister Mary Alabaster, 'a beautiful saintly nun – but a demon in her heart!' We all recognised Sister Mary. She was the kindly teacher who comforted you when you were in a state, arriving late for school without your homework and your pants wet. Yet behind the steel-rimmed spectacles there was a glint of a harsher, unknown, world. We all had aunties who were nuns, some of them appearing regularly for a fortnight's stay from a remote mission in Tanganyka. Many children in Ireland today have never met a nun. Those that are left seem to have entered a subdivision of society that is not despised but is definitely disregarded.

Sebastian Barry's Anna and Beatrice in *Fred and Jane* are nuns of impeccable probity. They are wonderfully contrasted. Anna is thirty, somewhat reticent, and was brought up in well-heeled Monkstown. Beatrice is sixty, amusingly direct, and, coming from the midlands, can appreciate the old joke about beef to the heels – in fact, she is the opposite of the physical stereotype. After fourteen years in the same convent, Beatrice and Anna are separated by a decree discharged like a bolt from somewhere higher up. They have been investigated. They were seen to be too close. Anna is sent on a mission to England. They do not understand what has happened and they deteriorate as people. 'Misery changes you,' says the Beatrice-less Anna. 'It adapts you to itself.' Then the stony, academically distinguished Reverend Mother – a Goldsmith scholar! – suddenly has a change of heart.

There is a motif throughout the play of Hollywood remembered from local cinemas, and this motif is renewed when Reverend Mother experiences a vision of Anna dancing and calls her home. Immediately Beatrice's physical disabilities – even diabetes – vanish through the power of love.

In Isobel Mahon's *So Long, Sleeping Beauty* there is no madness, there are no histrionics, and life's surprises and wounds are ultimately controllable. Glynis has found a bundle of letters in her late husband's effects. She reads them and understands that they are love letters from a man called Neville. She braces herself to contact the writer. When she does, she meets a pleasant and unassuming businessman whose chief interest is in amateur musicals. With tact and gentleness,

Neville tells Glynis as much as she needs to know about his long-standing and entirely unsensational relationship with her husband. Glynis comes to understand that in not fully knowing her husband she has not fully known herself. The situation is delicately explored, the characters are drawn with restraint and humour, and the playwright dextrously catches the distinctive quirks and patterns of speech of these two very 'ordinary' suburban people.

A piece in which the choice of language is especially telling is *Two for a Girl* by Mary Kelly and Noni Stapleton. It is set among tinkers – the euphemism 'itinerants' had not been coined in the 1940s when much of the play's action takes place – and has to do with the pain and dislocation occasioned by rigid ethnic or tribal customs and allegiances, and their effect on the destiny of those who step outside the accepted patterns of behaviour. The language here has the rich and raw feeling of authenticity.

Frances is the child of Josie, a tinker who did household jobs for a settled farmer and became pregnant by him. His wife agrees to bring up the child as their own, but for the mother there is ostracisation from her community, and she only knows her daughter from occasional visits. It is a play fraught with sadness and regret, but not in the least sentimental.

The recording of the naturalistic dialogue proper to a particular sector of society is also a strong feature of Donal Courtney's *Election Night*. Here we witness the intermingling rancour, bombast, backbiting and plámás behind the scenes while votes are being counted in a provincial parliamentary election at which Tomás Cahill, the outgoing deputy, may well lose his seat. Tomás is half drunk and sorry for himself. His humiliation will be particularly severe because he topped the poll when only twenty-eight. Tomás is attended by Denis, his experienced adviser, and Henry, his cocky PR man. Gradually we learn of the probable reasons for his anticipated fall. There were hushed-up incidents, and word has got out. The returning officer's voice drones on. Tomás has lost by only twelve votes, helped by unexpected transfers from another party. It's up to him to call for a re-count. He may yet win. Funny old game, politics.

Among Bram Stoker's many lesser-known prose works is a collection of stories called *Snowbound* in which members of a Victorian touring theatre company pass the time recalling backstage events while their train is halted in a snowdrift. One of these is recorded as the horrific 'The Star Trap'. How, one wondered, could a Victorian tale of love, jealousy and murder, in which the handsome Harlequin Henry dies in view of a packed pantomime audience, be adapted to the pocket-sized Bewley's performance space? Michael James Ford uses the effective device of allowing the macabre events to have taken place three years before his play begins. The still-heartbroken Loo Halliday, Henry's chorus-girl lady friend, and a young stage apprentice, Billy Hempitch, who knows what must have happened, meet. It gradually emerges that Loo's husband Jack Halliday, the theatre's master technician, tampered with the flying mechanism, thus sending his rival dramatically to his doom. Hempitch has lost the vital piece of mechanical evidence, and, as Halliday has died of apoplexy, the embittered Loo has no means of retribution. The piece is replete with period atmosphere, created by hysterically murky recollections in full-blooded language.

'Is there balm in Gilead?' is one of those unanswerable questions of the vaguely rhetorical variety that, when considered, really do not seem to expect a response. Michael Harding's two-person play of the same name is full of equivocations and ambiguities. It is inspired by something in Poe – than whom there could be no more highly programmed purveyor of the mystifying. The play has a haunting otherworldly quality, as if The Woman and The Visitor were moving in a world that is situated halfway between waking and sleeping. The Woman, Harding suggests in the stage directions, 'might be a person in the life of Poe, or might be a character in his fiction'. The Visitor, he says, 'might be Poe himself.' Who, of the pair, is disturbing who? – clearly they knew each other at some time; perhaps they are even related. Whatever about these uncertainties, the play is psychologically gripping. In fact, it is the uncertainties that make it so. It is also satiated with spellbindingly sardonic observations – such as when The Woman remarks, 'It's the sound of someone being dragged to an unwanted destiny', and, later, 'Even when the one you're most familiar with looks you in the eye you really don't know what you're dealing with…'

One wondered, relishing Donal O'Kelly's magisterially funny and heartrending delivery of his own magical script *Jimmy Joyced!*, if it was a case of performance transcending text. On reading the latter, however, it becomes clear that the one is as strong as the other. The challenge would be for another actor to take on the show. Kelly brings us on a journey observed by one J.J. Staines, the keeper of the 'Joycebox' (an old trunk in Rathmines Market), whose father told him that Joyce must be rescued from the tortured and tortuous labyrinths into which he and his works have become sloughed by the academics. Staines observes Joyce's perambulations, his ambitions, his frustrations, his disappointments, the decline of his family, his mother's death, his meeting Nora Barnacle and their ultimate removal from Ireland and their arrival at the Gasthaus Hoffnung where 'at last jiggle jiggle bedstead huffa-puffa just like… just like… NO not just like because Nora is not just like! Jimanora not just like John Stanislaus and May…'

'Intricacies of pain,' as Yeats wrote in another context; yet pain laced with abrasive laughter. In different hands this could be yet another quasi-academic attempt to 'interpret' Joyce to a wider public, but fortunately the hands are those of a theatrical wordsmith who knows where to elide, where to disconnect, where to let language run amok and where to halt the shenanigans with a wry riposte.

The contemporary dysfunctional Dublin family makes an appearance in Mark Wale's *Bad Sunday*. (Were it not first produced in 2000, one might take it for a riotous send-up of Anne Enright's *The Gathering*.) Da is a closet exhibitionist and wishful matricide; Ma is a thief, cooly robbing whatever she needs from the grocery store; Granny is a religious maniac; Son is an arsonist, aka 'the Phibsborough pyromaniac'; and Daughter is a 'sex mechanic'. Da has the lend of a Zephyr for a Sunday outing, so Granny is baulked of going to Mass. A twisty trip to Howth follows, with bizarre incidents along the way interspersed by the exchange of coarse epithets. Da kills Granny, but, witch-like, she flies home; and he is reincarnated as the Great Beast. When they return to Phibsborough they learn from the radio that 'the most unbelievable things had been happening' – 'An entire Kerry village had disappeared into a bog leaving no visible trace… A statue of Eamon de Valera in Limerick had been seen to weep tears of blood before crashing into the crowd… narrowly missing a Little Sister of Charity but killing her black poodle dog… The match at Croke Park had ended in a draw, two opposing teams of supporters… reduced one another to pulp with miniature hurleys, shillelaghs, Guinness bottles and rolled-up copies of the 1916 proclamation…' At no great stretch of the imagination all these reported events are perfectly possible – though perhaps not all on the same day! – but in the world of Da, Ma, Granny, Son and Daughter everything is possible at any time, for they are cartoon characters, their exploits drawing attention to and exposing the absurdities of 'real life'.

The fact is, nowadays, anything can be done on the stage that would have seemed impossible at the time when the Abbey Theatre was producing its 'great' one-act dramas like *The Rising of the Moon* and *Crabbed Youth and Age*. Far from film, television and radio putting an end to stage drama, stage drama has borrowed techniques from those media. More importantly, the theatre has come to understand that its audience does not need to be told that it is gathered together for the purpose of – among other things – suspending disbelief.

In 1931, at the time when radio drama was beginning to take a hold, Thornton Wilder wrote a short stage play in which the members of a family go on a trip by automobile: four chairs represent the car, and the scenery and roadside incidents are 'seen' by the audience because the actors see and experience them. It is no step at all from Thornton Wilder's *The Happy Journey* from Trenton to Camden to Mark Wale's *Bad Sunday* journey from Phibsborough to Howth. What is fortunate is that we have Bewley's Café Theatre to continue the tradition of bringing short sharp dramas so professionally to the stage before our eagerly astonished eyes.

Christopher Fitz-Simon
Dublin, September 2008

Foreword by Mark O'Halloran

Plays From A Room

THE CAFÉ THEATRE OPENED ITS DOORS in the Oriental Room of Bewley's Grafton Street in the summer of 1999. The management team consisted of Michael James Ford and Kelly Campbell and their remit was to produce a rolling season of lunch–time theatre to be enjoyed by the viewing public over a bowl of soup and a hearty sandwich.

The room itself was not a purpose-built theatre but one of the many tea rooms in the sprawling Bewley's premises. Perhaps not what could be called an ideal theatrical location, but with the inclusion of a raised stage in one corner, a lighting bar above and some heavy drapes to block out the mid-day sun, the space was transformed into a very atmospheric backdrop for the drama that was to follow. The next thing to be sorted out was what to put on.

It became clear pretty early on that to keep the programme of plays rolling along, new plays would have to be commissioned. I suppose to begin with it would not seem to be the most glamorous of commissions to get –'we want you to write a 50-minute play to be performed in the corner of a room on the second floor of a café on Grafton Street to an audience of people eating their lunch.' However Michael James Ford has powers of persuasion of a superhuman variety and, in the late summer of 1999, David Wilmot and I found ourselves commissioned to write a play. Neither of us had written anything before, but Michael had previously worked with me as an actor and thought I might have it in me to produce something of interest. And so 'Too Much of Nothing' was born and in the process I fell in love with that small room on the second floor.

There seemed to be something wonderfully liberating in the restrictions the space puts on you. Sometimes in the creation of a play, it is the absence of restrictions which can be the most crippling. If I am allowed to write a play about anything, of any length, with as many characters in it as I like, set anywhere in the world, well then how can I even begin? There were never such freedoms at the Café Theatre and those very restrictions liberated myself and David and allowed us to create our first piece. The piece in fact became about the room. If the theatre is in a café then let the play be located in a café and then its substance became about the chat that happens only in cafés and the characters that have always inhabited Bewley's of Grafton Street: poets and chancers and dreamers. The play itself was a great success and is something that both David and I look back on with huge affection and pride. We had written our first play and that small room had been the inspiration.

In fact, I believe it is the room itself that is the biggest inspiration to the majority of work that has gone on there. Its perceived restrictions and drawbacks have actually provided its greatest strengths. Its cosy intimacy has allowed first-time writers a wonderful opportunity not found anywhere else in the city to make a start and to get work produced. If David and I were entirely reductive in our response to the space, others took a different tack, transforming that room into a hospital or an asylum or a country pub or the parlour of a Victorian house – and each time that small room has responded and appeared to literally change itself to suit the circumstance of the piece. That room coupled with the sometimes anarchic and very open style of management employed by Michael and Kelly in the early years helped establish Bewley's Café Theatre as a venue which produces work of true quality, innovation and fun. It has also been and continues to be a venue that specialises in the fostering of new and emerging talent and I think I speak for many writers who started there when I say that without that venue, I don't think I would have written at all or continued to do so.

That small room has given a welcome start to a whole generation of not only writers (whom we are celebrating in this volume) but also first-time directors, young actors, musicians, stage managers and producers who have all worked heroically to get the plays staged. I am sure the writers featured in this book would like to thank all of them and also the many loyal customers who have filled that small room with laughter and applause over the last few years. And I hope you the reader will get as much pleasure reading this volume of plays from a room as we have had in making them. Thank you.

Dublin, September 2008

FRESHLY BREWED

TWELVE SHORT PLAYS FROM BEWLEY'S CAFÉ THEATRE

PHOTO BY KELLY CAMPBELL

Too Much of Nothing

By Mark O'Halloran & David Wilmot

TOO MUCH OF NOTHING WAS FIRST PRODUCED IN AUGUST 1999.

DIRECTOR: MICHAEL JAMES FORD
CAST: MARK O'HALLORAN AND DAVID WILMOT
LIGHTING: KELLY CAMPBELL

> ...when there's too much of nothing,
> No one has control.
>
> — Bob Dylan

A table in Bewley's Café on which is an old leather satchel. The front of house manager announces that all mobile phones should be switched off. Lights fade to blackout. A mobile phone rings from within the satchel. Enter CHRISTY with a tray carrying a mug of coffee. He attempts to answer phone. He is too late. The line has gone dead.

CHRISTY: Hello…hello…

He settles himself at the table, takes a notepad and pen out of the bag. Also a brown envelope which he places significantly in front of him. He glances around the room at pictures of great Irish writers. Lights a cigarette. Inhales deeply. Then he takes out a copy of The Little Book of Calm. *He glances at the book and takes a deep breath. CHRISTY turns to his writing. Enter DOMINIC, tray in hand. He looks around the café, spots CHRISTY, approaches.*

DOMINIC: Christy!

CHRISTY: Dominic.

DOMINIC: You're back.

CHRISTY: Yes. I was lying low for a while.

DOMINIC: I thought we'd lost you.

CHRISTY: No, no… no, no…

DOMINIC: I called in here a few times but there was no sign of you.

CHRISTY: A period of reflection was required.

DOMINIC: Ah yes… reflection.

CHRISTY: Deep reflection.

DOMINIC: It's a very lonely thing for a man to have to drink his tea alone… in a place like this.

CHRISTY: Well I apologise for any worry I might have caused. However the good news is… I'm writing again.

DOMINIC: Excellent… excellent.

CHRISTY: How have you been, Dominic?

DOMINIC: Just a little bit blue, Christy… just a little bit down. You know…

CHRISTY: The usual.

DOMINIC: Yah… the usual.
DOMINIC takes one of CHRISTY's cigarettes.

CHRISTY: You're smoking again?

DOMINIC: Yes. Do you mind?

CHRISTY: Of course not.

DOMINIC: I've had a very bad week. (*Pause*) What are you writing about?

CHRISTY: Paternity… maternity. Family. I'm just trying to finish it… but I can't seem to find the right… the right…

DOMINIC: Words.

CHRISTY: Indeed. Words!

DOMINIC: Yah well, you work away there, Christy. Don't let me disturb you.

CHRISTY: Thank you, Dominic.

DOMINIC strolls around the room. He picks up an ashtray and places it on the table.

DOMINIC: Ashtray. (*DOMINIC wanders again, looking over CHRISTY's shoulder.*) Words… words… wooorrds… wooorrrdddzzz…

CHRISTY: Yes. Words.

DOMINIC: You know, Christy, a word does not begin as a word. It is an end product, which begins as an impulse, stimulated by attitude and behaviour, which dictates the need for expression.

CHRISTY: That's a little sterile, Dominic.

DOMINIC: It is, practically speaking, just a series of clicks and vibrations, amplified by the sinus cavities in the cranium, made by the vocal chords and the tongue on an outbreath.

CHRISTY: Ah come now, Dominic, words are birds from the soul. And these great writers that surround us certainly wouldn't see it your way.

DOMINIC: No, I mean if you were to take your common or garden word… say the word giraffe, for instance, taken from the Arabic word *zarafa* and it immediately conjures up beautiful images of the horsey, spotty thing with the long neck, roaming free on the Serengeti. Yes?

CHRISTY: Yes.

DOMINIC: But, if you were to take that word and repeat it, say, fourteen times in a row, like so… giraffe, giraffe, giraffe, giraffe, giraffe, giraffe, giraffe, giraffe, giraffe, giraffe, giraffe, giraffe, giraffe, giraffe! There! All images of the spotty, horsey thing with the long neck have evaporated and you are left with what?

CHRISTY: What?

DOMINIC: A series of clicks and vibrations, in the cranium, made by the vocal cords and the tongue on an outbreath. Go ahead. Try it yourself. Try it with the word…wallpaper… for instance.

CHRISTY: Wallpaper?

DOMINIC: Comes from two separate words…the Latin *vallum* meaning rampart, and the Greek word *papyrus* meaning p… paper. Go on… go on.

CHRISTY & DOMINIC: Wallpaper, wallpaper, wallpaper, wallpaper, wallpaper, wallpaper, wallpaper, wallpaper, wallpaper, wallpaper…

DOMINIC: You see?

CHRISTY: Fascinating.

DOMINIC: Nothing but pure sound!

CHRISTY: Well thank God I'm not writing about wallpaper…or giraffes.

Pause. CHRISTY writes. DOMINIC is a little put out.

DOMINIC: I don't know why you bother writing in English in the first place. It barely exists. It's the magpie language, plundered from ancient cultures. Most of the words are foreign. Take the word mobile telephone for instance. It comes from three separate words… the Latin word *mobilis* meaning moveable, the Greek word *tele* meaning far off, and the Greek word *phono* meaning voice… the moveable far off voice. The word poem comes from the Greek word *poema*. Even the word *word* isn't an English word. It comes from the German *wort*. I think it shows a great lack of self-esteem in the English-speaking world that whenever it comes to naming anything new, they reach for a foreign word rather than making up one of their own. I mean the Greeks really have a lot to be proud of. I mean, their economy may be in tatters on account of the priapic tendencies of a certain Aristotle Onassis, who drove his shipping empire onto the rocks in his reckless pursuit of two goddesses… on the left Maria Callas, and on the right Jacqueline Bouvier Kennedy… then the whole thing was compounded by years of dogmatic socialism. Oh yeah they may have hyperinflation and mass unemployment, but still and all they can hold their heads up high cause they've named half the things in the known world. *(Pause)* What's your favourite word?

CHRISTY: Struggle.

DOMINIC: Struggle… don't know where that comes from… possibly High German. My favourite word is *gimp*. It's an old Dutch word for a length of silk fishing line… Gimp! Doesn't it just conjure up beautiful images… of the wide expanse of horizon over the Zuider Zee… and little Dutch boys with clogs on… fishing for their supper.

CHRISTY: Dominic please.

DOMINIC: Oh sorry… sorry. *(Pause. CHRISTY drinks his coffee.)* Coffee!

CHRISTY: No thanks.

DOMINIC: Coffee!

CHRISTY: No I'm all right.

DOMINIC: Coffee!

CHRISTY: I've just had one, thanks.

DOMINIC: You are drinking coffee.

CHRISTY: Yes.

DOMINIC: Exactly.

CHRISTY: Pardon?

DOMINIC: That's your problem. *(Pause)*. Rich roast?

CHRISTY: What?

DOMINIC: Is it rich roast?

CHRISTY: What, the blend?

DOMINIC: Yes.

CHRISTY: No.

DOMINIC: Java?

CHRISTY: No.

DOMINIC: Costa Rica?

CHRISTY: No.

DOMINIC: Brasilia?

CHRISTY: No. Colombia.

DOMINIC: Ah yes! Deadly.

CHRISTY: Yes… it was very nice.

DOMINIC: No, I mean deadly deadly, not deadly deadly.

CHRISTY: Your point?

DOMINIC: My point being that it is coffee that has you the way you are, so touchy, so nervy, and may I add so rude. What does coffee do for you, Christy? Why are you sitting here drinking coffee?

CHRISTY: It's relaxing.

DOMINIC: No, it is not relaxing. Quite the opposite, in fact. Physiologically speaking coffee induces a mild form of panic. It gets your mind whirling, unfocused, on edge, unhinged, and that is just the way they like it.

CHRISTY: Who?

DOMINIC: The establishment. It suits their purpose to have a large section of the population walking around unhinged, unfocused, unable to concentrate… because while everyone is a little bit freaked out, wondering whether to have a café au lait, alta rica rio, mocha, made with fresh cream and frothy milk with half a flake on the side, the government has a free hand to dismantle the Welfare State unnoticed. I can trace back the beginnings of the Celtic Tiger to an expansion in the range of coffees available to the consumer, the opening of a pavement café on every street corner… and the introduction of the cappuccino. And while we are being merely hoodwinked, the real victims of this gastronomic imperialism are the peoples of the Third World… eternally enslaved to The Bush of Beezlebub. Just look at any list of the main coffee producing countries in the world and it reads like a who's-who of the have-nots.

CHRISTY: True enough.

DOMINIC: Two types of coffee bean make up 95% of the coffee consumed on this planet. The first is the coffea arabica, elongated, oval and flat… grown throughout Central and South America… mild and aromatic, so they say. The second, however, is the most deadly bean known to humanity… the coffea robusta. A smaller bean with an irregular convex shape, it has two and a half times more caffeine than the arabica bean, and is the chief export of only three countries… The Ivory Coast, Angola and the country formerly known as Zaire… The People's Republic of Congo! Do you spot a pattern, Christy? Three of the most fucked up countries in the world… It can be said with all confidence that Lauren Kabila swept to power in the Congo on a wave of anarchy fuelled by the robusta bean. And who is the largest consumer of coffee in the world? The United States of America… I rest my case.

CHRISTY: I knew you didn't drink the stuff, but I had no idea your distrust was so deep.

DOMINIC: Oh no, Christy, it is more than just distrust. I once almost lost my mind to coffee.

CHRISTY: Really?

DOMINIC: Indeed. I was younger then, more foolhardy. I even had a job.

CHRISTY: A job?

DOMINIC: Yes.

CHRISTY: You?

DOMINIC: Yes, for three whole days… working in the kitchen of an Italian restaurant with a very strange man called Gringo. He was from Cabra. One night, after the restaurant had closed, he introduced me to a game called Coffee Roulette. Did you ever hear of an espresso, Christy?

CHRISTY: Of course.

DOMINIC: The heart of darkness. The game involves cutting a deck of cards and the person with the lowest card has to drink a double espresso in one gulp. Well, I had a bit of a bad streak… Gringo was a more experienced player and knew all the little tricks, and I ended up drinking twenty-seven double espressos in quick succession. That night I came within a hair's breadth of complete cardiac overload. My kidney went into spasm, and I thought I was staring at a life of enforced medication and group therapy, doomed to the day room of a high security psychiatric hospital. But I have reserves of mental strength, Christy, and I dragged myself back from the abyss. However, I have been left with extensive emotional scarring.

CHRISTY: I had no idea.

DOMINIC: So, after approximately ninety hours without sleep, and significantly grinding down most of my molars, it came to me as clear as day that coffee was an evil drug. It is the Bean of the Devil.

CHRISTY: (Pause) There's caffeine in tea too, you know.

DOMINIC: What?

CHRISTY: Yes. There's caffeine in tea… not as much… but there is caffeine… in tea.

They drink from their respective mugs. DOMINIC puts his down forcefully.

DOMINIC Shut up! (*Pause. The mobile phone rings.*) The phone, Christy?

CHRISTY: I know.

DOMINIC: Well, answer it.

CHRISTY: No.

DOMINIC: Why not?

CHRISTY: I'm not ready.

DOMINIC: What do you mean?

CHRISTY: I'm not finished.

DOMINIC answers the phone but keeps it at an arm's length from his ear.

DOMINIC: Hello, hello… You're going to have to speak up — I'm not putting this thing near my head for safety reasons.

CHRISTY grabs the phone from DOMINIC and switches it off.

CHRISTY: Don't interfere.

DOMINIC: Why won't you answer it?

CHRISTY: Not yet. If I can finish this work then the world will know why I can't answer this phone.

DOMINIC: Why… who is it?

CHRISTY: I don't know.

Pause. DOMINIC looking worried, places his palm over his ear. He leans over.

DOMINIC: Feel the side of my head.

CHRISTY: What?

DOMINIC: Feel the side of my head.

CHRISTY: I don't want to feel the side of your head.

DOMINIC: I don't want you to feel the side of my head… just feel the side of my head. No higher… more behind the ear. Now do you feel anything?

CHRISTY: Like what?

DOMINIC: Like heat!

CHRISTY: Well, you are sweating.

DOMINIC: There… I knew it… I've ended up with a hot spot on my brain now because of that stupid phone of yours.

CHRISTY: Don't be ridiculous.

DOMINIC: That thing gives off microwaves doesn't it? Did you ever see what happens to a tomato when it's exposed to microwaves… it blows up… I just cooked a part of my brain with that thing. They are a great danger to public safety, they are… I mean, just look around you, half the country's walking about with those things clamped to the side of their head, slowly cooking their brains… having hot spots and tumours and memory lapses and walking into lamp posts and trees and crashing cars, it is my belief that this country is on the verge of phonageddon.

CHRISTY: Well, why did you answer it then?

DOMINIC: Well, I had to choose between the lesser of two evils, the reality of noise pollution and the possibility of cooking my brain. (*Long pause*) Speaking of two evils, I seen that Brian Keenan fella on the telly last week. Do you know who I'm talking about?

CHRISTY: The hostage?

DOMINIC: I always thought there was more to that than meets the eye. I mean people don't just tie you to a radiator for no reason. And I was walking past that Lebanese restaurant the other day… lovely food, lovely people… (*Pause*) What time is it, Christy?

CHRISTY: It's twenty past one.

DOMINIC: No it's not… it's twenty-three minutes past one and my watch is exact. It's the exactest watch I've ever had… it's right by the atomic clock in Greenwich… the one on the radio that goes beep, beep, beep, beeeeeeep.

CHRISTY: Dominic!!

Pause. DOMINIC taps his knee nervously.

CHRISTY: Dominic, please.

DOMINIC: What?

CHRISTY: Don't start.

DOMINIC: Don't start what?

CHRISTY: Twitching.

DOMINIC: No, I haven't twitched in ages actually. I'm just very tense, that's all.

CHRISTY: Well, you know what I think.

CHRISTY produces a copy of <u>The Little Book of Calm</u>.

DOMINIC: What? No, *The Little Book of Calm* doesn't work for me! It just makes me more tense.

CHRISTY: I don't think you've opened yourself to it. It's changed my life utterly. I can honestly say that without *The Little Book of Calm* the last week might have crushed me.

DOMINIC: I don't know.

CHRISTY: Please… I honestly believe that somewhere in there is the key to your serenity.

DOMINIC: Alright… but I'm not doing that one where I have to pretend to be a windmill again.

CHRISTY: Alright, pick one randomly.

Passes the book. DOMINIC selects and reads out…

DOMINIC: Write it down. Write down your concerns and be surprised how quickly they dissolve when you read them on paper.

CHRISTY hands him pen and paper.

> No, I don't think so. I used to keep a diary you know, put all my darkest thoughts into it but then my mother read it and didn't speak to me for two years… I'm not going down that road again. However, I could channel my energies into a work of fiction. I once tried to write a formulaic type bonk-buster novel a la Jilly Cooper. I mean she has a winning formula — all she does is to pick a sport… say water polo or show jumping or opera singing or tennis and she observes them at play and then writes about them bonking each other. So I picked camogie, to give it that Irish feel, but then the characters began to grow in my mind and practically began to write themselves and there was one evil cow in the team called Mairéad, and what she did was towards the end of the first chapter, after a game in Carlow, she stripped her team-mates naked, tied them up in the shower room and flicked wet towels at them mercilessly.

CHRISTY: Here's a better one. Picture yourself… picture yourself on an idyllic

South Pacific Island. See yourself on the sun-bleached sands. Note what you're wearing… the relaxed way you're standing… the way the breeze blows your hair. The calm semi-smile on your face… now imagine what it's like to paddle in a crystal blue lagoon.

Pause. DOMINIC surveys idyllic island with closed eyes and CHRISTY goes back to writing.

DOMINIC: Aaaaaaaarrrrrrrrrrggggggggghhhhhhh!

CHRISTY: Jesus Christ, what?

DOMINIC: Jellyfish. There were huge Albanian Man O' War jellyfish everywhere. It was horrible.

CHRISTY: It's alright, it's OK. They're gone now.

DOMINIC: I told you, that book is useless.

CHRISTY: OK, once more, one last try… my personal favourite, never fails. Embrace nature.

DOMINIC reads while CHRISTY collects large plant from down stage right.

DOMINIC: Embrace nature… plants pour oxygen into the environment while soaking up CO_2 and pollutants. Keep plants where you work, sleep and live and you'll enjoy more oxygen. The more oxygen you get the calmer you will become.

CHRISTY: This is simple. In with the good, out with the bad.

They both place their faces amongst the leaves and take deep breaths. DOMINIC keeps taking deep breaths while CHRISTY lights a cigarette and returns to his writing.

DOMINIC: The leaves are quite dusty. It'll end up with its stomata blocked thus interrupting the process of transpiration. It's a *Ficus Ficus*, from the genus *Ficus* or fig tree family… Hardy enough, but prone to leaf drop if overwatered, aren't you? I love plants me, always did… That would be a lovely job that would, working with plants… gardening… driving from job to job in a van with Dominic's Landscape Gardening written on the side in big red… no, green letters. Working in the sunshine with your top off, getting a tan, using your muscles. Tackling a wayward rhododendron. That's my favourite plant, the rhododendron. It gets its name from two greek words… *rhodon*, meaning rose and *dendron*… meaning tree. As to why they didn't just call it a rose tree I'll never know. Still and all… a rosetree by any other name is still a rhododendron. They come from the Northern hemisphere… around Nepal and Tibet. A robust plant, but it can get out of control. You've got to show it who's boss. You must give it a good hard pruning in early April. I could graft trees as well. People hardly ever graft trees these days. It used to be a tradition in Ireland years ago when a Catholic girl and a Protestant boy or a Catholic boy and a Protestant girl got married, the families would graft two trees, say an apple tree and a plum tree, together as a sign of their love and unity and you'd end up with one big tree that grew both apples and plums…. I love gardening programmes… and fly-on-the-wall documentary programmes…and cookery programmes. I always thought there was a gap in the market for a new type of programme. A fly-on-the-wall gardening documentary program… in which celebrity chefs have to come around and do up your dump of a garden. I mean you could have Delia Smith coming round and she has a week in which to transform your dump of a garden into a paradise and if she succeeds she wins and if she doesn't she loses… And then as the credits roll she could cook up a sumptuous stirfry on the patio of the newly done up garden. That's a good idea for a program isn't it…

CHRISTY: It is.

DOMINIC: I should do that… shouldn't I?

CHRISTY: You should.

DOMINIC: I could do that, couldn't I?

CHRISTY: Dominic, I've always had the firm belief that you could do anything you wanted.

DOMINIC: Anything?

CHRISTY: Anything!

DOMINIC: I could… I could do anything… I can be very creative, you know… I could make things… I could make little things with my hands. Valerie always said I was very good with my hands. It's something I've always meant to ask her, if I was so good with my hands, how come she left me?

CHRISTY: No, not the past… the future. What would you make?

DOMINIC: Don't know.

CHRISTY: Would you, could you potter?

DOMINIC: NO!

CHRISTY: What then? (*DOMINIC turns away smiling coyly.*) Come on, what?

DOMINIC: Kites.

CHRISTY: Kites?

DOMINIC: Kites!

CHRISTY: Oh gorgeous. Aah, I really love kites.

DOMINIC: Yeah, me too. Beautiful handmade kites.

CHRISTY: Ooh!

DOMINIC: Yeah, really big beautiful handmade kites and really tiny delicate handmade kites and a range of kites in-between.

CHRISTY: I'd say if you went looking for a top quality handmade kite in this town you'd be looking a long time.

DOMINIC: Box kites.

CHRISTY: Well, there you go. You hardly ever see box kites these days.

DOMINIC: A real gap in the market that. I could make big box kites. Handmade box kites… and all my kites would be made with natural materials… no plastic in my pieces… because kite flying is a very green occupation. In fact kites could be said to be the bicycle of the aeronautical world.

CHRISTY: I remember when I used to fly kites as a child… It was a very spiritual experience.

DOMINIC: Oh yes. In China, the flying of kites is an integral part of their religious ceremonies part of their Zen aesthetic. Families get together and build kites and paint them with demonic faces and fly them as high as possible to keep their loved one's safe from harm. I could open a shop 'Dominic's Kite Shop' and paint the front with beautiful bright colours and have displays of my kites in the front window. And loads of kids hanging around inside thinking I was really cool.

CHRISTY: And you'll need a workshop space.

DOMINIC: Yes, big enough for me to work in and to store all my gear that I'll need cause I'll need an awful lot of stuff, I mean, I'll need thousands of yards of bamboo, which eventually I could grow myself… reams of crepe paper.

CHRISTY: Ribbons.

DOMINIC: Yeah, ribbons and one of those huge pairs of scissors, glue and some of that Dutch gimp string. And to help launch the shop we could have a kite festival; yes, a kite flying festival. They have one in India every year. Every single person on the subcontinent, and that's over one billion people, flies a kite for good luck!

CHRISTY: Where would you have the festival?

DOMINIC: In the Phoenix Park.

CHRISTY: It could be the biggest thing to hit the Phoenix Park since the Pope's visit.

DOMINIC: Oh yeah, because there would be grannies and granddads, ma's and da's and kids… and… traffic wardens and members of the Garda Siochána, and tax inspectors, and taxi drivers, and taxidermists… people from the north and people from the south, Catholic and Protestant, in one great act of reconciliation, all flying my handmade kites, and you and me, Christy, you and me launching the biggest box kite this country has ever seen.

CHRISTY: You'd need some wind.

DOMINIC: You would…

Pause. DOMINIC has been utterly deflated by the last comment.

CHRISTY: Dominic, I'm sorry.

DOMINIC: No, Christy. That's always been my problem. I suffer from crippling overambition.

CHRISTY: I think that's probably something we have in common, Dominic.

Pause. DOMINIC takes down a picture of W. B. Yeats from the wall and comes up behind CHRISTY.

DOMINIC: 'Romantic Ireland's dead and gone. It's with O'Leary in the grave.' Christy, stop writing… it's all been written already.

CHRISTY: For God sake. Put that back on the wall.

DOMINIC: I was only messin'.

CHRISTY: Do you want to get us thrown out… again?

DOMINIC: *(Pause)* What's wrong, Christy?

CHRISTY: What makes you think there's anything wrong?

DOMINIC: You're not yourself.

CHRISTY: It's just family problems.

DOMINIC: Your Da.

CHRISTY: No. Yes. Yes and no.Yes.

DOMINIC: What do you mean?

CHRISTY: Last week was his birthday…

DOMINIC: Come on, out with it.

CHRISTY: His fiftieth birthday. And Mother phoned to ask me to a party in the Royal Marine. A big do you know, lot of fuss. As well you know, Dominic, I had no desire to attend, but Mother kept phoning and insisted that underneath it all, father really did want me there. So I went with the possibility of burying the hatchet.

DOMINIC: In his forehead.

CHRISTY: Indeed, but in truth, Dominic, and surprisingly enough, I was happy to be there. So many people I hadn't seen in so long. Aunts and uncles, cousins and children. Oh Dominic, beautiful children I'd never met before. And surrounded by family I'd forgotten. I felt this movement, deep movement, do you know what it was?

DOMINIC: I could give a good guess.

CHRISTY: It was my writer's block shifting, lifting, leaving me. So inspired by the feast for my father. Words came pouring in, and on the back of a beer mat I wrote my first work in two years. 'Hommage à Mon Père'. I stilled the band and delivered my work. To a deafening silence. Broken only by a laugh, one laugh, a laugh I know well. The very man I had tried to honour was creased up on the floor. I was incensed, I went for him. It all gets a bit blurry but suddenly the word bastard froze the room. And my mother started to sob.

DOMINIC: Why?

CHRISTY: Because I am.

DOMINIC: What?

CHRISTY: A bastard.

DOMINIC: Not at all, you can be ratty all right.

CHRISTY: No illegitimate.

DOMINIC: What do you mean?

CHRISTY: My father is not my father. The whole story came out. He was in the army when they were first married, it seems I was conceived while he was in Cyprus with the UN. And when he came home he promised to stick by her. Him, a martyr?

DOMINIC: So who is your father?

CHRISTY: I don't know. My mother obviously does, and she has been phoning all week since. I haven't been able to answer it. But she left a message yesterday saying she'd written everything down and posted it to me. And that arrived this morning.

DOMINIC: It's unopened.

CHRISTY: I know, I can't, not yet. I'm using it to fuel what I hope will be my best work. To be honest, I've never felt so invigorated. And the fear is the minute I open it, all this will evaporate.

DOMINIC: I think there's a photograph inside.

CHRISTY: I know.

DOMINIC: This is amazing. I mean, I now have no idea who I'm talking to. And who would have thought it, eh?

CHRISTY: What?

DOMINIC: Your mother?! I mean he could have been anyone. He could have been anyone! You don't look foreign anyway. Though he could have been an English man or a Scottish man or a Welsh man or an American man of either English, Scottish, Welsh or Irish extraction… Do you know who it could be… Mickey the Butcher.

CHRISTY: I don't think so… for one thing, he has an enormous nose.

DOMINIC: You look like the guy from the telly.

CHRISTY: Who?

DOMINIC: The guy from *Steptoe and Son*.

CHRISTY: But his hair is dark.

DOMINIC: No, the old fella… Wilfred Bramble. He could have been over here doing a show in the Gaiety and one night after the show was over he was sauntering down Grafton Street and there was a full moon and a smattering of stars and suddenly he spots your ma and sweeps her off her feet and they go back to where he's staying… the Shelbourne or something and they do it in his room…

CHRISTY: Dominic… that's just not helpful… anyway it's not about who he is, it's about who I'm not.

DOMINIC: Christy, you're in shock… Do you feel numb?

CHRISTY: No.

DOMINIC: No?

CHRISTY: No!

DOMINIC: Classic case of denial… the second stage of grief or trauma.

CHRISTY: I'm not in denial. (*DOMINIC waves the letter in front of him.*) Oh, for God's sake!

DOMINIC: It's anger, stage three, very good just let it out.

CHRISTY: I want to forget about it, put it behind me.

DOMINIC: Stage four… disengagement or apathy, you're doing very well.

CHRISTY: Dominic, I'm fine, I'm fine.

DOMINIC: Recovery… this is remarkable… your powers of healing are positively athletic.

CHRISTY: Dominic, please I have to finish this.

DOMINIC: OK, I'm your man. We're going to finish this together… (*DOMINIC reads the poem.*) Hold on… isn't that supposed to rhyme? They don't rhyme Christy.

CHRISTY: Dominic, you are not helping here, you are not a poet and what would you know about it… the pain, the rejection.

DOMINIC: Nothing, I suppose. I suppose Valerie leaving me wasn't a rejection. Ah no, the only person I could have shared a life with, a normal life just leaving, going… no rejection.

CHRISTY: Dominic, I…

DOMINIC: No, And what was worse was that she used the working of my digestive tract as an excuse to bail out

CHRISTY: Pardon?

DOMINIC: She used my gut to go.

CHRISTY: I'm completely lost.

DOMINIC: As you know, I suffer from hypertension and ulcers, a side effect of which is that when I'm on edge my stomach swells with gas. Valerie was able to judge my state of mind by the amount my stomach was distended. When it reached a critical level she'd burst out crying and go for a walk to allow me time to relax… and then one day she just didn't bother coming back.

CHRISTY: Dominic, I…

DOMINIC: But it gets worse, Christy. You see I too received a letter this week.

A letter in a brown envelope and for the likes of you and me Christy, brown envelopes can mean only one thing... bad news, big bad news... I've been fucked off the dole.

CHRISTY: Why?

DOMINIC: Apparently cause I'm unemployed. The letter was an invitation to have a chat with the supervisor at my dole office. I thought they were going to suggest that I try another FÁS scheme...but no, it was worse than that. 'There are a number of irregularities with your claim,' says he. 'Hold it there,' I said. 'Check the record. Check this guy's track record and you will find that, as opposed to the civil service, which lost 240,000 man-hours last year due to malingering, I have never, I repeat never, in my 12 years in receipt of welfare payments, ever missed a signing on day. A clear indication of the seriousness with which I take my claim for Unemployment Assistance.' 'Yeah well, there are a number of untruths in one of the forms you returned lately,' says he, 'and according to my enquiries, you have never applied to be senior administrator to the Dental School of Trinity College nor to be Marketing Manager for Avoca Handweavers. Lies,' says he. 'They weren't lies,' says I, 'They were merely aspirational statements.' 'Yeah well, you no longer meet the requirements to be in receipt of Unemployment Assistance. And it is a very serious thing,' says he, 'to tell lies on official documents.' 'Only for some,' said I, 'because the people at the top, the rich people can afford to tell huge lies. Whereas the likes of me, at the bottom of the pile can't afford to tell lies at all.' 'Well, we've paid you for the last twelve years to do nothing.' 'Oh, I've done me quota of nothing,' says I. 'I've done too much of nothing,' says I. And with that he just pulled down the blind on hatch 15B. Simple as that Christy, the blind came down. And I was no longer a statistic on the live register. There's rejection for you, Christy. The people of Ireland have turned their backs on me.

CHRISTY: Dominic, why didn't you tell me?

DOMINIC: I could tell you had troubles of your own and quite frankly I couldn't get a word in edgeways.

CHRISTY: Blind... that's it... blind... that's it.

A very excited CHRISTY kisses DOMINIC and launches back into writing.

That's it. It's finished, it's done, it's complete.

DOMINIC: The poem?

CHRISTY: Yes. And, Dominic, I would like you to be the first to hear it.

DOMINIC: Why, gentle sir, I'd be honoured.

CHRISTY: Hello, hello, the message came
That shook the heart of me
A moving far off voice it was
That sought to set me free.

From all the joys of childhood days
When you would make me laugh
You seemed so gentle kind and strong
A benevolent giraffe.

The kites we flew upon the hill
Are sodden, sad and limp
And all that's left within my hand
Is a silken thread of gimp.

Unlike the plant that's grown from seed
And raised so lovingly
I reel right now to hear the news
I was grafted on to thee.

And in the April of my youth
You never let me ramble
But pruned me with your silver shears
Like a rampant woodland bramble.

A foundling boy, a bastard son
A cuckoo in the nest
Oh mother do you really think
You did (hid) it for the best.

You often said to me in rage
To get the finger out
Now this wee Dutch boy's done his best
And a deluge has come about.

A flood so fierce has washed away
My history from me
I'm left to sit, a boy alone
On the freezing Zuider Zee.

Your scorn has cut me to the quick
You've had your darkest wish
And felled me with the savage sting
Of a deadly jellyfish.

The Greeks know most, but never boast
Of empires ground to dust
And fatherless and blind I go
A modern Oedipus.

Pause. They are both deeply moved. DOMINIC picks up CHRISTY's letter and hands it to him.

DOMINIC: It's time, Christy.

CHRISTY: Yes.

CHRISTY opens letter and removes photo. He is shocked and hands it on to DOMINIC. More shock. They look at each other.

DOMINIC & CHRISTY: OH, FUCK!

THE END

PHOTO BY STEPHEN DELANEY

Bad Sunday
By Mark Wale

BAD SUNDAY WAS FIRST PRODUCED IN FEBRUARY 2001.

DIRECTOR: JOHN DELANEY
CAST: MARTINA AUSTIN, JESSICA FREED, BRENDAN MCDONALD, AOIFE O'BEIRNE
AND EOIN SHANLEY
LIGHTING: KELLY CAMPBELL

Author's Note:

Clowning by day, filmscript writing by night, suddenly this play pops out, a twisted flashback to Sunday afternoon drives of my childhood. Showed it to my Northside friends. Only Delaney responded. Any chance I could direct it, sez he. Why the f*** d'you think I gave it you, sez I. Rehearsed reading in Andrew's Lane, Bairbre Ní Chaoimh slipping a word in Michael Ford's ear and Bewley's signs up for the premiere. Next thing, I'm diceman-ing it up and down Grafton Street dressed as a Ford Zephyr distributing flyers, and we have a little hit on our hands. What I love about Bewley's is everybody's hands-on. That, plus the faces of visiting yanks when Da chucks Granny off Howth Head. Priceless!

—Mark Wale

A note to the reader:

This piece is not written for a literary theatre. If I was still in France it probably wouldn't have been written at all. As you read, think Commedia dell'Arte, *think Marx Brothers, think Ariane Mnouchkine, think Steven Berkoff, think Warner Brothers cartoons. If you can. If you can't, don't think at all. Just let the pictures happen in your head and leave the problems of staging it to whoever chooses to stage it. And hope, along with me, that they understand how a group of performers can work their magic with a few plastic elements and a willing public.*
—*Mark Wale*

This play can begin wherever you like. Let's say the story begins in a little house in Phibsboro.

DA: It being a Sunday morning.

MA: A fine, fine Sunday morning in the full heat of August.

DA: By God, it was a scorcher.

MA: The sun near burned the eyes out of your head.

DA: You were hung over.

MA: So were you.

DA: I took a strap to the slumbering kiddies.

SON & DAUGHTER: Aw, leave off, it's too early.

MA: Who tumbled down the stairs.

SON: I was pushed.

DA: Eat your bleeding breakfast.

MA: And after a swift dose of John Powers universal head remedy.

DA: And a chorus of Danny Boy on the arse bugle.

He cocks his leg and sounds the trumpet. The troops gag and retch and beat a hasty retreat.

MA: He made his announcement.

MA & DA: No Mass today.

SON & DAUGHTER: No Mass today?

DA: I have succeeded, through a combination of subtle negotiation, gentlemanly guile and downright moral blackmail, to acquire for a period of twenty-four hours, to the rich and undeserved benefit of youse whiners, cringers and apron strap hangers, the exclusive loan and disposal of my good comrade Sparky's vintage nineteen-sixty-six Ford Zephyr.

SON & DAUGHTER: Wa-hoo!

DA: Shut your gobs.

They shut them.

MA: You can't drive.

DA: I am full of hidden mysteries.

MA: You're full of a lot of things, but you can't drive.

DA: Don't confuse the issue with technicalities.

GRANNY: I've never missed Mass in me life.

DAUGHTER: Bring your beads. You can do them in the back of the car.

GRANNY: It's not the same.

MA: She wants her communion.

DA: Give her a Jaffa cake. That'll keep her happy.

SON: Where is the roaring beastie then?

DA: Fling wide the portals of this humble abode and prepare to feast your eyes.

The door is opened and they all emerge, dazzled by the glow emanating from the mythical vehicle in the diamond light of the summer morning.

MA: That's beautiful.

DAUGHTER: Look at the line.

SON: The colour.

DAUGHTER: Look at the curve.

MA: The fins.

SON: *(sniffing)* The seats are real leather.

MA: The speedometer goes up awful high.

DAUGHTER: Flat four engine with an overhead cam. I'd say this one drinks up the petrol.

DA: Leave that alone. Don't be messing with things you don't understand. Now, who'll be the first one in?

GRANNY: You'll not get me inside that thing.

SON: Go on, Granny, be a daredevil.

DAUGHTER: The speed will take years off you.

GRANNY: I may be old but I'm not daft. Here I am and here I stay.

MA: Ah, don't be so bleeding selfish.

GRANNY: Say what you like. I'm not budging.

They grab GRANNY and panhandle her into the back seat of the car, with one kid on either side to keep her in place.

I'm telling you, you'll regret this.

DA: *(to MA)* Hop in, make yourself comfortable.

MA: Don't mind if I do.

DA takes the driver's seat. There is a considerable pause as they bask in the status conferred by sitting in such a monstrous vehicle.

DA: How do you start the thing anyway?

MA takes the key off him and puts it in the ignition. DA turns the key and the engine springs to life.

First time. Not bad for an alcoholic. Now.

Tries various pedals with various feet. Guns the engine hideously.

DAUGHTER: *(leaning over from the back seat and pointing to the pedals)* Accelerator, brake, clutch. It's a cable clutch, so go easy on it when it starts to bite.

DA: Get back there and mind your Granny. Leave the controls to them that's in control. When I want advice I'll ask for it.

He lets up the clutch with a bang and they go kangaroo-hopping away up the road.

SON: So away we rolled, along the North Circular Road, belting out the old songs to make the road rise beneath us.

ALTOGETHER: He said I have a permit to travel near and far, To hell with your English permit, we want your motor car.

SON: And shouting out neighbourly greetings and dispensing free advice to the friends and acquaintances we passed on the way.

MA: *(to a bystander)* Get a new pair of legs, you bockedy-arsed old bar stool.

The rest of the family join in with taunting laughter.

MA: As we glided past Hanlon's Corner, a thought struck me. Where are we going?

DA: You're asking me where we're going? Is that what you want to know? You want to know where I'm taking you? Is that it? Is that the question youse are asking me? Is it? Is it?

Cries throughout of 'yes, yes,' tell us.

DA: I am taking youse all

[Yes, yes]

Up
Right up
To the very top
Of Howth Head.

Cheers, shouts of Yeah, alright, from the kids.

MA: Well, we're going the wrong bleeding way, aren't we?

DA jams on the anchors and a massive, unintelligible argument ensues, each one talking over the others to get their suggestion heard. The dispute culminates in MA, DA, SON and DAUGHTER getting out, grabbing a corner of the car each and physically turning it round.

And so, as we made our way back towards Doyle's, we came once more upon the friends and acquaintances we were after greeting so spiritedly, and they were swift to return those greetings in an equally fulsome and spirited manner.

The occupants of the car duck and fend off the jeers, verbal abuse and projectiles aimed at them.

DA: Mind the paintwork. This isn't mine. Have some respect for quality.

SON: As we cruised on past the Mater we observed a reverential silence.

DAUGHTER: All except the Granny.

GRANNY: Hail Mary full, of grace etc…

MA: Keep it down. Have a bit of respect for the sick and bereaved.

SON: And lulled by the steady hum of the motor, I slid into a dark pit of painful memories.

> *The others slowly turn round and look at him.*

GRANNY: Leave him alone. He's after sliding into a dark pit of painful memories.

MA: *(to DA)* And you keep your eyes on the road.

SON: I recalled how, for my fifth birthday all I really wanted was a fire engine. A metal one five times as big as my hand. It was in the window of a shop on Talbot Street. They told me all things come to him that waits, so I kept my mouth shut in the safe and sure knowledge that God knew my desires and would in the fullness of his wisdom make them known to the relevant parties. But come the big day, what the relevant parties had wrapped up and waiting in the kitchen were big and red alright, but they weren't for putting out fires.

The SON is confronted by a massive pair of boxing gloves.

DA: Go on, put your mitts inside them. They'll put hairs on your chest. Give us a look.

MA: You look a real little hero. Doesn't he, Mam?

GRANNY: He can barely lift them.

DA: A regular little Spider Kelly. Go on, son, put yer dooks up.

In an attempt to turn him into a man, DA persistently tries to raise the young fellow's hands into a fighting posture, and slaps his face to provoke him into an aggressive attitude. The greater the provocation, the more our young hero turns in on himself and silently suffers these slings and arrows of outrageous fortune.
The MA comes up behind him and begins trying to manipulate his arms, tosuch an extent that it soon becomes a battle between the parents in which the SON and his begloved fists become an unwitting and unwilling weapon.
The DA, taken in by the shouts of encouragement the MA is giving her SON, fails to realise what is going on until she, unable to hit her target efficiently with her SON's fists, resorts to using her own, pretending to be showing him what to do.
She lands a real stinger on the DA. The parents' eyes meet and the DA cops on immediately. He moves out of her reach, and disguises the real focus of his anger by giving out to the SON

for being a gibber and a nancy boy. The SON, standing centre stage, bursts into tears and is comforted by his sister.

DA: He's getting nothing off me.

MA: *(to SON)* You'll be getting nothing off him.

DA: He can stop snivelling for a start.

MA: Would you stop crying? Can you not just enjoy your birthday present and… just enjoy your birthday present.

The SON, meanwhile, is trying to take the gloves off—impossible, because with the gloves on he can't undo the laces.

DAUGHTER: Can he take them off now?

DA: He cannot.

MA: He's only after putting them on.

DA: He'll keep them on him until he starts learning how to use them properly.

MA: Did you hear that?

The SON looks as if he is about to burst into tears again.

DAUGHTER: He heard you.

MA: Ah, would you not just go over and give your old man a sock in the puss and we can get on with the birthday celebrations?

GRANNY: It's unnatural, so it is.

MA: What was that?

GRANNY: Grown men beating each other senseless and doing untold damage to each other for no good reason at all only the amusement of a few empty headed gobdaws.

MA: Sit down and have a mint.

GRANNY: But to subject a young lad to that kind of mindless violence, and him nothing but a child.

MA: Sweet Mother of God, would you shut her up before we're all driven to distraction? *(to DAUGHTER)* Give her a cup of tea quick. I think a cup of tea would do us all good. Nothing like a cup of scald to soothe the troubled soul, what? And we can cut the birthday cake.

They all sit down for tea. The DAUGHTER pours it out. They start to drink, but their attention is drawn back to the SON who is getting into all kinds of trouble trying to sugar his tea, stir it and drink it with boxing gloves on. They offer no help, but watch as his frustration builds, and just when he seems to be at breaking point, the DA leaps up.

DA: Come on, son, hit me. Give it to me square on the chin.

MA: Come on, son, now's your chance. Let it all out. Let him have it.

The SON, now totally confused and unable to act, bursts into tears again. The DA doubly disgusted, the MA doubly disappointed, they all walk away and leave him.

SON: It took about a week for the fuss to die down so the sister could take them off for me. I was getting quite handy with them at that stage. *(He demonstrates some of the skills he has developed with the gloves on before the DAUGHTER takes them off him.)* When they came off, my hands felt real little and cold. It was another six months before the old man started to talk to me again.

MA: *(to SON)* He meant no harm. He only wanted you to grow up properly. You can't blame him for how he ended up. It's the way he was reared. *(To DA)* Come here, do you remember what you said to me the week after we got married?

DA: *(thinks)* Was it to do with never giving me liver for dinner?

MA: You told me you knew you had become a man when you weren't afraid to use your fists to protect your reputation. I'll never forget that.

DA: Did I say that? God, I'm smarter than I thought I was.

GRANNY: I need to go.

DAUGHTER: She needs to go.

MA: Stop the car

DAUGHTER: It's the pedal on the left.

DA: Shut up.

DA brings it down far too hard on the brake, the vehicle screeches and skids to a standstill and the family are thrown forcibly together in an untidy bundle in the front of the car.

MA: *(to GRANNY)* Did you go yet?

GRANNY: Not yet.

MA: Good. Where are we?

SON: We looked around. We had passed through the shady groves of Ballybough, where kids tumbled over one another chasing crippled dogs and raced each other round the flats in stolen buggies. We had passed by the long, straight runway of Clonliffe Road, that pierces to the heart of Drumcondra, and now to our right lay the mature shades and verdant sports pitches of Fairview Park.

DA: Bring her into Gaffney's. I'm going to stretch my legs.

SON & DAUGHTER: *(in a chorus)* Get us a picnic, get us a picnic.

MA: Will I get them a picnic?

SON & DAGHTER: Ah go on, go on.

MA: What do you want, dog mess sandwiches and a bottle of your granny's water?

SON & DAGHTER: No, get us a proper one.

DA: Go on, get them a picnic.

GRANNY: They shouldn't be eating before their communion.

MA: They've had their breakfast already.

DA: There won't be any communion today.

GRANNY: Still and all, it's the principle of the thing.

MA: Get out of that. Come on away and do your business.

DA: Come here till I give you some money.

MA: Ah, I don't need your money.

The two women head off. DA and the kids get out of the car to stretch their legs. They play a game in which they are constantly trying to get ahead of him without him noticing, and he is constantly trying to stay ahead of them so as not to have to look at them. This goes on throughout the leg stretching.

DA: Ah, she's a good woman, your mother. Do you know what I mean? We've had our differences, but at the end of the day, do you know what I'm saying? She's a real, honest, straightforward, honest-to-God, straight down the line kind of, d'you know? She would never take advantage, in the way of, she never ever, to my knowledge, and I should know, sure haven't we been married for, oh, we're married that long and I can tell you in all that time she never once ever, well put it this way, she is utterly, completely and utterly straight up and down the line, fair and square the only woman, no the only person I can honestly say is honestly, honestly, em, honest.

DAUGHTER: I wouldn't be so sure of that.

DA: What?

MA and GRANNY enter flying, carrying a bag of picnic.

MA: Get in the car *(womanhandling the GRANNY into the back seat.)*

DA: Me legs aren't stretched yet.

MA: Don't argue, just get in the car

DA: What's the hurry? I was just starting to enjoy the day, the view, the trees.

MA boots DA into the driving seat, gets into the passenger seat, fishes the car key out of his pocket, starts up the engine

MA: Put the clutch down.

DA: Hold on. Wait a minute.

MA: Put the bleeding clutch down.

DAUGHTER: It's the one on the left.

DA: Thank you. I have that worked out by this stage.

MA: Then put it down.

He puts it down. MA puts the car into gear, pushes DA's accelerator leg down, smacks up his clutch leg, and they take off. She steers until they are on an even keel, then hands over to him. At this point she looks over her shoulder to check they aren't being followed.

DA: What's the story? Where's the fire?

MA: *(to the kids)* There's a pan loaf courtesy of Pat the Baker, cans of Coke courtesy of Pat the Barman, six individual pork pies, a bag of funsize Mars bars…

SON: Deadly.

MA: A packet of cheese and onion crisps, two more packets of cheese and onion crisps, an economy packet of crisps, flavour cheese and onion, a pair of tights, a tub of HB ice cream, a tube of toothpaste.

DAUGHTER: Toothpaste?

MA: Oh yeah, give it here, that was a mistake.

DA: Why did you get toothpaste?

GRANNY: She's after robbing half the grocery store.

DA: What?

MA: Keep you eyes on the road.

DA: Did I hear you correctly?

MA: Do you want the ham and the cheese in the one sandwich or shall I put them in separate?

DA: If I have not misinterpreted the message coming through to me from the rear of the vehicle as communicated by your recent companion in an excursion to, amongst other things, acquire food, the means by which you acquired the said food were, to say the least, nefarious.

MA: Probably.

DA: Illegal.

MA: I don't doubt it.

DA: You purloined it.

MA: You could say that.

DA: Took it in a clandestine manner with no intention of settling the bill.

MA: If you like.

DA: You robbed it?

MA: Yes, I robbed it. I went in and robbed it. It is robbed. What's that to you?

DA: Why did you rob it?

MA: Because I did. Because I'm good at it. Well, I used to be good at it. My God, why are you so interested in where your food comes from all of a sudden? You never normally even look at it before you shove it in your face.

DA: Do you mean to say that wasn't the first time?

MA: Oh you poor holy innocent. Janey, there's none so blind as can't see.

DA: Did the rest of youse know about this?

SON & DAUGHTER: Of course.

They tut and hum and hah to emphasise his stupidity. There is a silence as the revelation sinks in.

DA: Let me get this straight.

MA: *(reaching for the steering wheel)* Get the car straight first.

DA: You have for some time now been robbing, what, food?

MA: Sometimes.

DA: What do you mean sometimes? Did you rob other things? Clothes? Jewellery?

MA: Do I have any jewellery?

DA: Only that necklace with the pearly bits and the gold clasp. Ah, you didn't, did you?

MA: I only robbed what was strictly necessary for the family's health and well being. Physical or mental.

DA: How long have you been at it?

MA: God, would you ever drop the subject?

DAUGHTER: She started when Mooney's got burned down.

SON: And you were out of a job.

DA: When I lost the job at Mooney's? Things was alright then. I never heard you complain about it.

MA: Bleeding right you didn't.

DA: So why did you start robbing then?

MA: Jesus wept. Have you no recollection at all of what happened at that time?

DA: I was in a state of shock.

DAUGHTER: You were unbearable.

MA: Do you not remember the times you came rolling in blue blazing blind drunk at two in the morning, piss running down the front of your trousers, pulled a stack of old betting slips and a two bob bit out of your pocket and told me that was what was left of the week's housekeeping? Do you not? Do you not remember sitting like a great streak of misery by the fire day after day without a word of greeting for any of us, making no contribution to the running of the house? You never bothered to ask where the food was coming from then. You never bothered to ask how the fire stayed alight. You kept eating the rashers and drinking the tea and doing what you liked with your welfare money. You only ever saw what it suited you to see, and you're no different now.

DA: You only had to tell me.

MA: And what? Tell you and what? You would have become even more unbearable.

No way. I dealt with it in my own way and that's no business of yours and never will be world without end, Amen.

SON & DAUGHTER: Amen.

GRANNY: *(fingering her beads)* … now and at the hour of our death, Amen.

DA: But robbing things?

MA: Well what do you suggest?

DA: Why didn't you go out and find a job?

MA: Why didn't you?

They stare aggressively at each other, noses almost touching.

SON: Break.

He breaks them apart and they stare out of their respective side windows, arms folded. Slowly the car begins to veer off the road. Everyone in the back seat panics. The DAUGHTER grabs the steering wheel and takes effective control of the car.

DAUGHTER: Would the pair of youse ever grow up?

DA: But I mean to say, am I the only one? Does everybody else approve of her… her activities?

DAUGHTER: No.

DA: *(relieved)* You don't?

DAUGHTER: I think it's disgusting.

MA: Now listen, you.

DAUGHTER: No. You listen. You shut up and listen for a change. You think you're so great, robbing things and we'll say no more about it. You think you can solve it all that easy. Well it's not that easy. You always take the easy way out. Anything for a quiet life. You say you want the best, but you're not prepared to stick your neck out for it. You didn't want to help him. You only wanted to help yourself.

During the preceding speech the DAUGHTER has worked her way into the front seat and ends up driving the car sitting on her father's knee.

MA: Get out from underneath your daughter.

DA wriggles out, a bit ashamed, and into the back seat.

MA: Have you had your say?

DAUGHTER: I have not. And I'm damned if I'm going to let you get the last word in, tie it all in a neat little bundle and feck it out the window as if it had never been said. You wanted us to be the best kids in the street. You wanted the neighbours' kids to be jealous of us. What did you do?

MA: I did my best by you.

DAUGHTER: You sent me to dancing classes. For God's sake, look at me. I couldn't dance.

MA: Of course you couldn't. That's why I sent you to classes.

DAUGHTER: You won't even begin to listen to me, will you? I can see no point in carrying on. I'm running my head into a brick wall here. That's it. This is where it stops. I've had enough.

She stops the car.

SON: As we slowed to a halt, we all looked outside of the car and saw we had reached Raheny. Steam was coming off the tarmac and the trees were full of cats, eyeing us up as they digested their dinner. Along one side of the road the carcasses of recently sacrificed shopkeepers were hanging up to dry, on the other the parish priest was pumping the lees of the local gentry out of the tail end of eleven o'clock Mass.

GRANNY: Mass? Where?

DAUGHTER: I'm off. I'll see youse all later.

The DAUGHTER and the GRANNY get out of the car.

DA: Can I get back into the driving seat now?

MA: *(to SON)* Don't let your Granny get into that church.

The SON grabs hold of the GRANNY and holds her back.

GRANNY: I won't be long. You can wait out here if you want. I'll be out once communion is finished.

MA: *(slamming door of car so DA can't get in)* Would you ever wait until they are all back inside the car? *(to SON)* Bring your granny back here before she gets inside that church. *(to DAUGHTER)* Come back here and finish what you've started.

DAUGHTER: Leave me alone. I've had enough of your small-minded maternal manipulations. I've said I want to go and I'm going.

SON: *(to DAUGHTER)* Would you come and help me with Granny? She's stronger than she looks.

DA: Come on back here all of youse. Shake hands and make up like men and we can go off on our day out.

MA: Shut up you and get your daughter back into the car.

DAUGHTER: I'm not getting back in.

GRANNY: *(to SON)* Come in with me if you want. They can wait for us out here. We can come out once the communion is finished.

MA: Don't you dare go in there with her.

SON: I'm not. Come on back to the car, Granny. *(to DAUGHTER)* Come here and give me a hand.

DAUGHTER: I'm sorry, I'm not moving.

MA: Move.

SON: Please.

DAUGHTER: No.

GRANNY: Come on.

SON: No.

DA: Please.

DAUGHTER: I'm not moving.

MA: Up yours then.

DA: Ah lads, lads, lads. For the sake of all the sacred saints. We only have the use of the car for the one day. If we don't do it today it may never get done. *(He gets down on his knees.)* Look, I'm on my knees pleading to youse, mend your differences and climb back in again. You're breaking my heart.

They are all moved to hear this touching speech, including the GRANNY, whose defences drop.

DAUGHTER: Since you put it like that.

She walks back to the car.

MA: *(to SON)* Grab your Granny now, quick.

The SON wrong foots the GRANNY and in a twinkling all five of them are back in the car in the positions they first occupied. The DA starts the engine no problem, engages the gear and starts off.

DA: There now. I'm getting the hang of this alright.

DAUGHTER: We're going backwards.

DA: Oh yes. My mistake.

He changes gear again and they head off forwards.

GRANNY: That's it. My last chance is gone now. I did my best. I can only say it wasn't my own responsibility. I was coerced.

The others all start to give out, complaining that it isn't their fault. They end up all agreeing that it is the DA's day off and he deserves to be able to choose what he does with it.

SON: Where is it you're working now?

DA: Ah, you know, up there on Thomas Street.

SON: Where exactly on Thomas Street?

DA: You know, Des Kelly's.

SON: Des Kelly the carpet man?

DA: Yeah.

SON: That's very strange, because I was in there the other day and they hadn't heard of you.

MA: Wind the windows down, would you? This heat is choking me.

They all roll down the windows.

SON: How come they never heard of you?

DA: Ah well, they, eh, they wouldn't have. I don't exactly work in Des Kelly's.

SON: Not in Des Kelly's?

DA: No. More kind of around Des Kelly's.

SON: Do you drive for them?

MA: Him drive?

DA: No no no no. It's more like, I work near to Des Kelly's.

DAUGHTER: You work in the art school.

MA: You never mentioned the art school.

SON: You don't work in Des Kelly's at all.

DA: I work over the road from Des Kelly's.

SON: Yes, but you don't work for Des Kelly.

MA: Why didn't you tell us you worked in the art school? Do they have you caretaking? Sure they wouldn't let you teach, would they? Sure what do you know about painting? You can't even emulsion the ceiling.

DAUGHTER: Tell them what you do.

DA: I just do a bit of modelling

MA: You what?

SON: Like making little aeroplanes?

DA: No. Modelling. You know. They draw me.

MA: They draw you? Who'd want to draw you? I can't stand to look at you too long and I'm married to you. You've a face like the rear end of a public refuse collection vehicle. What do you mean anyway, they draw you?

DA: You know. They draw me. With pencils and things.

SON: In the nip?

MA: Ah no!

DAUGHTER: Go on, tell them. He takes his clothes off and stands there in front of a bunch of strangers till they stare at him.

MA: You do not. Do you?

DA: I do life modelling. They draw my body. They couldn't draw my body if I was wearing clothes.

MA: You stand there in your nude?

SON: Do you ever get excited?

MA: You never stand in front of me in your nude.

DA: You never ask me to. And you certainly never pay me.

GRANNY: So I'm well into my Fourth Decade, doing my best to ignore the foul behaviour being discussed all around me, when I notice that the car has slowed down to a stop on a quiet and well-to-do little stretch of the Howth Road. The windows of the houses are open and the local residents are all hanging out and bending their ears to hear what the heathens in the funny car are talking about.

They all suddenly look outside of the car in surprise.

DA: Close the windows for God's sake.

The SON and DAUGHTER close the windows as the MA is speaking.

MA: So you're ashamed now, are you? It's more than you are when you're displaying yourself to people in public. If they want to listen, let them listen. Let them get an earful and see what they think. Open them windows. I'm not suffocating for the sake of this hypocrite.

DA: *(whispering)* At least keep your voices down. Don't be giving these leeches anything they don't have to pay for.

MA: My God, I didn't realise I was married to a sick and sorry little pervert.

DA: I am not a pervert. It's a job. I do it for a job and it pays to keep youse lot. Anyway, what's wrong with taking off your clothes? Everybody has a body. It's perfectly natural and normal and there's nothing there that hasn't been seen before. Why should I apologise for myself? I'm not ashamed.

MA: Then why did you hide it from us all this time?

DA: Because I knew you would react like this.

DAUGHTER: Take your clothes off now then.

DA: No I will not.

DAUGHTER: I thought you said you weren't ashamed.

DA: Don't be so stupid. I'm not going to take them off here.

DAUGHTER: You'll take them off in front of a load of complete strangers but not in front of your own family, is that right?

DA: No.

MA: Go on then, get them off.

DA: Stop it. Would you ever cop yourselves on?

MA: We are copped on. It's you, you pathetic exhibitionist, getting up in front of a room full of Mary Janes from Blackrock with their pencils sharpened and flashing your packet. God knows there's little enough to see, but you might at least keep it to yourself and go and find a man's job.

DAUGHTER: One you aren't ashamed to admit to doing.

DA: I'm not ashamed. I'm not. If I didn't have to keep you lot I wouldn't be doing it anyway. If Mooney's hadn't burned down I wouldn't have had to do it.

MA: You're ashamed, and you damn well should be ashamed. Look at me. *(He doesn't)* Look at me when I'm talking to you. You're a bundle of filth. I feel sorry for you. Have you nothing more to say? You're pathetic. Pervert.

DA: Thief.

Silent and grim, DA starts the engine and drives off. All are tight lipped, bar the GRANNY, who resumes her devotions.

SON: I burned down Mooney's.

MA: Good lad. You what?

DAUGHTER: Did you just say you burned down Mooney's?

SON: Did you not know that? Strange that. You seem to know everything else. Yeah, I burned down Mooney's.

MA: Don't kick your Da while he's down.

DA: He'll have to do better than that. You couldn't burn a slice of toast.

MA: Yes, he could. He's great with a box of matches. *(To SON)* Do you remember that time you nearly burned the end off your thumb playing with matches,

and it came up in a big blister like a ping pong ball, and I had to write a letter to the school and tell them you did it on the cooker?

DAUGHTER: I don't believe you burned down Mooney's.

SON: Well, I did.

DA: You never burned down Mooney's. Don't make me laugh.

SON: I did so. I did. I climbed in through the little side window by the bakery and I went into the foreman's office and emptied all the drawers I could open into the middle of the floor, and I went and got a plastic bottle of meths from beside one of the machines and I poured it all over the heap of books, then I got a match and lit it and dropped it on the pile, and then I climbed back out of the window. I did it all before dinner, and I tore my trousers on the way out and told you I did it on old man Comiskey's fence, do you remember?

DA: You made all that up. You got it out of the newspaper. All that about the bottle of meths. You were talking to one of the lads that worked there. We're not taken in by your stories.

MA: Shut up you. If he says he burned down Mooney's then he burned down Mooney's. He's my son and he can do what he likes. *(To SON)* Don't be minding him now.

SON: You don't see, do you? Do you not remember what happened to Hayden's? To the Spar shop round the back of Croke Park? The fire in the Health Board in Charles Street? I did that. That was me. I started them fires. They all burned down because of me. Think of that. Think of what I wrecked and destroyed. Doesn't that make you tremble? Doesn't it make you sick? The senseless waste. All the time you spent on the dole. Aren't you angry with me? Take me to the guards, I don't care. I can face it. I'm ready for the likes of them. Hand me over. I don't care.

DAUGHTER: Are you telling us you were the Phibsboro pyromaniac?

SON: Hah!

DAUGHTER: We have the Phibsboro pyromaniac in the car with us.

DA: Yeah, and Jack the Ripper, too.

MA: Were you Jack the Ripper? Well listen here, I'm the Blessed Virgin Mary, and I can tell you now, your man upstairs takes a very dim view of your activities.

DAUGHTER: Well, you want to watch out the pair of youse. You've got Ulrike Meinhof in the back here and I'll sort you out with my Kalashnikov if you don't get your act together.

DA: Listen you, stop using them long words and behave yourself or Grandmother Christmas in the middle there won't be bringing you any presents this year.

SON: Stop it all of you. I've done terrible terrible things and you don't seem to realise what terrible terrible things I've done.

DA: Don't worry. Calm down. Your secret's safe with us. Just sit back and enjoy your holidays.

The car splutters and dies. DA tries the ignition a few times but there is no response. In a fit of anger he gets out to look under the bonnet, but comes back to shout into the car at his son.

DA: This is all your fault. If you hadn't started playing stupid games I would have been concentrating on my driving.

SON: I never did anything.

DA: You're a bleeding liability, you are. We should have left you at home. Come out here and make yourself useful.

The SON gets out and the two of them try and open the bonnet, but are unable to do so. As they are fiddling, the DAUGHTER calmly leans over from the back seat and pulls the bonnet release knob, which causes the bonnet to pop up and hit the DA and SON on the nose. They both immediately begin to blame each other for releasing the bonnet without warning the other. The DA lifts the bonnet and starts to fish around. He clearly doesn't know what he's doing, and disconnects various things he shouldn't before coming back round to the car with the SON behind him. They both get back in and the DA tries the ignition again, to no avail.

DA: I don't know what's wrong with it.

DAUGHTER: You're out of petrol.

MA gets out in disgust and slams the door. DA gets out and slams the door.
DAUGHTER gets out, slams the door and walks off. SON, not to be outdone, gets out and slams the door. Each time the door slams the GRANNY leaps withfright. Only the GRANNY is left in the car. As she goes on saying her rosary, the others, unable to speak with frustration, wander round outside the car wordlessly expressing their anger and annoyance with each other. When they are at each other's throats and about to commit silent murder, the DAUGHTER calmly walks through with a can of petrol and empties it into the car. The others watch in amazement. When she has finished and the cap is back on, the DA rushes to get back in the driving seat, but she stops him, reaches in, pops open the bonnet and starts putting back the pieces he took out and disconnected. The others keep watching in surprise and delight.

MA: Aren't you great? *(to DA)* Isn't she brilliant?

DAUGHTER: *(to DA)* Turn it over.

DA climbs in and tries the engine. It starts first time. They all applaud.

DA: Fair play. You're a better man than I gave you credit for.

MA: She's very handy. You've earned your dinner today anyway.

SON: That was amazing. Where did you learn to do all that?

DAUGHTER: Mister Dowling.

DA: Dinny Dowling? No better man. He's great, old Dinny. A great old skin. A real sport.

MA: He'd give you the shirt off his back.

SON: Did he teach you to drive as well?

DAUGHTER: No.

SON: Where did you learn that?

DAUGHTER: Dilip.

SON: Who?

DAUGHTER: From St. Peter's Road.

MA: Philip?

DAUGHTER: No. Dilip.

SON: What sort of a name is that? Dilip.

DAUGHTER: It's Indian.

MA: What's he doing with an Indian name?

DA: You mean the coloured feller whose parents keep the shop opposite the church?

MA: You had driving lessons with him?

DAUGHTER: Yes.

MA: What did you go to him for?

DAUGHTER: I didn't go to him. I met him in Doyle's. He said he was a driving instructor and I asked him would he teach me.

MA: Well, where did you get the money to pay him?

DAUGHTER: I didn't.

DA: You didn't pay him? By God, you're the hairy one and no mistake. Fiddling the free driving lessons. Fair play to you.

DAUGHTER: I didn't say I didn't pay him.

MA: So where did you get the money?

DAUGHTER: I didn't pay him with money.

DA: What did you pay him with?

DAUGHTER: Sex.

EVERYBODY: What?

DAUGHTER: I often wonder what my parents' honeymoon must have been like. In a caravan. In Bettystown. In the land where the sixties never swung.

In a trice we are in that very caravan. DA is in bed, under a blanket, trembling with fear. MA is at a safe distance, dressed to do battle.

MA: I'm not taking this off until you put that paraffin lamp out. (*DA reluctantly does so.*) Jesus, I can't see a thing. (*She bangs her shin against an unseen obstacle.*) Ah, me shin, ah, ah, ah. Where are you?

DA: I'm over here. (*MA feels her way over and into the bed.*) Are you ready now?

MA: Wait till I get my socks off. Now. Come here to me, lover boy. Ooh yes, ooh, I can feel it now. Ooh, it's very long. It's kind of floppy. It has tassels on the end of it.

DA, who is looking increasingly worried the more she feels, on hearing about the tassels decides to do some exploring himself.

DA: That's my pyjama cord you have in your hand. Here, let me show you.

He gently guides her hand to the correct spot. As soon as she hits it she lets out an almighty scream and leaps from the bed. In her haste to get away she bangs her leg once more against the hidden obstacle.

MA: Ah, ah, ah, suffering Jesus, my shin.

DA: What's the matter? Come back to bed, will you?

MA: No way. I'm not coming near that thing.

DA: Why not?

MA: It's like some little animal.

DA: *(hurt)* It's not that little.

MA: Listen, throw us over the pillow and I'll sleep here on the floor. Just for tonight. We can try it again tomorrow when we're sober. (*DA reluctantly throws her the pillow.*) Night then.

DA: Night. I'll just play with it myself so.

MA: Don't you dare!

DAUGHTER: But of course we can never really know what happened on our parent's honeymoon, can we?

SON: Are you saying you slept with him?

GRANNY: *(educationally)* You can't have sex when you're asleep. You have to be awake.

DA: You did the dirty with a darkie? Are you saying you're no longer a virgin?

DAUGHTER: Get real.

DA: Who'll want to marry you now?

DAUGHTER: Who says I want to get married?

DA: But with a darkie.

MA: I think he's very good looking. Lovely bum on him.

DA: There's a name for girls like you.

DAUGHTER: Yeah. Liberated.

DA: I didn't sweat blood raising my only daughter to… to…

DAUGHTER: To what?

DA: To have sex.

DAUGHTER: You make me laugh, and you waggling your langer at all and sundry up in the art school.

DA: At least I don't, you know…

DAUGHTER: What?

DA: Do the business.

DAUGHTER: Well, more fool you.

MA: I should hope not. A married man, and well past your prime. I don't know though. I think it's very romantic to have your first experience with an exotic Eastern potentate with beautifully formed features.

DAUGHTER: I never said it was my first.

DA: Do you mean there are others?

MA: How many others?

DAUGHTER: God, I don't know. I don't keep a record.

MA: Too many to keep a count of?

DA: I don't believe this.

MA: Like who? Give us some examples.

DAUGHTER: Well you don't think I learned about car maintenance for nothing, do you?

DA: What?

MA: Dinny Dowling?

DA: He's older than me.

MA: He's married.

DA: I knew it. The filthy scut. I knew he was never to be trusted. I'll kill him.

SON: What was he like in bed?

DA brakes the car to a standstill.

DA: That's it. Get out of the car now.

DAUGHTER: I'm not moving.

MA: Do as your father says.

SON: Leave her alone.

DA: *(to SON)* You can get out as well.

DAUGHTER: What's he done?

DA: Shut up, you whore.

SON: *(to DA)* Pervert.

MA: *(to SON)* Coward.

DAUGHTER: *(to MA)* Thief.

MA: *(to DAUGHTER)* Now listen you…

DAUGHTER: *(to MA)* No, you listen…

DA: *(to DAUGHTER)* No, you listen…

SON: *(to DA)* No, you listen…

MA: *(to SON)* You listen…

DA: *(to MA)* Be quiet all of you and listen…

DAUGHTER: *(to DA)* You shut up and listen for once.

MA: *(to DAUGHTER)* Just listen.

SON: *(to MA)* You listen.

GRANNY: Shhhhhhhhhhh. *(All four of them look round at the GRANNY, still and quiet in the centre of it all.)* It would do no harm if we were all quiet and just listened for a while. *(For once they all just do as they are told and keep quiet. The silence begins to dissolve their anger.)* We'd arrived at Sutton Cross. Very cross indeed, and I have to say, it looked like that was the only cross I would be seeing this Sunday, bar the one on the end of my beads. But everyone seemed to realise we were at a crossroads so we sat in contemplative silence and listened.

SON: To someone cutting grass with a manual lawnmower.

MA: To a child with allergy-related asthma coughing her throat raw.

DAUGHTER: To bees pollinating clover.

DA: To the sea, away in the distance, relentlessly wearing away at the shoreline.

GRANNY: Why not cut our losses and turn back now? We can be home for a nice early dinner, and I'll be able to get to Mass this evening.

DA: No. The sea is calling us. I said we were going up Howth Head, and I am a man of my word. We've come this far. We're going all the way.

With measured precision he eases the car into gear, accelerates gently and executes a perfect take-off.

SON: And over Sutton Cross he drove, straight and true. The traffic lights were even green. A man in control of his destiny.

DAUGHTER: Well, in control of his vehicle.

MA: Well, in control of someone else's vehicle.

The car hits a pothole and bounces them all two feet in the air. They are all winded but before they get their breath back to complain, the DA raises his hand defensively.

DA: It wasn't me. It was the road. Blame the Corporation.

They all rub their injured self-esteem, regain their composure and start looking around them .

DAUGHTER: Above and to our right lay Howth Castle and demesne.

SON: Below and to our left, past the railway, the dark waters of the Irish Sea.

DAUGHTER: And ahead.

MA: Ahead.

GRANNY: Ahead.

They all close their eyes, raise their noses to the air and sniff deeply.

SON: Fried cod and chips.

MA: Baskets of reeking fishermen's socks being carried into Sally O'Malley's laundry.

DAUGHTER: Old ones and kids slowly baking in suntan lotion.

GRANNY: Incense and pennies in collection plates.

DA: Pints of porter and balls of malt.

MA: Steady on. You're driving.

SON: And there she was.

They all open their eyes together and view the promised land.

SON: Howth Harbour.

DAUGHTER: Scarred and hoary fishermen scratched their crotches and sang songs as they stitched up holes in their nets.

MA: Happy holiday families with rakes of kids dripping ice cream and snot wandered aimlessly across the road.

DA: Ireland's Eye winked at us in the sunlight.

GRANNY: There's a lovely little church. We could just take a quick peek inside.

MA: Well, here we are. Our final goal and destination.

DA shakes his head grimly.

SON: Ah go on, let's park up, get out and enjoy the sunshine.

DAUGHTER: We're in Howth, aren't we? That's good enough.

MA: I for one don't intend to go an inch further. You can do what you like. I'm going to get a cup of tea and a sambo and relax.

DA: We are going all the way.

DAUGHTER: All the way where?

DA: All the way up to the very ben of Howth. The pinnacle. The summit.

They all consider this for a second.

SON: Strictly speaking that's doubling back on yourself a bit, going round through the village.

DAUGHTER: Considering the direction we've been going, all the way would really be to the end of the pier.

SON: Which pier?

DAUGHTER: The East pier. The other one would definitely be going backwards.

SON: You're wrong there. The East pier goes nearly directly north then takes a ninety degree turn back to the West.

MA: Lookit, if we stay here in the harbour you can walk down whichever pier you want and I can sit down on the grass there and get a bit of colour to my legs.

DA: I said clearly from the very beginning. The top is the top and that's where…

GRANNY: Balscadden.

Having sat in a semi-trance-like state through the preceding discussions, the oracle in the back has spoken. She is accorded the customary respect.

DA: Who said that?

MA: What's she on about?

DAUGHTER: Balwhat?

SON: Push your teeth in further and say it again.

GRANNY: Me teeth is fine. Balscadden.

They await further clarification with open mouths. None comes.

MA: Well if that's that then, I'll hop out if it's all the same to you and start sunning myself.

GRANNY: No, no, no. If you're determined to go all the way. The road there past the end of the pier. The Balscadden road. Up to the cliffs.

SON: The little road to the right?

DAUGHTER: I often wondered where that went.

DA: Up to the cliffs?

GRANNY: To the very end and beyond. You can't go any further than that. You stand there with the whole of Ireland at your back.

DA: The whole of Ireland.

MA: Looking out to the east. The exotic east.

DA: The Irish Sea.

DAUGHTER: Wales.

SON: Liverpool.

DA: London.

MA: Europe.

SON: Eastern Europe.

DA: Russia.

DAUGHTER: China.

MA: Japan.

SON: The Pacific Ocean.

DA: California.

DAUGHTER: New York.

MA: The Atlantic Ocean.

DA: Galway.

SON: Athlone.

DA: By Jesus, if we look hard enough we'll be able to see ourselves from the back looking out over it all.

That's one to consider. So they do. Hmmm.

GRANNY: Well?

MA: I'm game.

SON & DAUGHTER: Why not.

DA: Right so. Balscadden it is.

He takes the right turn and follows the snaking path of the road up towards the cliffs. The family crane their necks eagerly and follow the car's progress. All apart from the GRANNY, whose reminiscence button has been pushed.

GRANNY: It was never easy being little. Most of my younger sisters were bigger than me by the time they were eleven or twelve. There was only one older and she died of the pneumonia before she was old enough to give me a bit of moral support. At family gatherings I'd sometimes get beaten down under the table in the rush for the food. When I tried to push my way up again people would think I was the dog and kick me back. Big gombeen men of uncles with heads like heifers would heave me up against the wall with their hairy sausagemeat hands, ah you must be the baby of the family, then reach down and try to feel my behind when they thought nobody was looking and worse than that even sometimes, with breath on them like stale porter and Sweet Afton and stumpy yellow and black teeth smiling and slobbering over you, nnng nnng nnng. And sharing a bed with two others, the only way to stop being pushed out onto the floor was to be sure and get in the middle, and every time one of the others moved I'd be choked in a blast of bad gas and feet smells and praying all the time neither of them would roll over on top of me and crush me to death. Sometimes they forgot about me completely. They went off shopping by times and locked the front door so I couldn't get out. I realise now I could have climbed out through the window. Not then though. I thought that was just the way of it. I sat there at dinner with a poxy spoonful of cabbage and two spuds in front of me and watched while the men were dished out fourth and fifth helpings, great wedges of cow meat and steaming heaps of vegetables and them laughing and stuffing themselves and laughing again. God help me, I had to choke it back in spite of the hunger was on me. But choke it back I did. And going to confession hoping to share it with someone and you know the priest isn't listening to a word you're saying because he gives you the same penance every week, no matter what you tell him. Then I went to a dance in Glasnevin and a fellow told me I reminded him of Betty Grable. So I married him. And do you know what? (*The others ignore her.*) Do you know what? (*They still ignore her.*) He took no notice of me either.

The DA finally registers there is some noise coming from the back. He looks round.

DA: Did you say something?

GRANNY: Stop the car.

DA: What?

GRANNY: Wall!

He puzzles, realises, turns round again but it is too late. With a gentle THUD the car hits the end wall of the Balscadden road. The passengers are shaken but not stirred. The DA is sheepish.

DA: Sorry lads.

MA: They might have let us know the road was going to run out.

SON: Where do we go from here?

GRANNY: Up the path. We have to do the last leg of the journey under our own steam.

They hop out, slamming the doors behind them. The DAUGHTER goes round to check the damage to the car.

DAUGHTER: Nothing there a bit of rubbing compound won't sort out.

DA: You've talked yourself into a job there.

She shoots him a look.

And don't be expecting payment in your usual manner neither.

MA: Well, are we ready?

The family line up, the GRANNY in the middle, MA and SON on one side, DA and DAUGHTER on the other. As a unit they start on the final upward haul.

DAUGHTER: So we started off towards the cliffs.

SON: Hopping over the rocks that had tumbled onto the path.

MA: Scratching our legs off of the gorse bushes.

GRANNY: Son.

DA: What?

GRANNY: Did you love your father?

Bang. This stops them all dead in their tracks.

DA: What?

GRANNY: Your father. Did you love him?

The DA looks around to the others for some help. He clearly isn't going to get any.

DA: That's a very tricky question. Love him. I mean, it depends what you mean.

DAUGHTER: Mean by what?

DA: You know. Love.

DAUGHTER: You can't get much clearer than that.

DA: Ah, but things was different back then. You didn't do that kind of thing back then.

SON: What kind of thing?

DA: You know, love and all that. I mean, not your father anyway. I mean I hardly knew the man. He used to cross over the street and avoid us if he saw us coming. I don't think he ever said more than five words in a row to me in his whole life.

GRANNY: What's your abiding memory of him?

DA: Sitting in the chair with the strap on his lap waiting for one of us to move so he could lather us with it.

MA: He was a bully.

DA: That's unfair.

MA: He was a bloody big selfish thug of a bully.

DA: He was a man.

MA: Exactly. It's no excuse.

DA: He did what he could.

MA: Bollocks he did. He did what he wanted.

DA: Well, he died anyway, so that's that.

GRANNY: Son, my old legs is tired. Will you carry me the last bit of the way to the cliffs?

As a conclusion and finale, he sweeps the old girl up in his arms and the family advance once more towards the edge of it all.

SON: We were close now. Very close.

DAUGHTER: We could see more sea than land.

MA: More sky than sea.

DAUGHTER: The mailboat was steaming away towards the horizon.

SON: A seagull kacked on my head. Sploop.

DAUGHTER: Ha Ha. That's full of acid. You'll end up with a bald spot there.

GRANNY: You know when your father died.

DA: Of course I do.

GRANNY: It wasn't his heart like they said. Somebody killed him.

DA: Killed him?

GRANNY: Poisoned him.

DA: Who killed him?

GRANNY: His mortal enemy.

DA: Who? Who was he?

GRANNY: Someone who hated your father bitterly. Someone whose life your father made unbearable.

DA: He poisoned him? The old feller? My own father? Why did you never tell me?

GRANNY: I wanted to tell you. I wanted to wait until you were old enough. But son…

DA: Ma?

GRANNY: You never really grew up.

MA: This is it. We can't go any farther.

SON: Mind you don't slip on the loose rocks.

The SON and DAUGHTER peer over the edge with much trepidation.

DAUGHTER: Jesus, that's a long way down.

DA: Tell me who did it.

MA: Mind your mother.

DA: Tell me who did it, Ma. Tell me and by God and the blessed Saint Patrick and Saint Martin of Porres and little Saint Theresa and little Saint Bernadette and the blessed Holy Child of Prague and the blood and body of our blessed saviour and by the bleeding sacred heart of Jesus and the Blessed Virgin and all the Angels and Saints, and on my life mother and on your life, I swear I will seek them out and by these hands I will revenge the death of my own Da with their very life.

DAUGHTER: And then it happened.

GRANNY: Son, I killed him.

The action whams into slow motion to enable us to appreciate the full complexity of the DA's reaction.

SON: A hideous warp spasm the like of which we had never seen gripped him.

DAUGHTER: The muscles of his body knotted and bulged out like potatoes in a plastic sack.

MA: His eyes swivelled round in their sockets.

SON: His beer belly trembled and vibrated hideously as if it was about to explode and spew forth bile and venom and poorly digested convenience foods.

MA: Every hair on his body stood on end.

DAUGHTER: Every hair?

MA: Even the ones not visible to the eye.

SON: And then, gathering every ounce of his inconsiderable strength, marshalling all the force his belaboured body could muster…

A fierce PRIMAL ROAR emerges from the depths of the DA's being.

SON: He fucked his mother out into the sea.

MA: Language.

SON: I'm sorry. That's what he did though.

And that is precisely what he does. Except…

DAUGHTER: But then something happened.

SON: Beyond all human understanding.

MA: Before our very eyes.

SON: Instead of tumbling downwards.

MA: She just hovered there for a moment.

DAUGHTER: And out from her back, from somewhere underneath her cardigan, a magnificent pair of white feathered wings appeared.

SON: Began to beat slowly, majestically.

MA: And lifted her up, spiralling up into the firmament, up and away out of sight in the glare of the noonday sun.

DAUGHTER: And all we could do was shield our eyes trying to watch her ascent, feeling the pufts of air from the beating of her wings get softer on our faces as she disappeared above us.

DA: Oh, lads. Oh, Jesus.

MA: Meanwhile the quare fellow, having realised what he had done, suddenly found himself right on the cliff edge, the balance of his weight, due to the force exerted in throwing his Ma, inclined fractionally too much in an easterly direction, leading to the one inevitable consequence.

DA: Whoop.

Delicately, balletically, he tumbles over the cliff. The other three watch, grimacing with each impact as he bounces, tumbles, spins, woof, doof, bif baf bof and lands with a miniscule splash far below in the ocean.

MA: And all we could do was watch as he disappeared among the foam of breakers around the rocks.

SON: She'd gone up.

DAUGHTER: He'd gone down.

MA: And we were left standing in the middle.

So that's where they stay momentarily, uncertain as to what to do next.

DAUGHTER: I suppose we'd better go back so.

MA: I suppose.

SON: So we went back to the car and headed home.

DAUGHTER: I drove.

MA: Slowly.

SON: Very well though, I thought.

DAUGHTER: On the opposite side of the road there was a mighty tailback of cars full of families like ourselves on the way to Howth for a nice day out.

MA: They'll be lucky if they ever get there with traffic like that.

SON: As we went back through Raheny it occured to me that… (*He notices the MA has gotten out a handerchief and is dabbing her eyes.*) What's the matter?

MA: Ah, nothing. It's alright. It's funny though, I kind of miss him in a way. You know, he wasn't the worst.

SON: Maybe we should have let her go to Mass.

DAUGHTER: It won't make any difference to her now.

SON: It was a big match day and the streets around Croker were full of smiling culchies staggering about poking each other in the eye with flags and singing totally unintelligible songs, tongues lolling out of their mouths like half chewed hamburgers.

DAUGHTER: I winged a few of them with the bumper, but they were only flesh wounds so we let it go and ploughed on along the North Circular and back to base.

MA: And as we came through the front door who should we discover sitting at the dining table?

The three survivors part and reveal, seated pontifically at the head of the table, fit to judge the living and the dead, the GRANNY.

GRANNY: What time's dinner? I'm starving.

MA: Jesus, Mary and Joseph.

SON: How did you get here?

GRANNY: I flew.

DAUGHTER: But how did you get in with the front door locked?

GRANNY: Ah, us old girls have a few secrets you lot don't know about.

SON: Where are the wings?

GRANNY: Is it roast beef and spuds?

DAUGHTER: Ah, come on, show us your wings.

MA: What happened to himself?

GRANNY: Couldn't tell you. We didn't part company on the best of terms.

MA: And now you want your dinner?

GRANNY: It's Sunday.

MA: What about you lot?

SON & DAUGHTER: Dinner, dinner.

MA: (*Considers the options for a nanosecond*) Well, life goes on, I suppose.

DAUGHTER: So the oven was lit and the preparations began.

MA: (*Barks commands to her offspring who leap into action*) You, peel the potatoes and you, lay the table.

DAUGHTER: And yes, it did seem as the sun slanted down into the west and the shadows of evening began to take over the house, that there was some new and almost imperceptible radiance emanating from the venerable old lady sitting at the foot of the table with the knife and fork in her hands.

GRANNY: And it was the first time in my life I'd missed Mass.

SON: No evidence of the wings though.

He sneaks up behind the GRANNY and starts feeling her back.

MA: Leave your Granny alone. Any wings she's got she'll show you when she's good and ready. Turn on the radio. Let's find out what's going on in the world.

SON: So I turned it on, only to discover that in our absence the most unbelievable things had been happening.

DAUGHTER: A cow had given birth to sextuplets in Mullingar.

SON: An entire Kerry village had disappeared into a bog leaving no visible trace.

DAUGHTER: A statue of Eamon de Valera in Limerick had been seen to weep tears of blood before crashing down into the crowd watching beneath it, narrowly missing a Little Sister of Charity but killing her black poodle dog.

SON: The match at Croke Park having ended in a draw, two opposing teams of supporters had met outside of Gill's pub and reduced one another to a bloody pulp with miniature hurleys, shillelaghs, Guinness bottles and rolled-up copies of the nineteen sixteen proclamation. Even as we prepared dinner the guards were scraping their remains from the pavement and shop fronts.

DAUGHTER: And a hideous green beast had been seen proceeding from the Liffey up Church Street towards Phibsboro.

MA: (*Tuts and clucks knowingly*) It's the end of the world.

DAUGHTER: How do you know?

MA: All the signs are there, for God's sake. Haven't you read John of Patmos?

SON: It's no worse than what happens in New York every day of the week. We're just entering the twentieth century.

DAUGHTER: Yeah. Ninety years too late.

MA: No. This is it. You heard them. The great beast of the apocalypse is heading this way, dripping green slime and coming to claim all sinners.

With a mighty CRASH the door of the house bursts open and there stands the GREAT BEAST, roaring like an elephant.

He's here. We've had it now.

The SON and DAUGHTER run for cover. The MA drops to her knees and starts praying. Only the GRANNY doesn't move.

GRANNY: There you are. You took your time.

DA: (*For it is he*) Somebody put on the immersion. I need a bath desperate.

MA: Is that yourself?

DA: Who else would it be?

SON: We thought you were drownded.

DA: I swam for it. The old currents sucked me under at first but I popped back up again, thank God. Swam all the way round Howth Head, breast stroke, of course, down through the bay, along by the North Wall, past the Custom House, all the way up to Father Matthew Bridge, hopped out and walked up Church Street. They nearly arrested me only I don't think they liked the look of the slime.

MA: Come here, you big bowsey. You smell like a dog's posterior.

The MA and DA hug one another.

GRANNY: And so in spite of all the indications, the full complement sat down to dinner.

They sit down in their customary places.

SON: And we laughed heartily as we recounted the various misadventures of our day out.

DAUGHTER: Not forgetting, of course, to lament the sad if superficial damage inflicted on the fine vintage vehicle which had been the conveyance and catalyst of all that had befallen us.

MA: And in the end…

DA: We had to agree…

GRANNY: All things considered…

SON: That all in all…

DAUGHTER: It hadn't been a…

ALTOGETHER: BAD SUNDAY.

THE END

THE HEAD OF RED O'BRIEN

BY MARK O'HALLORAN

THE HEAD OF RED O'BRIEN WAS FIRST PRODUCED IN SEPTEMBER 2001.

DIRECTOR: MARK O'HALLORAN
CAST: CIARAN MCINTYRE
DESIGN: KELLY CAMPBELL
LIGHTING: KELLY CAMPBELL

Author's Note:

The commission to write The Head of Red O'Brien happened upstairs in JJ Smyth's on Aungier Street one late January evening. The story for it had been in my own head for a number of years and as Michael James Ford and I listened to some Jazzers do their thing, I told Michael the story and he commissioned me there and then to write the play as a Bewley's Fringe Festival show. It was my first solo piece of writing and I decided to direct it myself. The main thing that happened in the rehearsal process, besides me nearly driving the actor Ciaran McIntyre around the twist, was the 9/11 atrocity. I had to do quite a heavy edit of the piece in light of those events as there were lots of references to explosions and American intelligence. The play and those events are now inextricably linked in my mind. It is interesting how lunch-time theatre and major world events can sometimes cross over.

—Mark O'Halloran

> ...the native Irish are obsessed with heads.
>
> — Paul Durcan

A hospital room, with bed, table, etc. Strange music. Coloured swirling lights. Images being projected onto back wall—an orange, a fish, a knife, a battered car, a television, etc. Red is seated at end of bed. He is wearing pyjamas of some kind and sports a large bandage on the crown of his head. He appears to be in some sort of trance, moving to the music. Images and music fade. RED holds hands above head. Eyes closed. A beat.

> Aphonia, Aphemia,
> Aphasia, Alexia,
> Apraxia, Agnosia,
> Amnesia, Ataxia.

Like dead villages in my head. Forgotten pit stops on the road from catastrophe back to her, back to myself. Sometimes, during my recovery and reconstruction, by way of a sedative, a meditation, I'd recite the list of my ailments to myself. I'd always end up pissing myself laughing. That it should come to this.

> Anablepsy, Aprenia,
> Ophthalmoplegia, Orexia,
> Blephorospasm, micrographia,
> Echolalia...

Echolalia. Now I think that one was a misdiagnosis. Echolalia is the forced repetition of someone's words over and over again. Sometimes coupled with catalepsy, the forced repetition or echoing of postures, but I showed no signs of that. You see what I was saying wasn't forced or compulsive like they thought. It was chosen. I was imagining he was here and saying what he'd have said. Repeating it over and over again.

> 'Hold... hold... hold... hold'

But try explaining that to doctors.

> Micrographia, Erethism,
> Hypophonia, Parasia,
> Myoclonus, Festination.

Festination is a right queer one altogether. It's the forced, gradual speeding up of steps or talking or movement or whatever. It's like as if you get into a weird, compulsive race with yourself or as if the world suddenly tips forward and you find yourself getting faster and faster, putting one foot in front of the other faster and faster and faster, unstoppable, until some kindly nurse rugby-tackles you to the ground or you slam into a wall at the end of some corridor. Sometimes I'd even start racing myself to the ends of sentences, no reason at all only that the words were coming fast and furious and I had to get them out.

Twas always a draw in the end.

'What's wrong with me?' I'd ask the Doctor when an attack had passed.

'Festination,' he'd say, smiling like a bastard.

'I know that. But what… What's wrong with me?'

'I just said: Festination,' and off he'd go – lord of all he surveyed.

Words seem to be the cure-all of modern medicine. Used like some kind of primitive sticking plaster to cover up your woes. But the words that doctors used never really put my mind at ease. In fact, to tell the truth, doctors always gave me the creeps. I reckon too much golf has blunted their love of humanity and from what I can gather all they seem to be doing on their rounds is throwing words around and practising putting in their heads.

Once I was in an A & E all night. It would have been one of the first times that she punched the head off me – an argument over some book or a telly programme, 'Blankety Blank' probably. And my face is all puffed up and I'd been sitting there for hours with herself 'longside. Jesus, I'd never seen someone look so sorry in my life and eventually the doctor gets to see us and he's looking me up and down and checking my eyes and ears and she shouting at him—

'he fell down the steps'

– and he isn't even listening anyways, the way doctors don't, like, and he scribbles something on my chart and goes off to get a gauze or a bandage or something for the cut on my forehead and she picks up the chart and reads out loud –

'Dual Circum Orbital Haematoma.'

Dual Circum Orbital Haematoma? Well to the likes of her and me it sounded horrific. A slow and agonising death. So we hold and squeeze each other's hands and we make our peace there and then and I ask her to say goodbye to the lads for me and whatever. When the next thing, your man, the doctor waltzes in and begins applying his plasters and whistling away to himself and throwing his gruffness about and suddenly he stops and he looks at us and says—

'What the fuck are ye crying for?'

'Well' – says I, hauling myself up to my full shambles – 'As a man with Dual Circum Orbital Haematoma, I think I'm entitled to a few emotional moments with the one that I loves.'

It was then that he explained that Dual Circum Orbital Haematoma was in fact two black eyes. I pretended that I'd known all along, that we were crying about something else and that I was just being ironic or cynical or something clever like that. But the episode never left me. It stuck in my head, like. I mean why didn't he just write down two black eyes as opposed to Dual Circum Orbital Haematoma. It's shorter for a start – twelve letters as against twenty-six. I've asked every doctor I've met since and the ones that do answer say that it's to stop patients reading their own charts. To keep them from worrying, like. But surely doctors must realise that for me and hundreds like me, imagination can do far worse things than reality has ever tried. So I know it's not entirely that. I mean what is true is that doctors do try to take control of a patient's illness by covering it in exotic words. And so this is the advice I give to anyone poorly—: Take pride in your sickness. Own it. It is as unique and special as you are.

And, well, to put it politely, all this got me a bit worried.

So one day I bite the bullet and I unload all my worries to my surgeon – Mr Markham – an unfortunate name for a surgeon I think – and anyways he sits himself down at the side of my bed and he puts his head to one side and he smiles down at me in a fatherly kind of way – kind of like that angel fella from 'Highway to Heaven' – and he starts to tell me the history of surgery. About how, back in the 17th century everyone hated them, and other physicians wouldn't allow them to be called Doctor, and how they had to work out of barber shops, and how a barber's red and white pole got to be that colour because the surgeons used to hang their bloodied sheets off them after an operation and—

'Can I stop you right there, Mr Markham,' says I, 'you're turning me rigid with fear.'

I suppose that's where the word barbarism comes from.

Anyways, bonkers the lot of them.

And sure, at the end of the day, if you are going to get better, the recovery is already there, inside your head. If not, you better start saying your prayers; cause there is nothing no surgeon can do for you. And I should know, I've gotten better loads of times.

Aphonia, Aphemia,
Aphasia, Alexia,
Apraxia, Agnosia,
Amnesia, Ataxia.

Music again. Strange and funny. Images again. Also a bit strange. RED is in a trance or reverie of some kind.

My arrival in hospital this last time was some hoopla. Not like before when I was just a no one left on a trolley with a few broken fingers and a bit of concussion. Maybe in overnight for observations. Whose observations? I wasn't ever asked for mine.

'This hospital is a shit hole and is an epidemic waiting to happen'— I'd've said if I'd been asked, but I never was.

Oh but this time it was different. I was head boy, top of the class. I parted the people at Casualty like Moses at the Red Sea. People gasped and screamed, blessed themselves – and one junior doctor when presented with me turned white, got sick in my lap and passed out. There was no two ways about it— I was a class A fucking star specimen.

Did I tell you what was wrong with me? No.

Well, you see, my wife had stabbed me through the top of the head with an 8 ½ inch stainless steel carving knife with a beautiful ornate wooden handle which now protruded through a hole in the top of my cranium. The knife had been my Christmas present to her. I'd gotten it from a catalogue. I think that's what hurt the most. Emotionally, that is. Obviously getting stabbed in the head hurts like fuck. But emotionally, I'm saying. To have used my Christmas present to her as a weapon against me. Well, I thought it was rather thoughtless is all. And I shudder to think what would have happened if I'd bought her a cardigan.

But as can be seen, I've made a full recovery. I've always been lucky, I guess.

As for herself. Don't think the worst of her. I drove her to it. She didn't have much choice. We've always brought out the wilder side of each other I suppose. Maybe we should never have stuck together, I dunno. It's all academic now anyways.

Mary.

Boys oh boys, it's some temper she has. I'd spotted her ages before we started going out and christened her Mary Motorhead because she was so mad and the name kind of stuck around the town and that's what everyone calls her now. We met when we were in our late teens, nineteen or something. She was a fine looking thing back then, strong and fiery. And although I'm no Quasimodo here – I had the majority of my hair til my mid-twenties and was a bit slimmer then— still. I felt that maybe I was getting the best of the bargain here. That she was settling for less. And that annoyed the shit out of me for years. Drove me mad.

We had what you'd call a long courtship. I don't know when we started going out.

We kinda fell into it.

Talked about nothing.

Years of weekends in lounge bars and fairgrounds.

Always harbouring the thought that maybe this isn't right for either of us but we just kept going.

Occasionally Mary Motorhead would start ragin and roaring and would peg a huge rock at me or something and I always managed to get out of the way.
I should have read the warning signs I suppose. We even tried splitting up once. A ferocious row outside a chipper during which she called me a useless 5 foot stack of shite and stormed off. We didn't see each other for two weeks and—

—and I think I fell apart a bit. I felt a black nothing inside me and there wasn't anything new or beautiful and I stopped eating and terrified everyone in town by driving me Cortina too fast.

She apparently was the same.

'Like living with a briar'— her mother said. Stopped washing, nearly lost her arm to a machine at work. There just didn't seem any reason for anything and it was obvious to everyone that no matter how bad we were together, we were worse apart.

I spotted her the following weekend at the dance and I looked over and they were playing 'Do You Think I'm Sexy' by Rod Stewart and I wiggled my arse over at her and she broke her shite laughing and that was that. We got married by the end of the summer. I guess that's how I asked her—I wiggled my arse—cause neither of us popped the question or anything. We just presumed.

The wedding was a disaster from start to finish. It had been the wettest summer on record and all our photos look like shots from the trenches. Mud to our armpits. It was a small do. About 30 people. Aunts and uncles that neither of us knew and a few close friends. Later, for the afters crowd, there was a band called "Country Fever" but by that stage me and Mary Motorhead were so legless we couldn't have cared what they were called. And then fights broke out and the Guards were called—

Not the right way to start.

We woke up in our room the following morning and the place was in tatters. Everything was spilt or broken and there was an empty wheelchair there in the corner and to this day we have no idea where it came from and apparently we had thrown most of our clothes out the window into the garden below. The hotel crowd had picked them up and put them into a bag for us. And when the owner was handing it over, when we were leaving like, she just looks down her nose at us and says –
Ye're nothing but tinkers.

That's not the way good things start.

We did have good times though, oh Jesus, we did. Our pre-marriage course was a case in point. A weekend retreat with nine other couples and Fr Padraig. Now I'm not being mean here but Fr Padraig – if gay was an Olympic sport, he'd win gold for Ireland. Bent as a hook. And here he was trying to teach ten couples, who'd been riding each other on the sly for years anyways, how to have sex. Mary was priceless that weekend. Drinking and singing and cursing and taking the piss and saying the word vulva every chance she could in front of the poor little Priesteen. Sure, he didn't know what to do with himself. And I think we still get Christmas cards from one of the other couples every year.

Happy Christmas from Pat and Nancy, or something like that. I wonder has either of them stabbed the other?

So, we settled into a small flat near the post office field and got on with our lives. She had her job in the factory until it closed and I did odd jobs. Or to tell the truth I sat on my arse and watched the telly. These, now, were the golden years of mass unemployment when daytime television was top notch. Oprah was in her prime and the future was certain.

Shite, but certain.

We went out to the local about four nights a week and on special occasions and I played pool with the lads and Mary sat at the bar, like the queen of the silver dollar and took the living piss out of everyone in town.

We'd go to the cinema about once a fortnight, depending. Adventure stuff and anything with himself in it.

Mary was never one for the films really. She'd get bored easy and often slept right through them. Just to spite me I reckon. That had become our favourite pastime – spiting each other. The more I liked a thing the more Mary decided she disliked it and visa versa. Pushing each other into frenzies of loving and loathing. It appeared that we were beginning to define ourselves in opposition to each other. And so the more I loved films, the more she hated them. The more I hated Gay Byrne, the more she thought the sun shone out his arse.

And the more time she spent reading books, the more I realised that they were near enough the root of all evil.

I never really got the hang of it. Reading. Never really took to it that easy, I suppose. At school there was always some little Christian Brother hanging over my shoulder just waiting for me to be stupid so he could lay into me and consequently books have always given me the heebees. Just the size and the feel – just holding one and I'm immediately back in that that little classroom and the auld smell of dry rot. And I don't know what else. Books have always been used by people to make me feel bad about myself or that I don't belong and I explained all that to her and the next thing is, she's reading for Ireland. Rubbing my nose in it. Watching 'Folio' on the telly – which without doubt was the most boring programme RTÉ ever made and that's some claim to fame. But sure as time goes by it gets worse. Books everywhere. I'm sick of it. And the worst of the lot, the one that really gets me going is James Joyce. You'd swear he'd invented a cure for TB the way some people go on about him. They have Joyce cafés and Joyce days and museums and recitals and parades. They've even gone and named the largest car ferry in the world after him.

The Ulysses.

Twice daily between Dublin and Holyhead.

Rather apt when you think about it really because the only thing he ever did for his country is leave it. No sign of him in the GPO in 1916. Oh lord Jesus no. Too busy sitting on his hole in Italy tanked up, living off handouts and writing dirty books about his wife's arse.

But try saying that out loud. Bord Fáilte would have you lynched.

And no one has read the damn thing anyway – except for your man in Dublin, David Norris and sure, that's the reason he's a celebrity.

No, I don't read. I can't. I can't be bothered.

So when people come around saying:

'Have you read such and such, it's fabaless.'

'No,' I says, 'I'm waiting for the movie.'

Auld books. Auld dry rot.

And so time ambled on. The two of us beginning to grate on each other. Spending our time either going to the local or sitting at home, her reading a book and me watching the telly with the sound really loud so as to put her off or else me at the cinema, on my own mostly since she discovered literature.

And then one weekend it arrived and changed my life forever. The greatest film ever made, staring the world's greatest actor. *The Hunt For Red October*.

Music swells. Images are projected again. RED goes into his trance.

Me and Sean Connery had been through a lot together and in a way he's probably the best friend I ever had. To watch him struggle in public with premature baldness, well, it put my mind at rest. And I don't think anyone actually realises the pain you go through when you lose your hair, again I'm talking emotionally. Certainly Mary never did. Or if she did she sure as shite never let on. She just couldn't let go. Thought it was hilarious. It was baldy this and auld slap head the other... And you see, I never thought it would happen to me, you never do I suppose, but it's just that I was always a bit – hirsute, as they say. I mean in primary school I'd been kept back so often that by sixth class I already had a moustache. I mean that's a real achievement no matter what way you look at it – and then by the time I hit sixteen I already had a bald patch the size of a grapefruit on my poll. Just not fair. Never even got to enjoy a proper childhood. And you can console yourself with all your: I'm not bald – it's just a solar panel for a sex machine type bravado – but it's still a blow. Post-follicle stress disorder, I reckon I have. Anyway one of my only consolations in life was to watch Connery go through the same thing as me. I mean if Sean Connery can go through the same thing as myself, well, it just meant that life wasn't such a pain in the hole after all.

And there's just something about him that inspires absolute confidence. I don't know what it is, a twinkle in the eye or something, I dunno. There he'd be getting bet into Pussy Galore or whoever and he'd have this look in his eye as if he's looking straight out at you and saying—

'Here, Red, just give me five minutes with this Pussy Galore wan and I'll follow you down to the local and we'll have a rake of pints.'

A man's man, I suppose is what I mean.

And then there's one other very important aspect. You just know there is no way on God's earth that Connery is going to go Gaylord on you. See, I'd been let down very badly in the past. In my younger days I'd had a great devotion to Rock Hudson. Looked on him as a kind of Daddy figure. Turns out himself and Doris Day had been laughing at us all along.

But with Connery it was different, absolute confidence, you just knew where you stood. So, when *The Hunt for Red October* arrived in town I was nearly bursting with excitement. Even the name gave me shivers up my spine – my name being Red too like. And I races down to see it, herself staying at home, too busy with a book, she said, an auld sneer playing across her chops, and from the first frame I'm… I'm… I'm just there. I'm on that submarine.

Everything was right from the word go. His first line was in Russian—

'Biche albo nea biche'

An answer to a question about how shit the weather was, which translated as yes, cold and hard, which he delivered in a rumbling Scottish burr, which I thought was fantastic.

And he's standing on the top of this span new Russian submarine, waiting to set sail, staring out at the Baltic middle distance, with a full beard and silver crew cut (he wore a toupee which I wasn't entirely happy with but there you go) and there's this haunted look in his eyes.

This man has been through the ringer says I to myself.

Anyways, in the film he plays Marcus Rameus, famous submarine commander and trainer of Russia's navy elite.

'A near legend in the submarine community'— one of the Americans says about him. And he's just gotten control of this big, new, top secret Russian submarine called The Red October. And, you see, the big innovation with this new sub is that it moves through the ocean in complete silence, not a peep, undetectable, invisible. The Russians now are as smug as bejaysas. They think that all their Maydays have come at once. We have the cold war won, they're thinking to themselves, done and dusted.

The Cold War. Makes you nostalgic just saying it. Things seemed simpler back then. At least back then, you knew why you feared for the future.

So Connery sets sail, strangles a KGB guy and exchanges significant looks with his second in command, a man so nice that you just know that he'll be dead by the time the credits roll and slowly the plot unfurls.

It turns out that Connery is just a nice guy pushed to the limits by those bastards in the KGB and the Kremlin. So twisted are these lads now that they didn't even turn up at the funeral of Connery's beloved wife the year before.

That, now I think is unforgivable. I even go to funerals of people I don't know – it's the done thing like.

Anyways, that was the final straw for Connery and he decides to defect to the States. So when he's given control of this silent sub he starts to put together his plan.

I have to say at this point now that even though it says that the sub is silent, this is the movies like and not reality and in the movies silence doesn't exist. Even silence has a sound. So the sub sailed through the ocean like this—

Whish ishy fish mmm whish ishy fish.

So what Connery does is this. He hand picks the officers to serve under him and, of course, having trained them himself they love him like a father and would go to the ends of the earth for him. And off he goes. Undetectable. Not only to the Americans now, but to the Russians too and so all he has to do is race across the Atlantic in complete silence—

Whish ishy fish mmm whish ishy fish.

And then give himself up in his own time, leaving the red bastards behind wishing that they'd been nicer to this legend of the sea and his family.

But he can't just ring ahead to the Americans to say he's on his way like, no, cause the KGB would be listening and then they'd have him bumped off. What he has to do is sail to America in complete silence and then make himself known and Sam's your uncle. But as in all such endeavours it turns out that there's a double crossing spy on board who goes and shoots up the engine and knocks off the subs silencer and so Connery finds himself halfway across the Atlantic going—

Beep, beep, beep.

Detectable to the world and his wife, with the entire Russian navy closing in on one side hoping to blow him out of the water and the entire American fleet on the other hoping to do the same. (The Russians had told them that Connery was a rogue commander with plans.) But did he flinch? Did he freak out? Did he even break into a sweat? Did he fuck! He just kept his nerve, kept his goal in mind and ploughed on in pursuit of his dream and freedom.

And then, right at the climax, when the Russians shoot one of their heat seeking missiles at him and all around him are freaking out, he just calmly orders them to turn the sub around and sail straight for the torpedo.

But this is suicidal, Captain.

Hold.

This is crazy.

Hold.

But, Captain…

Hold… hold… Hold… Hold.

And the missile whizzes right past them.

Whooooosh.

He knew, he just knew that if he faced the danger head on, they'd get by.

Of course, it wasn't entirely without casualty. Connery's super loyal second in command was shot by the double crossing spy and died in his arms saying—

I guess I'll never see Montana.

Someone had to pay the price, I suppose.

Music swells. A break.

As films go it had it all and by the time the credits rolled I was just sitting there with my mouth hanging open. And for the first time in ages I wished that Mary was there beside me so that I could turn to her, there and then and say—

'Oh holy Jesus, that was fucking fantastic.'

But she wasn't and so as I sat there in the dark I decided that I was going to go home and suggest that the two of us go and see it together.

So I ambles back and says to her—

'That film was fantastic Mary. It'll knock you sideways. It's just fantastic. Will you come tomorrow night?'

'No,' she says. 'I don't think I'd like it.'

'But I'm telling you, you will like it.'

And I give her a short rundown on the storyline and she stops me halfway through and says that she hates the cinema and she doesn't care what it's about and that she hates Sean Connery and go shove it up my hole or something like that. And like, I wasn't going to take the rise off her now. So I explains that I just wanted her to see the film so that she could enjoy it as much as I did and that I'll be going myself anyways and sure won't she be just sitting around doing nothing anyways and she said that she will be doing something, she'll be reading her book.

Like a slap across the face that last statement was delivered and she looks at me, bold as brass, willing me to go ape, trying to push me over the edge, but I wasn't going to rise to it.

'Well, maybe the day after tomorrow so?'

'No, I'm enjoying this book too much and afterwards I have another lined up.'

'Well, whenever you want I'll go.'

And we both stayed silent for the rest of the night, the smell of dry rot everywhere – her reading her book and me watching the telly. The both of us seething.

I went to *The Hunt for Red October* every night it played in town, three weeks I think in all and each time I saw it I understood more of the hidden depths. Like when Connery said – hold – he was talking about a hell of a lot more than just the direction of the submarine, he was talking about his struggle with the KGB and his dead wife and his plan to defect – and it was Mary and me too.

She never came to see it and she knew that it was driving me mad. I wasn't going to let her know that though. There are ways and means and I wasn't going to let her off that easy.

So each night after the cinema I'd head home, stop at the front door, take a deep breath, and walk in with a big smile on my face.

Hold.

And she'd have her book in front of her face.

Hold.

Laughing, I'd say she was.

Hold.

And I'd pull up a chair and I'd sit real close, facing the side of her head and I'd tell the story of the film, in the minutest detail, from start to finish – every single night.

Towards the end of the three weeks I nearly had whole scenes off by heart that I could act out for her – and she continued to ignore me completely and tried to keep reading. Neither of us showing any annoyance.

I was just bringing the mountain to Mohammed, as the man said and there was no way I could be stopped.

Hold, hold, hold, hold.

So the film finished in town but the more I thought about her pigheadedness at not having seen it the more annoyed I became and so I continued to retell the tale every night, start to finish. She just kept on reading away and ignoring the fact that I existed and then one day I hit on a plan.

I traipsed into town and bought her a copy of the book.

I don't know why i hadn't thought of it before. She'd read the book, love the story, demand to see the video and we could try and settle back into some kind of normal abnormal.

I practically ran home and flung the book at her.

'Here, horse, read that and tell me what you think.'

And she looks at it and she turn to me and I think there are tears in her eyes and she says—

'I'd rather choke myself.'

And she throws it onto the fire.

Onto the fire!

Now, admittedly, I did get it half to annoy her. But this was an act of war. Time to get clever. I bided my time. Watched the telly. Did my nightly retelling of *The Hunt for Red October*. Watched her read her books. And then one night I watched her put her bookmark in and head out to the kitchen to make herself a cup of tea. No offer of tea for myself. No way. The only things she gave me at that point were dirty looks and the odd few belts. So while she was out I just lent over, took out her bookmark and fucked it onto the fire. I was over the moon. One nil to me and I wait for her to come back in with her tea and her Penguin bar and as she's settling herself I'm about to burst my shite laughing. Hadn't felt so alive in weeks. And she picks up the book and there's a moment, just a moment, a tiny halt when she realises what's happened and I can see this rage roaring around inside her, but she hardly flinches, keeps the lid on, doesn't say a word and just opens the book again at page one, making sure I can see. There's no way you can stop me, she's saying.

And so we continued on. She's extra careful about bookmarks from that point on. Usually she'd curl a corner of the page or memorise the number when she was going out for her tea break but I did manage to catch her out a few times – usually if she had to get up quickly, to answer the door, say, or the telephone, or sometimes when my retelling of *Red October* would drive her over the edge, and she'd get up quickly and race into the kitchen and smash a few plates or bang pots together or else she'd storm around the flat, roaring, screaming, kicking walls and slamming doors and then when it had passed she'd quietly come back into the room, pick up her book and start all over again.

Sometimes when a scene like that had happened I'd want to stop it all and hold her in my arms and say that I was sorry for everything. But it was too late for that.

After she became fully immune to my little bookmark trick I went one step further. She'd just started a new book that night – *Flowers in the Attic* I think it was called – and as usual she memorised the number of the page she was on and places the book down and heads out to make a cup of tea, and I just leans across and takes up the book and I tear out pages 85, 98 and 107 and I throw them on the fire and place the book back where she'd left it. My very own private version of the boobytrap. Boom!

Some days she'd take to beating the head off me, pulling what was left of my hair and pummelling me with her closed fists and although I wouldn't really advise it as a pastime for anyone, it was more real than being treated as if I didn't exist for weeks on end and reassured me that I was right in all the things I inflicted on her – mental tortures and suchlike.

We continued like this for weeks and months and years. A war of attrition. Battle weary troops. Walking wounded. Lonely.

And then one day she did it. She took that step beyond. She went where neither of us had gone before. The land of no return.

She came home with a copy of *Ulysses* under her arm.

Ulysses!

She knew how I felt about that book. It was a sign of everything that was wrong with this country in my mind and here she was in front of me reading the damn thing.

Occasionally, she'd break into a laugh –

Ha, ha, ha, ha, from behind the book like.

Ha, ha, ha, it's just so funny. No one tells you how funny it is. Ha, ha, ha, ha.

And I'm going apeshit bananas and I decide to up the ante.

I start to recite *The Hunt for Red October* from the moment I wake till the moment I sleep. Acting out scenes. Using the furniture to illustrate tricky bits, the front room becoming the Atlantic Ocean, the settee becoming the Red October, over and over again, louder and louder – one day, two days, three days, four days.

> But this is suicidal, Captain.
>
> Hold.
> It's just so funny.
>
> We're all going to die Captain.
>
> Ha, ha, ha, ha.
>
> Hold.
>
> Such a good writer.

Hold.

Ha, ha, ha, ha.

I guess I'll never see Montana.

Hold.

And she just snapped. It had to happen to one of us sooner or later. Something had to give. And she plunged the carving knife into my head. And I went underwater.

Music, lights and images. RED moves in a trance.

I didn't really feel it going in. I just heard this deep rumbling sound, massive now, like two submarines scraping off each other and I could hear the sound of water, huge scary oceans being sucked down plugholes and intense humming. The kind of humming that only dogs or bats should hear and I felt as if I'd sunk to the bottom of the sea, floating. And then colour pulsed and flashed in front of my eyes, colour so wild I could hear it too and feel the weight of it in my hands and then whiteout.

The doctor told me afterwards that Mary undoubtedly saved my life by not pulling the knife out after she'd plunged it in. If she had I'd have bled everywhere and drowned what was left of my mind. It was the least she could have done, says I to him, seeing as she was the one who tried to kill me in the first place.

Apparently I never passed out. Just sat there in my arm chair with my eyes wide open, an inane grin on my face, a bit of dribble beginning to hang from the corner of my mouth, the big wooden handle sticking out of my crown and a trickle of blood rolling down my forehead.

The world is in some state, isn't it? We've made some mess out of it. Men, that is. With our brains. We're to be pitied really. If we're not being led around by our private parts we're desperate to inflict our brains on the world. Brains. We believe in them more then we believe in God. One and a half pounds of grey matter with the consistency of warm butter that has caused nothing but trouble since the time we climbed out of the trees. Better off to follow your heart. Solid red meat.

She drove me to the hospital after she calmed down a bit. The front seat had to be laid flat, otherwise I wouldn't fit in with the handle sticking out on top and all. Giggling away to myself I was and moaning a bit. She dumped me at Casualty and went on the run. Like some Clyde-less Bonnie. They found her four days later holed up in the Prince of Wales hotel in Athlone. Petrified.

The knife had slipped easily into the gap between the two halves of my brain, not doing much damage, severing the odd nerve or blood vessel and finally coming to lodge in the perisylvian region. The centre for language in the brain. And I was just wiped free of words. By the time I got to hospital I was suffering from Global Aphasia. Language had ceased to exist, words had come to a full stop. And not just that, I couldn't speak or couldn't hear – words had been wiped from my brain. Lost. Nor had I any understanding of this, no awareness of anything lost. I was alive in a wordless world.

It was the most beautiful place I'd ever seen.

Everything humming or singing, truly there. There, not because I spoke it into existence but because it just was. Colours bright and vibrant swimming around me and the world was as it should be.

A world of music.

Everything was music. Everything had its own song, people, birds, buildings, doors, floors, everything, and I was happy. For the first time ever I was happy— because I'd forgotten so much I just thought that this was the way things were and I'd forgotten myself.

And then one day I sees herself in front of me and I have no idea who she is at this stage. Even she had been washed away and she is with people, guards maybe and she began to talk to me and I don't know what it was she was trying to say, sorry maybe, but the music that her voice makes is like a … *(Pause)* … like a stream of Jazz, strange and beautiful, and I just knew and at that moment I'd have done anything to make her stay with me. I loved her.

Images on wall.

I stayed global aphasiac for nearly two months and then one day I was sitting here, happy, staring at a bowl of fruit that someone had left in, just looking now, not judging it or anything and suddenly the word orange rises up out of nowhere and at once I realised I'd lost something huge and I cried for about four days.

So slowly words came back.

Words.

Getting in the way, standing between me and the world. Always being less then they tried to describe, always falling short, never being able to make full sense, always undervaluing what was described.

You see I'd seen the world as it really was, as music – and words, well, words just rob the world of its music.

That's the truth; words are the heart of the problem. Without words the world is beautiful and with them there is doubt and fear and misunderstanding and anger and hatred and fights and and cruelty and loneliness and all because we don't fully understand each other, we don't fully understand ourselves because words can never say enough of what we mean.

> Aphonia, Aphemia,
> Aphasia, Alexia,
> Apraxia, Agnosia,
> Amnesia, Ataxia.

So I travelled my little road map to recovery and I thought about things. Lots of things. My life and what I done. Nothing much really except watch telly, marry Mary and then undermine her every chance I got. I thought about all the luck I've never had. About being bald, something I've never come to terms with. Why, God, why? Insult to injury. And I gets to thinking about my wound. My crown. And do you know there are some religions where the top of the head is considered the holiest place in the body, the lotus, the baby's fontanel beating its original sin, the pathway through which God's radiant love enters the body. That's what it said on the telly anyways. And as I sat there watching I thought, crazy now I know, but what if Mary knew this, deep down she just knew, and that when she stabbed me it wasn't just to hurt or maim or injure, but she saw this soul, this blocked soul and so she plunged in her knife to set me free. Act of love. Long shot, I know. But if all that is true then it might explain baldness as well. It could be that God makes some men bald so that the world can see their soul and if the world sees their souls it might overlook all the bullshit they come out with.

And now I'm nearly better, a few setbacks along the way but making progress and they say that I won't know it till I'm out there again in the real world.

What then? Well, I've decided to do a lot more listening from now on. And not selfish listening where I'm just drawing breath between sentences or thinking about the next thing to say but real listening, where you just sit with your ears open. It's one of the most important things you could do. Should be in the Leaving Cert, listening classes. Listening exams. It would be a great way to weed out all the swatty freaks. All the laid back decent kids getting A1s. Fantastic.

And besides that I'm going to wait for her. For however long it takes. And when she comes home I'm going to get down on my knees and ask her forgiveness and tell her about the stream of jazz and I'm going to ask her to give me a second chance and a third chance and a fourth chance and to let me spend the rest of my life with her and then while I wait for her answer, in my head like, I'll go—

> Hold, hold, hold, hold…

THE END

THE STAR TRAP
BY MICHAEL JAMES FORD

The Star Trap was first produced in May 2002.

Director: Michael James Ford
Cast: Amelia Crowley and Alan Smyth
Design: Emma Cullen
Lighting: Moyra D'Arcy

Author's Note:

When I read Bram Stoker's theatrical anecdote *A Star Trap*, I was much taken with the idea of a tale of jealousy and murder set against the tatty glamour of a Victorian theatre. But it was the characters of Loo Halliday and Billy Hempitch that most interested me. She was a tough, sexy, high-kicking chorus girl who had married Jack, the old master machinist, for the financial security he offered, but was soon seeking erotic diversion elsewhere. Billy was the gauche young apprentice who'd seen the tragedy unfold, but whose loyalties were divided by a sense of duty and by secret longings of his own. The play is about their meeting, and was brought to life by the wonderful perfomances of Amelia Crowley and Alan Smyth. I couldn't have been happier with the casting and fondly remember the laughter that went into the making of this dark little drama.

—Michael James Ford

A backstage workshop in a large theatre somewhere in the north of England. The year is 1900. Music from a solo cello. Mrs Halliday (LOO), a young woman in her twenties, comes in dressed in black. She looks around her, examining old props, flats and other bits of theatrical bric-a-brac. The music becomes darker, more insistent, almost frantic. A sound like a scream is heard. Lights up to full. HEMPITCH, a man in his early twenties enters. He is dressed in a formal black suit.

HEMPITCH: You found your way all right, Mrs Halliday? Course you did. Sorry about that. A mix up with the keys.

LOO: Not much changed around here. Same old dump it always was.

HEMPITCH: Sit yourself down.

LOO: I'm quite happy to stand, thank you.

HEMPITCH: Shall I make you a cup of tea?

LOO: Quite the man about the house, aren't you? But no. I'll just take his things and go.

HEMPITCH: Of course. I've put everything together in this box. It's tools mostly. Some lovely old ones too. Old Jack really looked after his things.

LOO: He did that alright. Kept a close eye on everything. Worth a few bob, are they?

HEMPITCH: I suppose so.

LOO: Or would he have wanted you to have them?

HEMPITCH: I don't know about that…

LOO: The loyal apprentice inheriting his master's tools… I'm sure he'd have approved.

HEMPITCH: He never said.

LOO: No. He never said much, did he?

HEMPITCH: You must be exhausted, Mrs Halliday.

LOO: For God's sake, stop calling me that. My name is Loo, just like it always was.

HEMPITCH: Sorry, Loo… It's been a long time, that's all. You must be very tired, after all the upset of today. Why don't you have that cup of tea?

LOO: I need something stronger. *(She takes a bottle from her bag.)* Gin, darling. It's what keeps us poor widows going. Will you join me?

HEMPITCH: No thanks, Loo. I'm not really a drinking man.

LOO: No? And you all grown up and all. You do surprise me.

HEMPITCH: I'll get you a cup.

He goes to get a cup.

LOO: Fine bone china if you've got it. *(She sits and looks around.)* Oh God, what am I doing here?

HEMPITCH returns with the cup.

HEMPITCH: There you are. It's the best I could find.

LOO pours herself a drink. Silence.

LOO: It must be three years since I was in this place. Three years of wedded bliss. I should get all teary eyed, I suppose, and reminisce. My life with a master machinist.

HEMPITCH: He was always good at his job.

LOO: Oh, he was that. Very clever with traps and levers and counter weights. Very bloody clever.

HEMPITCH: The best. He'll be missed around here, that's for sure.

LOO: Well, that's a comfort, I suppose.

HEMPITCH: He was a good man, Loo.

LOO: Good? I don't know about that.

HEMPITCH: He was mad about you.

LOO: Oh yeah?

HEMPITCH: Used to talk about you every day.

LOO: Every day?

HEMPITCH: In the old days, you know, when you first got wed.

LOO: Oh yeah, those days. How could I forget?

HEMPITCH: You were happy, weren't you? At the start?

LOO: I dunno. Maybe I was. He wasn't exactly Prince Charming, but he tried his best.

HEMPITCH: He used come in singing some days. Sit at his desk and sing to himself. Not that he could carry a tune too well.

LOO: No. Not in a bucket.

HEMPITCH: But he did seem happy.

LOO: Couldn't believe his luck, that's why. An old geezer like Jack getting a girl like me. Wouldn't you sing if you were him?

HEMPITCH: I suppose I would.

LOO: Aren't you lovely when you blush? I bet you were jealous of old Jack. Bet you wondered what I saw in him.

HEMPITCH: I wouldn't say that exactly. Obviously I was pleased for his good fortune.

LOO: Oh yeah? He wasn't such a bad looker. Still had a nice head of hair. And he behaved like a gentleman. Never cursed, never drank. Treated me respectfully. All those little courtesies and compliments. Who'd have thought he had it in him?

HEMPITCH: What do you mean?

LOO: To do what he did.

HEMPITCH: I'm not with you, Loo.

LOO: I think you are.

HEMPITCH: (Pause) It could have worked out differently.

LOO: Course it could. I thought we'd be all right together, even if he was old enough to be my father. Besides, there wasn't anyone making me a better offer.

HEMPITCH: No?

LOO: Sometimes a girl has to settle for what she can get. And it wasn't so bad, not at first. Didn't we have that lovely honeymoon on the Isle of Man? Five days. Looking out at the drizzle.

HEMPITCH: Jack said it was the happiest time of his life.

LOO: It probably was. Truth to tell I was quite proud of him then. All dressed up in his swanky suit. Spending all his savings on me. Hotel on the seafront. Clean linen on the bed. Grilled kippers for breakfast. And afternoons under an umbrella listening to the brass band on the pier. It felt nice, you know, sort of safe. I don't care what the other girls thought. I had someone to look after me and I felt safe.

HEMPITCH: It was a good turn out this morning, considering.

LOO: Yeah. It was an interesting assortment altogether. Didn't expect to see Horace Duxbury there for a start.

HEMPITCH: Great man for a formal occasion, Horace.

LOO: Them tragedians probably love funerals. Gives them a chance to practise their solemn poses. Do you know what he said to me? 'Jack was a consummate master of his craft whose untimely passing diminishes us all'. I didn't know where to look. And then that Flash Harry, Archie Sturridge, kept giving me meaningful glances over the graveside. He doesn't believe in hanging about, does he?

HEMPITCH: No. Archie always makes time for the ladies.

LOO: But all the while old Mrs Homcroft from wardrobe was sobbing and making these funny sniffling noises. I got quite dizzy from trying not to laugh. Thought I'd fall in the grave on top of him.

HEMPITCH: You were a model of composure. You did him proud.

LOO: It was good of them all to come.

HEMPITCH: Everyone respected Jack. It was a terrible shock when we heard the news.

LOO: Who are you telling? Wasn't I the one who had him die on me? And just before his dinner, too. Stew and dumplings. He never touched it. Just went deathly pale and slid off his chair without a word. He lay on the floor and trembled for a little while… and that was it. Gone.

HEMPITCH: What did they say it was?

LOO: Apoplexy. A blockage in the brain. At least it was quick.

HEMPITCH: Poor old Jack. We're all going to miss him.

LOO: Speak for yourself. He was a miserable old bastard for three long years. You know as well as I do that after that night everything changed.

HEMPITCH: The night of the accident?

LOO: Yes, Hempitch. What did you think I meant, the night they relieved Mafeking?

HEMPITCH: No of course not. It was a terrible tragedy. It was bound to change things.

LOO: He knew something. And I knew something worse. And we weren't ever going to trust each other again. We never spoke about it. We never really spoke about anything after that. We just rubbed along together, watching each other's every move.

HEMPITCH: Doesn't sound too cheerful.

LOO: Oh he tried, I suppose. Tried to get back to what we used to be. But I didn't want to be there any more and couldn't pretend otherwise.

HEMPITCH: Did you ever think of leaving him?

LOO: I thought about it all the time.

HEMPITCH: And why didn't you?

LOO: I was afraid.

HEMPITCH: Of what people would say?

LOO: No, Hempitch. I was afraid of what he might do.

Pause. LOO takes a long drink.

HEMPITCH: You should go easy on that stuff, Loo. It can't be good for you when you're all stirred up.

LOO: Aren't you the little Temperance crusader? Why don't you join me? I haven't had a proper drink in years.

HEMPITCH: No, I don't think…

LOO: Go on. Just a little one. When was the last time you got to comfort a widow in her time of sorrow?

HEMPITCH: Well, then. Just a tiny nip.

LOO: That's more like it. We'll have a drink to old Jack.

HEMPITCH: I'll get a cup.

He exits. LOO gets up and starts to rummage casually in the box. She takes out a shabby cap and an old apron.

LOO: Some Beau Brumell you were. I'm glad you didn't wear them around the house.

HEMPITCH returns. LOO picks out a few other item: a waistcoat, a scarf...

Aah, his favourite muffler. The last thing his old mother knitted for him. This is making me feel all creepy. I don't think I want any of this. *(She takes out a chisel.)* My God, you could really do someone mischief with that.

HEMPITCH: Easy, Loo.

LOO: Don't be so jumpy.

HEMPITCH: There's a picture of you there.

LOO: I am touched.

She takes out a framed portrait.

HEMPITCH: Very nice.

LOO: My last appearance on the boards. Before my enforced retirement.

HEMPITCH: You haven't changed a bit.

LOO: Such a charmer. I'll have to watch you. Do you think they'll have me back in the chorus?

HEMPITCH: I don't see why not. You could always kick higher than anyone else.

LOO: You should know.

HEMPITCH: Sorry?

LOO: Do you think we didn't know about you watching us rehearse? You was always snooping and spying on us, weren't you?

HEMPITCH: No, not really, I...

LOO: We were up to all your little tricks.

HEMPITCH: What do you mean?

LOO: Watching from the flies. Hiding in the prompt box.

HEMPITCH: I was only interested.

LOO: Course you were, dearie. Why wouldn't you want to see professional artistes at work? And you a young lad with hot blood in your veins.

HEMPITCH: No, it wasn't like that. I was...

LOO: You was having a good look. Don't deny it. You're an odd fish, Hempitch. Or may I call you William?

HEMPITCH: Billy.

LOO: How sweet. Well, Billy, I suppose you knew all about him and me?

HEMPITCH: Mortimer?

LOO: Henry Mortimer to you, darling. Well?

HEMPITCH: I knew a little bit. Same as everyone else.

LOO: And?

HEMPITCH: He was quite a swell.

LOO: He was that alright.

HEMPITCH: I used to think he was the bee's knees. Best Harlequin I ever saw. Everyone loved to see him come onto the stage.

LOO: Out of the trap you mean. Like a cork from a bottle of bubbly. Such a cocky bugger. Thought he could fly.

HEMPITCH: Do you know that he'd demand twice as much counterweight on the trap as anyone else. That's how he managed to shoot up so much higher than the others.

LOO: Doesn't surprise me. He was so sure of himself. Flying Henry Mortimer with his legs tucked up under him like a frog, and a look on his face like he was the eighth wonder of the world.

HEMPITCH: I can see him now, doing the splits in mid air and then straightening his legs before he landed. Remember the cheers he got some nights?

LOO: Course I do. They positively howled with delight.

HEMPITCH: Everyone loved Henry. All the girls seemed to be sweet on him.

LOO: Did they now? Who are you thinking of in particular?

HEMPITCH: Well… Kissie Montpellier for instance.

LOO: Kissie Montpellier? Surely not? That little trollop was sweet on anything in trousers. Or didn't you notice? I'm surprised she didn't give you the glad eye, Billy… or maybe she did.

HEMPITCH: Of course not. I was just a lad.

LOO: That wouldn't stop Kissie. She was that desperate to get herself hitched.

You've gone beetroot again! Well, I never. Tell us about you and Miss Montpellier.

HEMPITCH: There's nothing to tell.

LOO: I've stumbled on a little secret, haven't I?

HEMPITCH: No. Honest.

LOO: Go on, you can tell me. Did you have a liaison in the costume store? She did love to entertain her gentlemen friends up there.

HEMPITCH: No. It weren't anything like that.

LOO: Why are you all flustered then?

HEMPITCH: I'm not.

LOO: Did she live up to her name?

HEMPITCH: Leave off, Loo, will you!

LOO: Did she get you to help her with her corset?

HEMPITCH: Leave it.

LOO: Oh sorry! Very touchy, aren't you?

HEMPITCH: No… It's not that… it's…

LOO: Delicate. I understand. Anyway, did the lovely Miss Montpellier talk much about us? Henry and me?

HEMPITCH: Yes, she did a bit. They all did.

LOO: What did they say?

HEMPITCH: Nothing directly to me like. I never got involved in gossip and all that. But I heard things.

LOO: Like what?

HEMPITCH: They said that old Jack must be blind not to see what was going on.

LOO: He wasn't so blind. He'd be waiting for me at the stage door every night to take me home. I began to feel like a prisoner under escort. But there was nothing in it at the start. It was all just a bit of fun.

HEMPITCH: I'm sure it was.

LOO: Go on, Billy. What else did you hear?

HEMPITCH: Well… I remember Kissie talking to Jenny Postlethwaite one time…

LOO: Jenny Postlethwaite! We're really going downhill fast. What did she say?

HEMPITCH: That Jack was a fool cos he thought harm could only be done after work was over. And then they started sniggering and whispering stuff and I didn't like to listen any more.

LOO: Very sensitive for a snoop, aren't you?

HEMPITCH: I didn't understand what was happening… or maybe I didn't want to. Old Jack was my boss and I always liked him, but I could see he was getting strange and sullen and bad-tempered. And whenever you were with Henry you seemed so happy. I didn't know what to think. I was fond of you both.

LOO: Did you say anything to Jack?

HEMPITCH: Course not.

LOO: Nothing at all?

HEMPITCH: Not a word. I just hoped it would work itself out.

LOO: Well it certainly did that. *(Pause.)* Have another drink, Billy and tell me more of what you know. Please.

HEMPITCH: There's nothing more to tell. It was a tragic accident. You were at the inquest. You heard what they said. Mechanical failure, cause unknown.

LOO: How were they so sure? Everyone was in such a hurry to get the case wrapped up. So the show could go on as usual.

HEMPITCH: That's business, Loo. You know the way it is. But I can tell you that trap was impeccably maintained and still is. Every day the points of the star are checked and the hinges oiled. But they're dangerous things. Henry Mortimer wasn't the first man to be killed by a star trap and he won't be the last.

LOO: Is that so?

HEMPITCH: It's the moment of release that's so risky. When the weights are let go the platform comes flying up at a hell of a lick and when it hits the buffers it just catapults the artist onto the stage like a human cannonball. There was a Harlequin killed in New York a good few year ago when a grip… that's what the Yankees call a carpenter… this grip walked over the trap just as the counterweight was released. It was a shocking mess apparently. His whole head was burst open.

And it wasn't much comfort to the widow to know that the grip was killed as well. And then I've heard of cases where the sections of the trap don't fall immediately back into place, so the mangets impaled round the waist as he lands. In Drury Lane there was this bloke…

LOO: (*Becomes visibly distressed.*) For God's sake, Billy, give it a rest.

HEMPITCH: I'm sorry, Loo. I didn't mean to upset you. (*LOO weeps.*) That was stupid of me to go on like that. Forgive me. Come on now, you best be getting home. I'll get you a cab. Wouldn't that be the thing? (*HEMPITCH puts his hands on LOO shoulders. She turns and hugs him tearfully.*) There now. You just let it all out. It's been a difficult old day.

LOO: (*Continues to hold him close. Then she straightens up and takes his face in her hands.*) Oh, Billy. Why won't you tell me?

HEMPITCH: Leave it be, Loo. It's all in the past.

LOO: (*She kisses him very gently, very deliberately.*) Please, Billy, I have to know.

HEMPITCH: What good will it do?

LOO: It'll give me peace. (*She takes his hand.*) Now then, sit down here beside me and tell me what you know.

HEMPITCH: It's all mortised and clamped up by thinking. I don't know where to start…

LOO: This will help. (*She pours another drink.*)

HEMPITCH: Thanks.

LOO: Tell me about that night. Tell me about Jack.

HEMPITCH: He wasn't himself at all. He'd looked pale and sick all week and on that Saturday I thought he was really going down with something bad. But he kept working away as usual and after the first show he left the men to stack the scenery for the quick changes. There was some trouble with the wheels on the chariot and I went off to find him in the coffee shop over the road. But he wasn't there. I thought nothing of it and went back to the theatre where we managed to get everything sorted in time for the men to go off for their tea. Then I had a quick bite myself and came back to give everything the once over, especially the trap, for that was a thing Jack was most particular about. He'd overlook a fault for anything else but if a man didn't follow procedure along a trap he'd get his marching orders. He always said it wasn't ordinary work, it was life or death.

LOO: But where was Jack all this time?

HEMPITCH: I'm coming to that. I needed to get a rasp to smooth off a chipped bit of scenery, so I came back here to Jack's den. And there he was hunched over his bench and filing away at something so intently that he didn't seem to hear me. He was so preoccupied that I just cleared off.

LOO: What was he doing?

HEMPITCH: I couldn't tell. The next time I saw him was when the whistle sounded for the Get-Ready. He was there at his post but looking so white and ill that the company manager asked him if he wanted to go home. He said he felt a little weak but that he'd be well able for the job in hand. Then the doors were opened and the audience came rushing and tumbling in.

LOO: It was a great house that night.

HEMPITCH: It's still the same story, Loo. However slack it might be for the rest of the week, it's Saturday nights that pay our wages.

LOO: I remember it so well. All that noise and excitement on the other side of the curtain. I just couldn't wait to get out there and dance. I knew me and Henry were getting into some terrible old mash and that we'd have to sort something out. But when I was dancing it all felt right.

HEMPITCH: I never saw you look so pretty, or kick so high.

LOO: And then I was in the wings waiting for the harlequinade and Jack was standing there beside me...

HEMPITCH: He was still ghastly pale and he kept gazing at the star trap. I looked at it too in case something was wrong, but it had been checked twice over as usual. I remember seeing it shine where the limelight caught the brass hinges... and then the spotlight came on for Henry's jump and the counterweight was released...

LOO: Oh God... yes...

HEMPITCH: I heard the platform rushing up dead on cue and then there was that terrible tearing sound and splintering of wood and out he came in his spangled suit...

LOO: I knew he was dead the moment I saw him. The way he stood there gently swaying with his head slumped to one side. I've seen it a hundred times in my dreams and I hear the screams begin all over again, and they get louder and louder and I see him topple over like a sack with his legs all doubled up beneath him...

HEMPITCH: You were the first to get to him.

LOO: I don't remember.

HEMPITCH: It was old Jack that caught you when you fell.

LOO: So I believe.

HEMPITCH: He carried you to the wings and tried to bring you round.

LOO: And what did you do?

HEMPITCH: It was pandemonium out there. Screaming and shouting and whistles blowing. People were climbing up from the orchestra pit and the stagehands were trying to keep them back. I made it my business to gather up the pieces from the trap. All scratched and splintered they were. And I put a box over the hole lest anyone should fall in and break a leg or worse. And then I spotted this queer looking piece of metal…

LOO: What was it?

HEMPITCH: A bit of flat steel, bent and jagged. I knew it didn't belong to the trap but it had to come from somewhere. So I put it in my pocket.

LOO: And?

HEMPITCH: That was when the police arrived. There was a big crowd gathered around Mortimer's body and they had to clear everyone away before they could examine him. I won't describe how he looked. It was all too ghastly. After a while they carried him off and laid him out in the property room. Two of them stood at the door and wouldn't let anyone in without permission.

LOO: So that's where he was. The props room. I wanted to see him so badly. I remember finding myself on a couch in wardrobe with Mrs Homcroft and some of the girls gathered round me. They kept giving me brandy and holding me hand and telling me not to worry. What did worry have to do with it? I knew Henry was dead and all I wanted was to see him and touch him again. But when I stood up and tried to go to him, my legs went from under me. So they gave me more drink and Mrs Homcroft kept shaking her head as if she was disgusted by what she saw. Then Jack came in looking like a corpse and he knelt down beside me and I thought he was going to cry. Then, without a word, he lifted me tenderly and carried me down the stairs. There was a big crowd at the stage door, all noisy and excited. Your friend Kissie was there talking to a bunch of Harlequins, but when we came out they went silent and seemed to turn away. Jack helped me into a four wheeler and we drove home. I must have slept for an age… Why didn't the police ask me any questions?

HEMPITCH: You were far too distressed.

LOO: But in the days after? Why didn't they talk to me then?

HEMPITCH: They didn't need to. There were plenty of other witnesses.

LOO: Did they talk to you?

HEMPITCH: Just a few questions. They didn't seem too interested in me.

LOO: Why ever not?

HEMPITCH: I don't know. Probably thought I was too young to bother with. I showed them where I found the pieces of the broken trap, but I was all agitated and I dried up when I tried to talk. One of them muttered something about an idiot asylum which wasn't too nice.

LOO: No. Coppers can be very unkind. So they let you go?

HEMPITCH: Yes. And I was never subpoenaed for the inquest either.

LOO: That doesn't surprise me.

HEMPITCH: Anyhow, I hung about for a while to see if there was anything I could do. The crowds drifted off home and to the pubs, all still stunned by what had happened. After an hour or so, the coroner's officer came and they took Henry's body away to the City Mortuary in a white van with no windows. It was hard to believe that the man in the spangles was lying dead inside.

LOO: You're a lovely way with words, Billy. But get to the end. Tell me how he did it.

HEMPITCH: That night, when I was undressing, something scratched my leg as I was taking off my trousers. It was the piece of flat steel which I had picked up off the stage. It was in the shape of a star but some of the points were bent and twisted. I stood with it in my hand wondering what it was for and where it had come from, but I couldn't think of anything in the whole theatre that it could have belonged to. So I left it on the table and told myself to bring it in the next day to see if any of the men knew what it was. I turned out the gas and went to sleep. I must have begun to dream at once and all the terrible events of the day gone by were mixed up in that dream. Mortimer in his spangled suit flying out of the trap. The broken piece scattering all around. Old Jack as pale as death looking on. And then you screamed and I woke in a cold sweat and I knew.

LOO: The steel star.

HEMPITCH: That was it. That's what Jack had been filing so intently at his bench.

He'd fixed it over the star trap where the points of the star joined. That's what I'd seen glinting in the limelight and that's what stopped the trap from opening and broke Mortimer's neck as he was driven up against it.

LOO: *(Pause)* So that's how the master machinist settled his score. What did you do with the piece of metal? What did you do with the murder weapon?

HEMPITCH: That was the dreadful thing. I realised that that twisted star would be enough to get Jack Halliday hanged. I thought about it long and hard. Jack was my master and you were his wife and he only did it because he loved you so much and couldn't bear to see you with another. And now Henry was dead and I thought you and Jack deserved a second chance.

LOO: A second chance! You're some fool, Hempitch. Did you really think it would all work out that easily?

HEMPITCH: I didn't know. I did what I thought was best.

LOO: So where is it?

HEMPITCH: What?

LOO: That damned piece of metal.

HEMPITCH: It's gone.

LOO: What do you mean gone?

HEMPITCH: Like I say, gone forever.

LOO: Explain yourself.

HEMPITCH: I was living up beside the quarry and there's a pond there so deep the boys used to say that at the bottom the water was boiling, it was so close to hell. I went outside and threw that metal star as far as I could into the dark water.

LOO: You never?

HEMPITCH: Yes, I did. As far as it would go.

LOO: Oh, Billy, you should have thrown yourself in while you were at it.

HEMPITCH: Don't say that, Loo. I did what I thought was right.

LOO: You've no idea, have you?

HEMPITCH: I wanted what was best for you. If it had come out… if there'd been a scandal and Jack was found guilty and… who'd have looked after you?

LOO: And what about justice? What about Henry? The man in the spangles? How do you live with that, Billy Hempitch?

HEMPITCH: I didn't know he meant so much to you. I thought it was just a passing thing.

LOO: And would that have made it right? To do what you did? *(She stands up.)* You know what you are, Hempitch? An accessory to murder. How do you feel about that? Does it not keep you awake at night? *(Pause.)* I'm sorry but I can't bear to look at you. I've got to get away from here once and for all.

HEMPITCH: Where will you go?

LOO: I dunno. I might meet some of the girls. Have a few drinks. Who knows, maybe Archie Sturridge will be sniffing around. Goodbye, Billy. Try to be good.

HEMPITCH: Loo, please.

LOO: Look after his tools for me.

She starts to leave.

HEMPITCH: What about your picture?

LOO: Keep it to remember me by.

She exits. HEMPITCH left alone. Music. Slow fade to black.

THE END

PHOTO BY KELLY CAMPBELL

FRED AND JANE
BY SEBASTIAN BARRY

FRED AND JANE WAS FIRST PRODUCED IN AUGUST 2002.

DIRECTOR: CAROLINE FITZGERALD
CAST: MARY MCEVOY AND COLETTE PROCTOR
DESIGN: EMMA CULLEN
LIGHTING: MOYRA D'ARCY

Author's Note:

This play was originally written to be played by my late mother Joan O'Hara and my wife Alison Deegan – but that plan came to naught. However, there remains something of them both in the characters. Caroline FitzGerald had the little play for a few years and finally put it together for performance in Bewley's in 2002, an entirely pleasant experience, and one I treasure in memory.

—Sebastian Barry

Day. The ante-room of a convent. Slow milling of sunlight. Rich polish of wood. Sense of care. Two nuns seated, Anna about thirty, Beatrice in her sixties, vigorous, bony. Expectant, like horses before the off. They are being interviewed, the questions as if edited out.

BEATRICE: *(midlands accent)* No assumptions, that would be the main thing.

ANNA: *(Middle-class Dublin accent).* Yes. I'd agree with that. No assumptions. We'll just go from the start for you. But if you thought you knew about it already... For our part, we'll be as candid as possible, as open as we can, after all these years of relative...

BEATRICE: A good layer and a bad hen are often found in the one bird.

ANNA: There's a proper country background for you. I wish I had that!

BEATRICE: A good layer and a bad hen... She'll give eggs, but she'll hide them. If you want to find them, you've to learn to think like her. And under old tractor parts you'll get them, old traps that were pushed aside in the fifties for the motor car.

ANNA: I think I especially was drawn to her because she was from the midlands.

BEATRICE: Lord, don't mention the midlands.

ANNA: She thinks there's no respect for the midlands in Dublin. We have a joke about that.

BEATRICE: The whole country has a joke about that. Unless you're from the midlands, you know.

ANNA: But Meath was the centre of Ireland once. The midlands were once considered the sacred part of Ireland.

BEATRICE: Dublin's revenge on Tara – Mullingar heifers. A phrase to terrorise you.

ANNA: As you can see, she's no heifer.

BEATRICE: Well, now. I've seen some pretty heifers in my day. I've seen heifers would put Lauren Bacall in the penny place. My own father had heifers he doted on. We used to worry about that. My mother and me, in the kitchen.

ANNA: Usually in a Dublin family you'll find a farm somewhere. But not in ours. Before Finglas was built up, my great-grandmother… But aside from that. And of course now…

BEATRICE: That's the why we wouldn't want assumptions. Because it's generally believed among the people that nuns, like guards, are country people. But Anna, as you can see plainly…

ANNA: People think also that country families love their daughters to go off being nuns.

BEATRICE: Oh, God. If only.

ANNA: She had a mighty struggle, a mighty struggle. She says she had to bribe her father… Tell her, Beatrice.

BEATRICE: Oh – well, it wasn't just only the heifers. I'm afraid, just between ourselves, and Lord love him, he's dead now, of course, and I hope for his sake he managed to… square things with Father O'Malley… what a man he was for scarves. Oh, dear. Was it Mullingar or Gomorrah, you are thinking now. But yes, I believe in a fair picture of things, but there were things I knew about him, I'd seen him at the edges of the darkness, you know, those little spaces of the country after dark, when light from somewhere unexpectedly… That's when you see the secrets.

ANNA: He was handsome like Beatrice.

BEATRICE: Handsome? I suppose he must have been. Or they thought so. Various shop girls, nothing too ambitious!

ANNA: She had the dope on him.

BEATRICE: Aye – and when I got the yen… To tell you the truth – I could go into that later, in a minute. You see, I had a sort of vision. *(After a moment)* Yes.

ANNA: A vision, she had. A real one. Like Saint What-Are-You-Having in Lourdes. Bernadette.

BEATRICE: Oh, I was fourteen. There wasn't a boy would go out with Beatrice Dunne because she was as tall as a dray horse. Well, to them. They were only little boys that time. That's all that was going those days, with the diet. Well, I was keen for a boyfriend and the pictures. I could have made a decent use of one. Not a bit of it. The devil wouldn't play. So one Saturday I asked my mother for a penny or tuppence or whatever was the asking price, and I went off to town and the pictures on my own – like a gangster!

ANNA: There's style for you.

BEATRICE: This would be the thirties, you see. Fred and Ginger were all the talk then. The couples in those primitive times modelled themselves on Fred and Ginger. Well, we were all there, the youth of Mullingar and outlying districts – huffing and puffing at each other they were. I felt like a lamb amongst wolves. I was that envious, that kissing going on, that wonderful rich noisy kissing Mullingar couples perfected at that time. Because it didn't do just to press the lips together. It was quite complex, you know, there were styles of arm-wrestling…

ANNA: Isn't she great?

BEATRICE: But the thing I don't think they saw was when Fred and Ginger were dancing and… A balcony, and that white light and the white floor… Fine music someone had got up for them… Oh, and I saw a dove came down from the top of the picture and sit on Fred Astaire's head…

ANNA: The Holy Ghost it was called then.

BEATRICE: Aye, aye, the Holy Ghost, Lord love us. I was sitting there. Fred paid no heed to it. Didn't mind one way or the other. Kissing went on. But for myself… Decisive. So I blackmailed my father to let me go to… to the cats he called it. He had his wits about him. Lord, he was angry though. Fuming. But he was a bit stymied, because of the dope I had on him, as Anna says.

ANNA: They might have made a fair go out of it, with pilgrims and such like, in Mullingar, out of Beatrice's vision.

BEATRICE: But you couldn't make a shrine out of the Capital Cinema, girl, the people wouldn't like it.

ANNA: But wasn't Ballinspittle a garage?

BEATRICE: I didn't hear that. Was it? Oh, but where would the couples have gone then? The last thing they'd want is some spotty girl getting the cinema dismantled, and holy terrors milling around after miracles… It was a private vision. My own.

ANNA: Of course it was. I was joking with you. I'm ashamed to have joked with you, Beatrice.

BEATRICE: Of course you're not ashamed. Why shouldn't you joke? It was a ridiculous vision. Fred Astaire, I ask you. But it suited me at the time. I was glad it wasn't that dreadful Cesar Romero, with the grease he used to put in his hair.

ANNA: She had the cream of the cinema at her beck and call.

BEATRICE: I used to wake up when I was a novice in the middle of the night and see Fred standing in the corner of the room, smiling very nicely. I must say he did always smile very nicely. At the back of my mind I wanted Gary Cooper to turn up, just the once, for the effect. Or Henry Fonda. Do you remember the time Ingrid Bergman left her husband and went off with the Italian director? Hollywood was very annoyed with her. Hollywood! Gomorrah itself. I was delighted for her. Because, I think my father imagined he was married to me, in a manner of speaking. Oh, how he went on. He used to drool when he was angry, because his head tilted forward and all the juice ran out down his chins. Hmm. I ran off anyhow, to the great Italian director in the sky!

ANNA: Beatrice!

BEATRICE: Oh, well. You're not shocked, are you? Not a bit of it.

ANNA: She's neither sense nor discretion betimes.

BEATRICE: I have plenty of both, thank you very much. You're a one to rebuke me, that fancied herself as Jane Fonda in *Klute*, as you're always saying, and were intent on being an actress. A fine example. A prostitute, no less. In the film, I mean. Oh, yes, I've had to sit through it a number of times. I've nothing against prostitutes as a matter of fact, but I can't let her away with that, that self-righteous…

ANNA: She was fantastic in *Klute*. Imagine seeing that at fifteen. I was with my brother. He was nineteen and got me in as his girlfriend. That was it. Flash of understanding. Jane Fondahood. Acting.

BEATRICE: She could have been an actress. She had the figure and the voice.

ANNA: Jane Fonda, I worshipped you. I have the tape. The fitness tape? She's fifty or something like it. Fifty?

BEATRICE: Thank you.

ANNA: Sorry, Beatrice. Fifty, and fit and shapely as a fiddle, I meant.

BEATRICE: Her father Henry never put on weight. I doubt if he danced about like that. In the blood.

ANNA: I'd have killed to be an actress. Wanting to be an actress at that age – a disease. A fire. You sit in the fire, not burning up. But burning.

BEATRICE: You still hanker after it. She still hankers after it, believe me, the poor girl. And she has the face and the figure and the voice still. Maybe we should encourage her to try her luck.

ANNA: I see. Now you can do without me all of a sudden.

BEATRICE: I'll come with you and be your dresser. I can be that splendid black actress, what was her name? Used to play the dresser in all the films. Like that chap lives in Ireland used to play all the bellhops and desk clerks, Hoagy Carmichael.

ANNA: O. Z. Whitehead, Beatrice.

BEATRICE: Yes, him. Dublin naturally is and was the haunt of famous actors. Did you know all the stars I've mentioned visited Dublin down the years? And where was I? In a nunnery in the midlands. Coming to Dublin was the making of me, though I missed the stars I was interested in. Fred was here a few years back, but not the same Fred. He looked like a survivor. A man who had survived being Fred Astaire. I mean, he looked grand. But not for visiting out in Collinstown.

ANNA: Dublin airport.

BEATRICE: Whatever they call it now. I was there the one time in the fifties. They had little tables out on the tarmac where you could have tea or, would you believe, coffee, and the planes were fat and silver. It was when the Bishop of – of – well, he was coming back from Africa. We were there, all the dames in black, waving. It wasn't the same as a film star, as you can imagine. A Wicklow man, the bishop, Dunne by name. No relation. He was said to be avuncular. He didn't get a chance to avunculate me, though. Too lowly, I must have been. Back to the midlands that night, on the train. The lot of us exhausted. Girls we were. Ignorant, but full of life and speculation. But not like Anna when I met her.

ANNA: You rogue. Not like Anna. Really.

BEATRICE: Anna Nagle, will I ever forget her, seventeen years old, a streak of misery.

ANNA: Oh, well!

BEATRICE: But very nice, you were lovely. A Monkstown girl. Lovely. Everyone admired you for taking the plunge, in an era when plunges weren't often taken, plunges of that sort.

ANNA: My acting career…

BEATRICE: My vision… *(They laugh.)* Aren't we the ones, with our carry-on? *(After a bit)* Of course, you had boyfriends galore. Before…

ANNA: A flood. When my mother would be going out, you know, to the theatre or whatever, in the evening, she used to say, 'Aprés moi, le deluge.'

BEATRICE: Louis the Fourteenth. Oh, you know…

ANNA: And sure enough, in they'd come, Simon and Gerry and the rest, and they'd drink her Bacardi. She hated Bacardi, so there was usually a bottle. You had to have it for – some drink grown-ups used to drink then. The fashion. The poor old deluge. Where are they now? They were good types. Then we'd hear her coming home, and away off out the back into the garden with them and over the back wall and into the old field. She didn't mind them in the house because she trusted me and she liked the deluge. But it was a point of honour with them not to be caught and identified by 'the conspiracy', as they called the parents. I was almost entirely Jane Fonda by then and would sit in the armchair looking like I'd just had a pretty demanding evening. All we did really was drink tiny amounts of Bacardi and play don – do you know that game?

BEATRICE: My sinful Anna!

ANNA: Well, you see, I was very keen to be a nun the summer after that, but I was ferociously sad to lose the deluge. And that was why I was a streak of misery when Beatrice found me. The others thought I was a pious snob, but I was just missing the deluge. Then Beatrice, as you will have gathered, was obviously a sort of deluge rolled into one. A mate. So I cheered up. I got into gear. She put flowers on the alter of Anna Nagle. Bingo.

BEATRICE: I don't know why she refers to a dignified old woman like me as a flood. The day the Pope landed on Phoenix Park I thought I was going to have to beat her, drive her back over the rugby grounds to Parkgate Street. She was like a puppy that wouldn't obey the simplest commands. I had to hold on to her cord. She kept hugging me and then bolting away nearer to the cross, and all sorts of esteemed religious bumped in the process.

ANNA: All right for you, nine feet tall. I wanted to see him properly. A man like that. He gave up a career in the theatre to be Pope.

BEATRICE: Well, the sacrifice. And not exactly, Anna.

ANNA: To be a priest. And do you know, he was the spit of Jane Fonda. Or Peter, anyway.

BEATRICE: He's not the slightest bit like any of the Fondas. Such a thing to say about the Holy Father. My God, Anna, but you see what you want to see. You always did… *(After a bit)* Jimmy Cagney I might allow…

ANNA: That old gangster? I'm sure the Pope would much rather be compared to Peter Fonda than Jimmy Cragface Cagney.

BEATRICE: Cagney looked just fine when he was young. He played Shakespeare, on celluloid. *A Midsummer Night's Dream*. Beautiful diction.

ANNA: And what part did he play, Beatrice?

BEATRICE: Bottom.

ANNA: See? Bottom. Jimmy Cagney. The Pope.

BEATRICE: It was just after that that the trouble started.

ANNA: Yes, it was. I still don't know why they decided… They didn't care what we felt… They didn't even know we… It's like the civil service in here betimes. Words from on high. We must obey. The earthlings will do as follows. The Daleks.

BEATRICE: After my time.

ANNA: Bureaucracy for nuns.

BEATRICE: We considered… Various options…

ANNA: Well, we sat back that day we heard and we wept like kids.

BEATRICE: You do feel powerless. Quite the same sensation when my father died. Or when they told me he was, you know, dead. Apoplexy. It seemed to me an old-fashioned thing to die of, but apparently you still can – die of it, I mean. Apoplexy. A man that never let a day go by without practising for it.

ANNA: My father's still alive but he's stuffed into one of those homes. Run by nuns, of course. Too many years without my mother. Never a successful pairing. Anyway, he had anal cancer and they took it out in Monkstown Hospital. I don't know if my mother went to see him. He used to read old letters to me that he saw on the napkins, or thought he did. Hard drugs! Then he came back from that but he fell down the metal stairs of a 46A bus – the common bus, we used to call it, because it went through Monkstown Farm. The 8 went very sweetly by the sea road. Old nonsense. The conductor caught him but he banged his old head. He's happier now than he's been for years, with his little room and Tennyson and Kipling for company. Not dogs, the real thing, books. Me and Beatrice go in to see him with chocolates.

BEATRICE: He's my age. Which goes to show. One sandwich short of a picnic, but a splendid man. Knows reams of poems off pat. A kind of cake mixture of Tennyson and the other fellow – but captivating. The most charming man on earth.

ANNA: So she says. You're a charmer, Mr Nagle, she says to him. And he goes red with elegance and pleasure. Anyway, we wept like kids.

BEATRICE: We'd been together for fourteen years. It did frighten me, that – there was too much feeling there. Wasn't there? Too much stored up. Too many good times. The daft little girl who came in as a novice, my little actress, had flowered into a friend.

ANNA: At first we thought it was a punishment, because Beatrice told me there had been some sort of meeting, a tribunal, but we found out later that that's quite normal.

BEATRICE: They hold a tribunal for everything. If a loo breaks down they hold one. But this tribunal decided they were sending Anna to a mission in England.

ANNA: England. You'd think it was a land of savages. A mission to England. As if England couldn't do without Anna Nagle.

BEATRICE: I thought it was a bizarre decision. But of course the English cities are – this was Manchester, and that's in a right state, so Anna says.

ANNA: You never saw such desolation and withering of the spirit. I believe things have improved lately.

BEATRICE: They had you for two years, dear.

ANNA: We lived in a terrace house, me and two other nuns. One was a very nice woman from the Gambia. The other was a witch from Glasgow. We tried to minister to old Irish expatriates down on their luck. Was there any other sort in Manchester? Not that I saw. Good women once from Irish towns done for with drinking, and half on the street, and marrying jailbirds for the company. You might as well marry a sailor for all the company you get. Meanwhile, back at the ranch…

BEATRICE: I was here blowing sorrow up the chimney.

ANNA: If you read her letters today. Huge big things like sliced pans, and the best thing since. I almost ate them for news. I was very afraid.

BEATRICE: We knew something was up with us. It was too severe and it didn't lessen.

ANNA: I started to imagine I was being punished after all, and I wrote to Mother Superior in Dalkey and asked her what I'd done wrong and that I missed home dreadfully. She wrote me a lovely letter, full of surprise and tenderness. But what use was that to me, when she didn't call me back? You see, I thought maybe they imagined – no, they just considered that me and Beatrice were...

BEATRICE: Wonky. No, they do go wonky sometimes, nuns. And the boys are prone, too. The poor boys. It's a great deal worse for the boys because they're not exactly tactile at the best of times. Did you ever see a priest embrace another? They're like diplomats at airports. But nuns don't heed all that. They're sisters. If they like each other. But we began to think we'd been investigated. Someone had been looking into us. That was the madness in the business.

ANNA: We were so lonely without each other we imagined all sorts of things.

BEATRICE: Like spies must do when they hear nothing from Moscow for a few months. But it was just a straightforward mission. It's normal for our order. We kept knocking our heads on the phone over it and in my sliced pan letters. And we never actually said the real crux of the matter. We never actually said the truth – we didn't know it.

ANNA: My whole system went out of kilter. It was like a menopause and a pregnancy rolled into one. I ate so much bad food I couldn't think for calories. My hair began to thin out – to fall out, for heaven's sake. I had more aches than a soccer player. The doctor thought I was an hysterical young nun and gave me barbiturates. I used to cry – you know those ornamental ponds? There'd be one in the middle of my pillow. You'd be surprised how much moisture you can produce. But I was a young woman. Beatrice started to come apart like an over-boiled onion. Not that she ever told me. I thought she was doing fine, aside from mere grief.

BEATRICE: I did deteriorate a little.

ANNA: Ha. The lobster speaks. Look at me, I'm alright. Bubble, bubble, bubble. Just going a little red. Hey diddle diddle.

BEATRICE: I asked a little child once – he was on O'Connell Street, a Sunday. It was an All-Ireland final, in the afternoon. Meath was playing, so I went out to hear the accents. He was a skinny little fella, seven or so, with a bag of glue. I don't usually stop. The city is so full of... But I did, and asked him if he was all right. You know, a foolish nun, stooping down to a little gangster. 'I'm bollixed, mister,' he said. Mister! Still, it was a powerful expression of his situation. After a year without Anna I might have said the same. First the lining of my stomach started to ball up and then the doctor said I had ulcers. I thought that elderly racing men that drank whiskey and drove across Ireland in their cars to get to meetings got ulcers. Fellows with rolls of ready bills and purple faces. But no, ordinary sixty-year-old nuns too.

ANNA: And she never said a mumbling word, as Odetta used to sing.

BEATRICE: After my time!

ANNA: The way I found out was, I was back for a few days – leave, to see my family. I don't even remember seeing them. All I remember is this one here, a vision of miserable – you see her now, a hale woman, a young woman…

BEATRICE: A young woman!

ANNA: She was like the old woman of the roads after a particularly bad winter. Thank God it's funny now, but I remember thinking, Mercy of God, she looks like an old banana in a habit.

BEATRICE: A charming…

ANNA: Well, you did, Beatrice.

BEATRICE: I had a little stomach trouble.

ANNA: That's right.

BEATRICE: Oh, I did, I looked like hell.

ANNA: The ghost of Fred Astaire.

BEATRICE: Poor Fred.

ANNA: If you can imagine now that we had another year and three months to go, and no guarantee I'd be brought back to Dublin at the end of that. I remember at Dun Laoghaire, those dreadful early-morning sailings, when half the country seems to be going home to England.

BEATRICE: Christmas, the government's shame.

ANNA: And poor Beatrice among the taxis, at the iron gates. 'Look after yourself, dear,' she says, and hands me the *Independent*. Jesus Christ!

BEATRICE: Did you not want the *Independent*, dear?

ANNA: Then back to sunny Manchester. Did you ever see the bleakness of Manchester? I swear to you, a vision of revengeful hell. Old factory chimneys, old black streets, poor ashen-faced citizens. Totally and utterly without God.

BEATRICE: You can't say that, dear.

ANNA: No, I can. God is a transforming light. Totally and utterly without God.

BEATRICE: But, dear…

ANNA: It is possible. There was nothing for me to do there. Totally and utterly. If anyone here thought that I, Sister Anna, the wrong side of thirty, was the person to bring God to Manchester – God wouldn't come. I did ask him a number of times. I begged him. But no, no. He wouldn't. 'Manchester?' he said.

BEATRICE: She exaggerates. Dublin people are excitable.

ANNA: Dublin. I used to dream of it. What is that softness of Dublin you dream of far away? Of course, these country politicians have destroyed the old city, but what is that – that mystery which remains? The complete grace of it? The politeness of the servers in the shops, the lovely way older people have of greeting you. I don't care if young people think I am mad to be a nun, or couldn't get a husband, or parts of me were sewn up, or whatever they think. That's all just temporary. We're a new nation now, and everything's being looked at. They're right, most of our old ways are antiquated. But they don't know yet that so many religious are looking at things anew and trying to adapt, and trying to get back… not the respect of the people, but the – you know, the feeling that a nun is a citizen too, a kind of fellow worker. That she has a place. Oh, this is my hobby horse. Nothing more tiresome, I know.

BEATRICE: You see, she exaggerates. The other day she said to me that nuns were like Travellers, that you'd be refused a drink in a public house. I pointed out that she didn't drink anyway. Then she said we were like those boot-boys in the sixties. I must say I don't remember them. Then she said I was like an angel, given an off-putting human guise.

ANNA: I didn't mean off-putting, I meant…

BEATRICE: Vanity, I know.

ANNA: Everyone knows you're handsome, Beatrice.

BEATRICE: Handsome. Clark Gable was handsome. He had bad breath, did you know that?

ANNA: Well, anyway, I wrote to Mother Superior again and told her I was – you see, you have to write delicately to a Mother Superior, because they tend to see through everything, like Superman – I said I was concerned about Sister Beatrice's ulcers and could she be sent after me to Manchester, where there was a world famous ulcer hospital, which there was. Mother wrote back saying she had looked into the matter and thought it best to keep Sister Beatrice in Ireland, where she was comfortable.

BEATRICE: If there had been a world-famous ulcer hospital on Mars and Anna was there, I'd have risked the space rocket. What took them longest to work out was how to deal with the body waste of the astronauts. In the end they were told to go in their suits. Anything, anything to be with Anna.

ANNA: But it wasn't to be.

BEATRICE: No. Everything got worse. Mother Superior came to see me herself and asked me directly what the trouble was. She looked at me very closely, stared at me kind of, you know, entered my mind. Well, I couldn't tell her. I didn't know, I still don't. I was falling apart like an old pair of shoes. You don't like to tell your Mother Superior that you can't get by without – without Anna. It would have sounded so adolescent to her. She's a very distinguished woman, a Goldsmith scholar. My God. I much preferred to suffer in silence. Dignity, anyway.

ANNA: It was a sobering year for us.

BEATRICE: Then I was diagnosed diabetic. Pernicious something or other. The doctor looks at you sort of pityingly. I could have told him better. I was suffering from Annalessness, a little-known-and-understood disease. You could tell from the way he sat in the chair that he thought my career as a pernicious diabetic would be a short and glorious one. The needles were fun. Hatpins.

ANNA: When you think of the ignorance of the wise.

BEATRICE: To a degree. But management has to keep a certain detachment. After all, the business of the order couldn't be disrupted because two of us were – were – suffering. But then the lovely thing happened. Fred Astaire to the rescue.

ANNA: After a long time of misery, misery changes you. It adapts you to itself. As I came to the end of my time in England, I thought – this is it, they won't let me go home, they'll send me on now to Africa. And I would have gone...

BEATRICE: The Mother Superior turns up one day. I do remember it, I mean of course I remember it, but I remember it exactly, because it was a day when I thought I couldn't go on, I couldn't go on with those injections, feeling awful, passing out, being shunted in the ambulance to hospital every so often, all the wretched drama of the diabetic – and it was in that light of illness, a flickering sort of light – Mother Superior, a Leitrim woman, the most sensible person on earth, she comes in quietly and sits near me, and she recounts this dream. She'd had this dream the week before, and it was on her conscience, and she didn't understand it but she knew what she had to do. She'd had this dream where I was dancing with Anna, a slow immaculate dance and Anna in a ballgown, and this clever Leitrim woman who never remembered her dreams ordinarily – wouldn't you think she'd be offended by such a dream, but no. She said no one knew the essence of things. Nobody, she says, can really say what represents what. What the meaning of things is, what the meaning of nuns is. She said it was her first and only vision, which she was going to nurture now for the rest of her life. She knew it was a good vision, she said. She knew there was something important in it, because when she cleared her mind it was still there, me and Anna dancing. So she was calling Anna Nagle home.

ANNA: So I came home.

THE END

ONE TOO MANY MORNINGS
BY MARK O'HALLORAN & DAVID WILMOT

ONE TOO MANY MORNINGS WAS FIRST PRODUCED IN SEPTEMBER 2002.

DIRECTOR: MICHAEL JAMES FORD
CAST: SEAN MCDONAGH AND MARK O'HALLORAN
LIGHTING: KELLY CAMPBELL

...'cos I'm one too many mornings and a thousand miles behind.
— Bob Dylan

Café. Afternoon. DOMINIC Enters. Fastidiously. Arranges table. Settles. Waits. CHRISTY enters speaking on mobile phone. He acknowledges DOMINIC.

CHRISTY: Passive… it can't be… read it to me. No passé… Watercolours 2002 is an exhibition so far past passé… no I don't think it's too harsh… I don't see what landscapes of the West of Ireland have to do with the people of Raheny. Well, I did like some things. Babin Ryan's Dublin doorways – you know, the doorways and window boxes – there was one with a cat in a boot. 'The youthful art of Babin Ryan' is positive. Yeah, I know she's seventy-six but she's a real artist and she has arthritis… (*Aside to DOMINIC*) The editor. (*Back to phone*) I don't think that's my remit. I'm a critic. I have to be truthful. Anyway, I can't do this now. I'm with a friend. OK Connor, thanks, I'll talk to you later. (*Switches off phone.*) Dominic!

DOMINIC: (*Stands.*) Christy.

CHRISTY: Hello.

DOMINIC: Sorry for your troubles.

CHRISTY: Ah, don't worry, it's nothing. It happens all the time. I'm too radical.

DOMINIC: No, I mean…

CHRISTY: Ah, you mean… thanks.

DOMINIC: It's a hard auld station. Sudden death.

CHRISTY: Yes… yes.

DOMINIC: I would have called you but…

CHRISTY: You weren't to know.

DOMINIC: No, I did know, I just didn't call you.

CHRISTY: Well, I'm sure you were with me.

DOMINIC: No, I wasn't.

CHRISTY: Well, you know what I mean.

DOMINIC: I did what I could but I should have done more but I didn't so I'm sorry.

CHRISTY: I understand. *(Pause.)* He was a lovely man.

DOMINIC: I'm sure he was.

CHRISTY: Yes. (*CHRISTY goes to sit.*)

DOMINIC: You must know, your father lost a father / that father lost, lost his, and the survivor bound / in filial obligation for some term / to do obsequious sorrow. The Bard.

CHRISTY: Lovely.

DOMINIC: 'How hard the winter / coarse and long / when your loved one's dead and gone.' Helen Steiner Rice. *(Pause.)* Half a league, half a league, half a league onward…

CHRISTY: Dominic. There's no need. Sit down…

DOMINIC: Tennyson.

CHRISTY: How have you been?

DOMINIC: More down than up.

CHRISTY: Ahhh. Really?

DOMINIC: Yeah.

CHRISTY: Anything in particular?

DOMINIC: Interpersonal difficulties.

CHRISTY: Right.

DOMINIC: Valerie.

CHRISTY: I didn't know you got back with Valerie.

DOMINIC: I didn't. This was a different Valerie.

CHRISTY: Oh right.

DOMINIC: A Valerie. Another Valerie. Tell you, Christy, there's something in that name. Karmicly speaking, Valeries' have it in for me. I should study it more deeply really. I mean, I know that it's a Latin name meaning healthy or strong and that it's the name of a second century Roman virgin martyr who was beheaded for loving Jesus and whose arms are to be found in a church in France, but it does not explain why two separate Valeries' have played havoc with my life. I should consult the Kabbalah.

CHRISTY: Indeed.

DOMINIC: How are things with you?

CHRISTY: Great.

DOMINIC: And Vivian?

CHRISTY: Fine.

DOMINIC: Is she still…

CHRISTY: Lets not go back there.

DOMINIC: Lets not. Bygones be bygones.

CHRISTY: Indeed.

DOMINIC: Lovely phrase.

CHRISTY: Beautiful phrase.

DOMINIC: Thanks for coming, anyway.

CHRISTY: No problem.

DOMINIC: You're looking great.

CHRISTY: Yes? I'm feeling fantastic… I'm cycling a lot, you know.

DOMINIC: I partly guessed.

CHRISTY: Really?

DOMINIC: Yeah, from your head. (*Indicates helmet.*)

CHRISTY: Oh, I always forget.

DOMINIC: Allow me.

They both take off his helmet.

CHRISTY: Thank you. Yeah, four miles in in the morning and then four back. Along the coast, sea breezes.

DOMINIC: That's a lot of miles.

CHRISTY: And the job itself can take me anywhere.

DOMINIC: Yes?

CHRISTY: Oh yeah, only yesterday morning I had a book launch in Crumlin and then after lunch I zipped across town to a fundraiser in Stocking Lane, Rathfarnham.

DOMINIC: Stocking Lane?

CHRISTY: Yes, the cats and dogs home.

DOMINIC: Ah.

CHRISTY: So that by the time I got home I'd notched up twenty-eight miles.

DOMINIC: Incredible.

CHRISTY: Sometimes I feel I'm never off the bike.

DOMINIC: Well, I hope you fare better than Paul Kimmage.

CHRISTY: Pardon?

DOMINIC: He spent his youth cycling around the low countries. Fifteen years on a bike and he got nowhere. He's a journalist now, you know. Blew the whistle with anabolic steroids and uncovered Tony Cascarino's Italian ancestry… but as to why anyone didn't guess at that, I'll never know.

CHRISTY: Sometimes journalists have to state the glaringly obvious, Dominic.

DOMINIC: You are part of a noble tradition my friend.

CHRISTY: Noble, but demanding.

DOMINIC: Responsibility.

CHRISTY: Responsibility to the truth.

DOMINIC: Pilger, Cameron, Kimmage.

CHRISTY: The Greats.

DOMINIC: The great cynics.

CHRISTY: Who?

DOMINIC: Journalists.

CHRISTY: I'm not a cynic.

DOMINIC: Well you should be. Any descent journalist has to be a cynic. Whether he realises it or not.

CHRISTY: No, no, no. Look, Dominic, *The Raheny People Freesheet* is a community newspaper. We are there to celebrate the extraordinary in the ordinary. It's more cups of tea and fairy cakes, but I love it. Just last week I met Maureen Potter at the opening of an adventure playground. For the kids. Wonderful. The sun broke through just as she was cutting the ribbon. It's as far from cynicism as I've ever been.

DOMINIC: Ah, I understand. But I believe our disagreement here is semantic rather than substantial.

CHRISTY: Go on.

DOMINIC: You are presuming that I'm using the word cynic in the pejorative sense.

CHRISTY: Of course, yes.

DOMINIC: Not at all Christy. The modern use of that word has nothing whatsoever to do with the noble philosophy of the founder of the cynics, Antisthenes.

CHRISTY: Antisnines?

DOMINIC: *Sthenes*, Christy. Antisthenes, the man who invented cynicism. The man who got the ball rolling, cynically speaking, back in ancient Greece. Cynicism, Christy… An ostentatious contempt for ease or pleasure.

CHRISTY: Ah! Now I'm with you.

DOMINIC: Yes, Christy. He just threw off the shackles of comfort and the re-emergence of his cult of the cynic could be just the thing to save this festering, post-opulence, Celtic-hangover of a country of ours.

CHRISTY: In what way, Dominic?

DOMINIC: Well, as a cynic I believe that you shouldn't value anything except virtue itself. Something this country needs to learn fast.

CHRISTY: Hold on. I thought that was what Socrates said.

DOMINIC: Well, the key ethical doctrines came from Socrates, but it was Antisthenes who sort of latched on to Socratic thought, so to speak, stuck it under his arm and ran with it. Eventually distilling it to a much purer form than his guru. Much to Socrates' chagrin, I might add, cause when Antisthenes formed his span-new school of cynicism, Socrates was there, barracking him saying, 'Why so ostentatious Antisthenes? Through your rags I see your vanity.' Is it any wonder he ended up poisoned?

CHRISTY: So, as a cynic, what is it that you believe in?

DOMINIC: Nothing. Except nature and virtue. As Antisthenes himself said, Christy, I would rather go mad than experience pleasure.

CHRISTY: Right. Kinda tough doctrine?

DOMINIC: Tough but rewarding. I lead a simple life now. According to nature, not convention.

CHRISTY: Right.

DOMINIC: Yes. Society has put value on many things, which I believe to have no value at all – hair-care products, anti-aging creams, the cult of celebrity. Materialism and money worship lead only to misery, greed and envy and as the great man said all those years ago, Christy, 'As iron is eaten by rust, so are the envious consumed by envy.'

CHRISTY: I see. So is there a group?

DOMINIC: Well, no. There's just me so far.

CHRISTY: Right.

DOMINIC: That doesn't worry me, Christy. I'm sure there will be others. And anyway, there have been many lonely cynics down through history.

CHRISTY: I'm sure there have.

DOMINIC: Diogenes the Cynic, for instance, was a solitary voice of truth and my all time favourite hermit. Lived his life to all intents and purposes as a beggar, in a barrel.

CHRISTY: In a barrel?

DOMINIC: In a barrel!

CHRISTY: He didn't live in the barrel.

DOMINIC: What do you mean, he didn't live in a barrel?

CHRISTY: I'm sure he was just in the barrel.

DOMINIC: Well, what's the difference between being in the barrel and living in the barrel?

CHRISTY: Well, he didn't cook or socialise in it.

DOMINIC: I don't know. He was an ascetic. Suffice it to say he spent a great deal of time in the barrel.

CHRISTY: Was it a big barrel?

DOMINIC: I don't know. But it was a significant enough gesture to draw the attention of Alexander the Great.

CHRISTY: Really?

DOMINIC: Oh yeah! So impressed was Alexander that he visits Diogenes one day as he sunbathed by the side of the road and says to him, Diogenes you may have from me whatsoever you desire, and Diogenes looks at him and says, Is that so? Well, will you get out of my light so, you're blocking the sun. He was a true great. With much to teach this modern age.

CHRISTY: Indeed.

DOMINIC: Except for his one small fault though.

CHRISTY: Yeah?

DOMINIC: Yeah. He was fond of masturbating in public.

CHRISTY: No. Could he not do it in the barrel?

DOMINIC: Obviously not and so the people of Sparta banded together and asked him to stop. To which he wisely replied: Would that I could cure my hunger by rubbing my belly.

CHRISTY: Well, as you know, I was always more of a man for…

CHRISTY & DOMINIC: The Stoics.

DOMINIC: Yeah, you were a stoic. Or the screamers.

CHRISTY: I was only a screamer for two days, Dominic.

DOMINIC: Three very long days if you were living in the adjacent bedsit.

CHRISTY: That's how we met. You screaming outside my door.

CHRISTY & DOMINIC: Shut the fuck up!

DOMINIC: Indeed. No. 163. The basement.

CHRISTY: Rathmines in the 80s.

DOMINIC: Our ancient Greece, Christy.

CHRISTY: Indeed. No. 163.

DOMINIC: No. 163.

CHRISTY: How is Squid getting on? I heard he was running a nightclub.

DOMINIC: Lapdancing.

CHRISTY: No.

DOMINIC: Yeah. Club called Girly Whurley on Parnell Street. Polishes the poles and keeps the punters in order.

CHRISTY: So he's given up the songwriting.

DOMINIC: He has turned his back on creativity. You two worked on some lovely stuff together.

CHRISTY: It was only two songs, Dominic.

DOMINIC: Indeed... Ahhhnnnmm... 'April Won't Be Here Till September' and...

CHRISTY: Ah... 'Snowdrops in Santry.'

DOMINIC: Beautiful words Christy. And how is the writing going at the moment?

CHRISTY: Well, well. I, well, I don't really have the time these days.

DOMINIC: For poetry?

CHRISTY: No, no. I still read a lot.

DOMINIC: Christy, any idiot can read poetry. I'm talking about writing it.

CHRISTY: I know you are. It's all different now, Dominic. Just, well, I don't know. Heaney winning the Nobel really knocked me back.

DOMINIC: Knocked us all back.

CHRISTY: Poetry shouldn't be about prizes.

DOMINIC: I know.

CHRISTY: I know you know.

DOMINIC: Well, that's all the more reason for you to be writing.

CHRISTY: Thank you, Dominic. You see when I started I felt I was being called to...

DOMINIC: Words.

CHRISTY: Indeed, but also to defend values, to promote beauty. Now it is just decoration. Wallpaper.

DOMINIC: Wallpaper.

CHRISTY: It's sold by the pound. Poetry by the pound.

DOMINIC: I know, Christy. All the more reason. You're still writing?

CHRISTY: No!

DOMINIC: What?

CHRISTY: No. I'm not writing. (*Dominic looks devastated.*) Look, Dominic, it's just not practical anymore.

DOMINIC: What? Poetry?

CHRISTY: Yes! I'm busy.

DOMINIC: Poetry?

CHRISTY: Yes! The paper takes up so much time.

DOMINIC: Poetry!

CHRISTY: And when I get home I'm tired and…

DOMINIC: Vivian!

CHRISTY: (*Pause*) I know what you're thinking. But it's not like that. Vivian's great, you know. She helped me see, that it wasn't good for me, you know. It upset her to see me descend to those lonely desolate places. Where only the beast of the blank page waited… and… and…

DOMINIC: Watched.

CHRISTY: Yes, watched and… and…

DOMINIC: Laughed.

CHRISTY: No, wrestled I wrestled with my… my… my…

DOMINIC: Writer's block.

CHRISTY: Yes, writers block. Sometimes now, when I look back on my years as a writer, I think that all I had was writer's block. And those struggles…

DOMINIC: Noble struggles.

CHRISTY: Yes, but exhausting. And Vivian, she hated to see me in that sort of pain. And one night, after a titanic struggle with my muse, I emerged from my room and she was sitting there, bags packed, coat on, an ultimatum on her lips. Poetry or me.

DOMINIC: Christy!

CHRISTY: No, no, no, Dominic, I was thinking too much. And you know, since… well, I'm happier. Things are more practical and sure everything's like that now. The whole of Ireland's gone practical. People ask straight questions and you give them straight answers and you go about your business and you keep yourself to yourself and that's that. There's no need for poetry any more.

DOMINIC: Wha… but… the…

CHRISTY: I know, Dominic.

DOMINIC: Life without poetry.

CHRISTY: Yes.

DOMINIC: Life without poetry.

CHRISTY: I know, Dominic.

DOMINIC: But what do you think about?

CHRISTY: Well, I don't really. I mean, I don't really have the time any more. Me and Vivian just sit at home or cycle places.

DOMINIC: And how long has this been going on?

CHRISTY: Well… about a year.

DOMINIC: A year without poetry?

CHRISTY: Yeah, Dominic, it was a compromise.

DOMINIC: But you were still writing the last time we met.

CHRISTY: Dominic, I haven't seen you in a year.

DOMINIC: Do you think I don't realise that… Christy, I hope that just because Vivian and me rowed that time we met, it has nothing to do with this crime against literature.

CHRISTY: Well, in a way it does!

DOMINIC: Christy.

CHRISTY: You upset her that night.

DOMINIC: She started it.

CHRISTY: You started it, Dominic. Look, she just can't stand the life poetry offered. The people. She just can't live life on the edge the way we used to.

DOMINIC: I see.

CHRISTY: And she's very healthy for me.

DOMINIC: Right.

CHRISTY: We lead a normal life now.

DOMINIC: I see.

CHRISTY: I'm happy. Things have just gone right since I first saw her.

DOMINIC: Right. And how did you first see her?

CHRISTY: Well, I was at the sea front in Clontarf one day, and the People In Need thing was on and I found myself being drawn in to the ladies slow bicycle race and there she was and I was just so impressed by her balance, her stability and it was just bang. You know? And we have a lovely flat together. Above a shop. And she is great with interiors. Everything matches. Curtains, carpets, tablecloths, tea towels, bedspreads, pyjamas. All Burberry. And we sit there of an evening. Not really saying anything. Maybe just holding each other's hand and just blending into the background. And that's very relaxing, you know. I don't even need *The Little Book of Calm* anymore.

DOMINIC: So I can see. I think we've all grown out of that book. But…

CHRISTY: And she's been a rock through all the family mayhem.

DOMINIC: OK. Well I'm glad you had someone there.

CHRISTY: Dominic, I think I'd have gone under if it wasn't for her. It was a terrible thing to find out that the man who raised me as his son, wasn't actually my father at all. Didn't want me around any more.

DOMINIC: I personally will never forget it, Christy. The day you discovered who your real father was. Deep psychic shock.

CHRISTY: Weeks and weeks of stasis. And then Vivian. And she encouraged me to make contact with my real Da, to be with him, as father and son, you know.

DOMINIC: I know…

CHRISTY: No, you don't know. You can't know. Meeting him for the first time was a… thing for me. To stand outside his shop. Just to revel in the…

DOMINIC: Smell.

CHRISTY: The smell and the…

DOMINIC: The blood.

CHRISTY: My blood.

DOMINIC: Your blood?

CHRISTY: My blood, my father, Dominic.

DOMINIC: Oh right.

CHRISTY: And surrounded by this…

DOMINIC: Horror.

CHRISTY: Dominic, I am aware of your beliefs around the subject of meat consumption but, please, this was my father.

DOMINIC: Christy, I'm sorry to offend your sensibilities but I have no intention of offending my own sensibilities by ignoring your biological father's participation with the beef holocaust.

CHRISTY: Dominic I know you're a militant vegan but just give this space. To me he was not just a run of the mill butcher but rather a master craftsman. And for a man who worked so gruesomely, he was incredibly handsome and tender and he won prizes up and down this country for both his spice sausage and his blood sausage and in the short time we were together he even named a new spiced burger blend after me. The Christy burger.

DOMINIC: Corpus Christy.

CHRISTY: Indeed. And when he died…

DOMINIC: So horrifically.

CHRISTY: He died of a heart attack, Dominic.

DOMINIC: But didn't he fall into his mincer?

CHRISTY: Only his arm, Dominic. Please.

DOMINIC: Sorry.

CHRISTY: Vivian was there for me one hundred precent. She's my rock and we made this decision to leave poetry behind together and we're both happy and there's no going back now. Poetry has come to an end.

DOMINIC: Right.

CHRISTY: Sorry.

DOMINIC: No, I'm sorry. *(Pause)* So how did you finish up?

CHRISTY: I beg your pardon?

DOMINIC: Well, what was the last poem you wrote?

CHRISTY: What?

DOMINIC: What was your final work?

CHRISTY: Ahhhhmmm… I can't remember.

DOMINIC: Your last work. Your final piece of art. You can't remember?

CHRISTY: Well, it's just…

DOMINIC: What?

CHRISTY: Nothing.

DOMINIC: You can tell me.

CHRISTY: Well…

DOMINIC: Come on. Out with it.

CHRISTY: I, ahhh…

DOMINIC: Yes?

CHRISTY: I wrote one for him.

DOMINIC: Who?

CHRISTY: For my Da. When he died.

DOMINIC: But he's only dead three months.

CHRISTY: I know.

DOMINIC: Ahhhh!

CHRISTY: Dominic, Vivian doesn't know.

DOMINIC: Well, that's fine.

CHRISTY: No, it's not fine.

DOMINIC: Well, why did you write it then?

CHRISTY: Because I had to.

DOMINIC: (*Pause*) I knew it. You are a poet, Christy!

CHRISTY: Well… I'm… no… just don't tell Vivian.

DOMINIC: Fine. So are you going to recite it for me?

CHRISTY: Ahhh… Jesus, Dominic.

DOMINIC: Our secret, Christy. Old times' sake.

CHRISTY: Old times' sake. Thanks, Dominic.

DOMINIC: Thank you, Christy.

CHRISTY: Right. Ahhh… it's a sonnet.

DOMINIC: Beautiful form, Christy. Comes from the French word *sonnett*. And may I add it is the perfect structure for such a formal dedication.

CHRISTY: Thank you, Dominic. Right. Poem for my Da. RIP.

> Mickey the Butcher
>
> Wire brush beside the block lies idle now,
> You'll see no more of meat swing to and fro.
> No more the carcass of the pig or cow
> Will loom above you entrails hanging low.
>
> An artisan with cleaver and with knife.
> A master with a fine array of meats.
> But never faithful to long suffering wife
> Oft women swooned and fell about your cleats.
>
> And when you found I was your long lost son.
> You nearly lost your arm to Grinders Claw.
> But oh, you soon accepted me as one.
> And overlooked my every little flaw.
> Mickey, man and butcher, rest in peace.
> You smelled of meat and now you are deceased.

DOMINIC: Strong, Christy. Very strong.

CHRISTY: Do you think?

DOMINIC: Oh yes. Really captures the man. Up there with your best.

CHRISTY: Do you think?

DOMINIC: Oh yeah. As good as you've ever been.

CHRISTY: Do you think?

DOMINIC: Oh yeah. Had me going there for a while you did.

CHRISTY: Well, in truth…

DOMINIC: Thought I was going to have to put my plan on hold!

CHRISTY: What plan?

DOMINIC: My plan to save our language.

CHRISTY: What? Irish?

DOMINIC: Not fucken Irish! English. (*He extracts bundles of papers from his bag and lays them on the table.*) In the beginning was the word and the word was with God and the word was God. Do you see, Christy?

CHRISTY: No.

DOMINIC: Antisthenes said it best, 'the investigation of the meaning of words is the beginning of education.' Words, Christy. We are going to investigate and invent words.

CHRISTY: Invent?

DOMINIC: We are going to endeavour to save the English language and prevent it from devouring itself.

CHRISTY: We?

DOMINIC: Up to this point, Christy, language has been sacred. But all that is going to change unless we act now.

CHRISTY: I'm sorry, Dominic, you've lost me.

DOMINIC: Did you know, Christy, that the beginning of language coincided with the domestication of the dog?

CHRISTY: No.

DOMINIC: Rather curious don't you think? I mean, why?

CHRISTY: Is it possible it's just a coincidence?

DOMINIC: There are no coincidences, Christy.

CHRISTY: Right.

DOMINIC: And I've wondered for a long time, Christy. What happened to mankind around the time they got their first pet that made words pour forth?

CHRISTY: I don't know.

DOMINIC: Well, I'll tell you, Christy. Before that for your average caveman it was just eating and procreating and you knew you were just another beast of the field and everything was groovy. But suddenly he gets a dog and he's sitting around the fire – him and his cave-wife and two cave-kids and the dog at his feet and he feels something, Christy.

CHRISTY: What?

DOMINIC: Something primal, huge but unseen, he feels like a human being and he has to mark the occasion and he lets out the first word, the holiest word

ever spoken and the foundation stone of all languages. He says the word OHM!

CHRISTY: OHM!

DOMINIC: OHM, Christy. The voice of God and man together. The sound of the human soul. And out of this other words flowed and grouped and moved and branched off. Arabic, Hebrew, Aramaic, Sanskrit, Ruratarian, Persian, Norse – all evolving from the sacred stream of OHM. Do you know where the word *orange* comes from, Christy?

CHRISTY: No.

DOMINIC: From the Sanskrit word *naranj*. And they passed it on to the Arabs and they passed it to the Spanish and then they passed it to the French and they passed it on to us and it changed to *naranjah* and *narangee* and *narenge* and eventually *orange*. Don't you see, Christy?

CHRISTY: See what?

DOMINIC: Words are sacred. They have been passed down to us. We are guardians of a linguistic heritage as old and precious as the pyramids. But we've ignored our duties and neglected our inheritance and now our language is about to devour itself.

CHRISTY: How?

DOMINIC: It has become tired. Stretched and meaningless.

CHRISTY: How, Dominic?

DOMINIC: (*Consults his paper.*) English began when the languages of the Angles, the Saxons and the Jutes crashed into one another in the fifth century and then it got mixed up with low German and Danish and Latin and old Norse and Norman-French and it became Old English and then Middle English and finally Modern English, like we speak today. But still sacred, still part of the stream of OHM. Holy words with history and lineage. Words that remind us of our humanity, Christy. That tell us we're not alone.

CHRISTY: Beautiful, so what's the problem?

DOMINIC: Because it is all changing, Christy. You are a poet, you must have seen. They're inventing new words. Words without history, without humanity, without divinity. Anti-poetry. Machine words. Work words.

CHRISTY: Like what?

DOMINIC: Wap, dotcom, gigabyte. Words to isolate and dehumanise and we have to fight back. Cause if we don't, we are all wapped, we're dotcomed. Over.

CHRISTY: But what can we do, Dominic?

DOMINIC: You, as a worker in words, Christy – you must join me.

CHRISTY: But I…

DOMINIC: Trust me, Christy. We can set about meeting and inventing words. Real words. New words. Words with history. Sacred words. Now to start, I'll just show you a list I've made. Here's our manifesto.

He lays his hands over his papers.

CHRISTY: Manifesto?

DOMINIC: Yes, Christy, we are going to form ourselves into a quasi-political grouping. The Language Party. Literatum et Verbatum. Campaigning initially on the language issue, but when that is sorted we can move more into the mainstream. I have lots of ideas. Cynicism in practice. Firstly, I would like to make the Good Friday Agreement an annual event, thus keeping the momentum going in the peace process.

CHRISTY: The words, Dominic.

DOMINIC: Right. This is our new dictionary. Test me.

He hands CHRISTY a scroll. CHRISTY reads.

CHRISTY: Pomposterous.

DOMINIC: One who is pretentious and absurd at the same time. Comes from a mixture of Latin and English words. And all these words you can use in your poems, Christy. Go on.

CHRISTY: Fundamotionalist.

DOMINIC: One who tries to oppress you with his own suffering.

CHRISTY: Paedofoil.

DOMINIC: A person who foils paedophiles.

CHRISTY: Mobollix.

DOMINIC: Someone who leaves their mobile phone on in art spaces.

CHRISTY: Tissers.

DOMINIC: A person who has their walkman on too loud on public transport. Onomatopoeia, Christy. Ts, ts, ts.

CHRISTY: Cassandroid.

DOMINIC: One who is paranoid but correct. I was thinking maybe that we could start drip-feeding the masses with a weekly article in your publication.

CHRISTY: The *Freesheet*?

DOMINIC: Yes.

CHRISTY: Dominic, I'd have to get approval for something like that.

DOMINIC: From who?

CHRISTY: Well, Connor, my boss, but he answers to—

DOMINIC: To who?

CHRISTY: To a board, you know. It's a community driven thing.

DOMINIC: *(Points at his scroll)* Commutiny – a collective turning of tables. So I think we should meet here again, say, tomorrow at 8 am. How are you set for the weekend?

CHRISTY: Me and Vivian usually go cycling on…

DOMINIC: Right, we can work around that. I think to begin with we will need to meet five days a week. I have the schedule here.

CHRISTY: But the job and all?

DOMINIC: Yes, there will be sacrifices we'll all have to make.

CHRISTY: Well, what if I can't afford to?

DOMINIC: What? Afford what?

CHRISTY: Well, the time I suppose.

DOMINIC: Afford time?

CHRISTY: Yes. I'm in a relationship. I share my time with someone else. It's easy for you.

DOMINIC: How is it easy?

CHRISTY: It's easier. You're single.

DOMINIC: How is it easier being single?

CHRISTY: From the—

DOMINIC: To be abandoned like that.

CHRISTY: Oh Jasus.

DOMINIC: Again and again.

CHRISTY: Valerie, still.

DOMINIC: Yeah. No, no.

CHRISTY: The other Valerie. What happened this time?

DOMINIC: I don't want to talk about it.

CHRISTY: Fine.

DOMINIC: Fine. *(Pause)* Well, we met because of our mutual dependence on public transport. The number 41. A beautiful route, Christy. One of the most beautiful in all of Dublin bus's many finely planned routes. And I seen her one morning on the way into town on the bus and her nametag read Valerie and it was just... I don't know. And she worked in a call centre in town and I used to get the bus with her every morning and we'd sit there, second seat from the front, comfortable and we didn't have to say a word to each other. Just...

CHRISTY: No, I know.

DOMINIC: Yeah enjoyed being there and looking out the window at the view.

CHRISTY: And where was she from?

DOMINIC: Do you realise you can see seventeen different types of trees along the 41 route. Oak, ash, laburnam, sycamore, spruce, elm, willow, roan…

CHRISTY: Where was she from, Dominic?

DOMINIC: I dunno.

CHRISTY: So what happened in the end?

DOMINIC: One day, out of the blue, she just turned around to me and she says, Would you ever fuck off and stop following me? And then she must have organised alternative transport for herself, cause I never saw her again. (*Rummaging in his bag.*) Have you seen my thesauruses?

DOMINIC pulls two bricks from bag, puts them on the table and continues to rummage.

CHRISTY: What are they Dominic?

DOMINIC: They are bricks Christy.

CHRISTY: I know they are bricks.

DOMINIC: Yes. Ordinary building blocks and the source of much of the insanity sweeping this country.

CHRISTY: But why are you carrying them around with you?

DOMINIC: I collect them, Christy.

CHRISTY: Bricks?

DOMINIC: Yes.

CHRISTY: Why?

DOMINIC: Well, to start with, I didn't know what attracted me to them. The colours, I suppose. Reds and such like. But then they began to mean something to me. I saw what they really were. You see, they're just like ourselves, Christy – just an accumulation of dust. Brick. Comes from the Middle-Dutch word *bricke*. And so I started collecting them. There was so much building going on all over I used just visit the various sites and tips and demolitions and liberate the bricks. Old ones, new ones, concrete, grey, red, ochre, brown, butterly yellow – a noble brick, Christy, lovely things. And I'd bring them home and stack them neatly in the back garden. I even believe I own one of the oldest bricks in Ireland. Liberated by a midnight visit to an archaeological dig. Little muddy brown thing it is. Beautiful. And I was collecting and stacking so hard that I didn't really notice what was happening to the community around me.

CHRISTY: What?

DOMINIC: Well, all the old neighbours were moving out or dead or dying and For Sale signs were springing up all over. Community in flitters. And then he moved in next door.

CHRISTY: Who?

DOMINIC: Ferdia.

CHRISTY: Who, Dominic?

DOMINIC: The first time buyer, Christy. Bought out Mrs Scanlan after she decided to opt for sheltered accommodation. A tidy enough fella. Twenty-six going on forty. Career Administrator with the dental hospital in Trinity College. And to start with, I kind of felt sorry for him cause he was clearly addicted to home improvement. Always hauling down walls or laying decking or buying things. Loads of things. Patio heaters and garden furniture and sliding doors and he lived entirely without curtains, which I found revolting. But then he starts to try and draw me into his lifestyle, tempting me to cross over to his consumerist nightmare of a life. Suggests various ways I can improve my frontage. Eggshell this and magnolia wash the other and I says thanks but the house has looked like this since I was eight years of age and I see no need to change it now and then he just changes his focus. Starts to mention the advent of summer and his pressing desire to entertain in his back garden, barbecues and the like, and he asks if I could tidy up the weeds and high grass and the bricks as it was spoiling his view and I says that I happen to find an untended garden both beautiful and relaxing and the pile of bricks were my business and my business alone and then I starts to give him a rundown on the perils of cooking meat on an open grill and he just walked away.

CHRISTY: That's rude.

DOMINIC: Exactly. And then things really took a turn for the worse and he's threatening solicitors' letters and court injunctions and quality of life surveyors and county councillors and one day we were on the street in front of our homes arguing furiously, and he said it. And he must have seen me flinch when he said the word cause he's looking delighted with himself and he says it again and again and again. You're nothing but a loon. A loon. A loon. And my plan just fell into place, it revealed itself. Cause I start collecting in earnest. Waiting for that magic number. 15,000.

CHRISTY: 15,000?

DOMINIC: Yes, 15,000. And I'm collecting night and day and it's neighbours from hell, shouts and dirty looks and loon accusations and then one day I get there. 15,000 bricks. And I wait for him to get home and I march over and knock on his door and he answers and I says, Do you know how many bricks it takes to build the average home? And he says, Pardon? And I says, Your average house. How many bricks? And he says, Excuse me? And I says A house like this. How many bricks? And he's looking kind of odd now and trying to close the door on my foot but I'm on a roll and I says, Well, will I tell you? 15,000 bricks give or take a few hundred. And do you know how many bricks I have in my back garden? 15,000 bricks give or take a few hundred. And do you know how much my bricks cost me? Nothing, gratis, free. And how much did your bricks cost you? I believe it was in the region of 300,000 euro. 300,000 euro. Now ask yourself. Who's the fucken loon? Who is the fucken loon?

Pause. CHRISTY struggles to respond. His phone rings. He answers. It is obviously Vivian. He has short conversation.

CHRISTY: I gotta go, Dominic. Vivian's waiting.

DOMINIC: Right.

CHRISTY: Good to see you.

DOMINIC: Yeah, great.

CHRISTY: Right.

DOMINIC: I'll be in touch about all this.

CHRISTY: Right, do.

Goes to leave.

DOMINIC: Hold on, Christy. Your helmet.

CHRISTY: Thanks. Protection.

CHRISTY leaves. Pause.

DOMINIC: Oh fuck.

THE END

PHOTO BY KELLY CAMPBELL

ELECTION NIGHT
BY DONAL COURTNEY

Election Night was first produced in May 2003.

Director: Joan Sheehy
Cast: Edward Coughlan, Emmet Kirwan and Micheál Ó Gruagáin
Design: Caitriona Ní Mhurchú
Lighting: Kelly Campbell

Author's Note:

For as long as I can remember, I have had a keen interest in politics and, in particular, local politics. My father is a town councillor and I have fond memories of attending election counts. It amazes me how close to the action one can get on election night. To see every vote being counted. The tension and the drama of an Irish election count has to be seen to be believed.

It was with this in mind that I sat down to write Election Night. I wanted to capture that drama. At the time of writing the play, there was talk of the abolition of manual counting. I felt an integral part of our democratic process was being eroded.

This play is my homage to the people behind the scenes on election nights. The foot soldiers, the canvassers, the tallly-men and all the amateur mathematicians who combine to create a drama more engaging than anything one might find on stage.

—Donal Courtney

A man sits forlornly on a chair centre stage. He is drinking a glass of whiskey. He is well dressed but his clothes are ruffled and his tie undone, like he has had a long day. DENIS enters. He is older, immaculately groomed. He has a sense of purpose, alert despite the lateness of the hour. The room is a small meeting room found tucked away at the back of almost any Irish hotel. DENIS sighs as he sees TOMÁS is drinking. They look at one another, each waiting for the other to speak. As this is happening, the audience hears the Returning Officer calling the latest Election Count results.

VOICEOVER: Returning Officer. The results of the distribution of Lennon Michael's surplus are as follows: Cahill Tomás, Fine Gael – Plus Three hundred and twelve, 3-1-2, total 3,197. Dempsey Maura, Non-Party – plus Three hundred and ninety-eight, 3-9-8, total 3,184. Gleeson Noel P., Labour – plus One hundred and forty-three, 1-4-3, total 2,653. Hannon Lower Lake Liam, Non-Party – plus Eighty seven, 8-7, total 2,112. O'Mahoney Brian, Fianna Fáil – plus Two hundred and twenty three, 2-2-3, total 2,701. As none of the candidates have reached the quota, I will now proceed with the elimination of Gleeson, Hannon and O'Mahoney and distribute their votes among the remaining candidates.

TOMÁS: Whiskey is highly over-rated, don't you think?

DENIS: In that case, don't drink it.

DENIS makes phone call on his mobile phone.

TOMÁS: Where have I heard that before?

DENIS: (*On the phone*) Have they counted Gleeson's transfers?

TOMÁS: Did we invent it or was it the Scots?

DENIS: Let me know when they have. (*He hangs up*) Sorry, what was that?

TOMÁS: I'm wondering if we invented whiskey or was it the Scots?

DENIS: We did.

TOMÁS: I thought so. That's what I like about having you around, Denis. You always have the answer. There isn't a question yet asked that you haven't an answer for.

DENIS: Tis my job to have the answers.

TOMÁS: Funny that. The public assume it's mine.

DENIS: That was Henry on the phone. They're still counting Gleeson's.

TOMÁS: And we invented whiskey. We should publicise that more. The Scots get the credit, same old story the world over. You do the work, someone else gets the credit.

DENIS: Stop feeling sorry for yourself man.

TOMÁS: We invented the kilt as well.

DENIS: Christ almighty will you stop ráiméising. (*Pointing to glass*) That stuff is doing you no good.

TOMÁS: You say kilt, everyone thinks of Scotland.

DENIS: (*Taking the glass*) You still have a speech to make.

TOMÁS: Don't remind me.

DENIS: If you lose, you'll have to come across disappointed but not bitter. Be gracious, humble. The public hold no *meas* on arrogant speech. All eyes will be on how you handle this defeat.

TOMÁS: They even filmed *Braveheart* here.

DENIS: Hah!

TOMÁS: The Scots.

DENIS: Sure, what about them?

TOMÁS: They filmed *Braveheart* in the Curragh. One of the few moments in their history they could feel proud of and when they had to re-enact it, they came over here. They used the F.C.A. in the battle scenes. That's a good one. The F.C.A. in a battle.

DENIS: Tomás, you may have a very important speech to make.

TOMÁS: What's the point?

DENIS: The point is, tis your duty.

TOMÁS: Not for long more.

DENIS: You're still a TD. While you are, you'll do as I tell you.

TOMÁS: If it's all over, I don't see what the problem is. (*He pours another drink.*) Want one?

DENIS: Don't spoil all the good work you've done by acting the eejit now. You've achieved a lot.

TOMÁS: If I did, it went unnoticed. One paper said I was competent.

DENIS: You are.

TOMÁS: I don't want to be described as competent, even if that is what I am. Competence won't get me re-elected. I'd have preferred dynamic. Energetic. Anything but being called competent. That's like when a girl tells you you're a nice fella. What good is that? It's not going to get you laid.

DENIS: You're a good politician, Tomás. There's no shame in losing your seat, for whatever reason you lose it. The shame is if you don't bow out gracefully. How you handle this defeat is vital.

TOMÁS: Vital for what.

DENIS: Your future chances. Think of next time. You're young, there'll be another opportunity.

TOMÁS: If I want one.

DENIS: Don't talk rubbish. (*Phone rings. Denis answers it.*) Go on? Down another twenty-three. That's bad but not as bad as we thought. Right. He's fine. How many of Hannon's are they counting? And O'Mahoney's? Get back to me as soon as you know any more.

TOMÁS: More bad news?

DENIS: We're down further after Gleeson's. Jesus, I knew we couldn't depend on those feckers in Labour. I'd better go down.

TOMÁS: Denis, I'm not sure I want this any more.

DENIS: The way things are going you might not have a choice.

TOMÁS: I mean ever again.

DENIS: So you're going to throw away years of attending functions, funerals, fundraisers, arse licking your way to the top, for what? To jack it all in the first sign of trouble. Get a hold of yourself man, tomorrow is another day.

TOMÁS: I thought I could make a difference.

DENIS: Ah for Christ sake, you're watching too many movies. No politician could have worked as hard as you.

TOMÁS: Then why have I lost?

DENIS: You never know what an electorate will do. Thirty years I'm in this game and I'm still at a loss to how the whole blasted thing works.

TOMÁS: Well, you should know. You're my adviser.

DENIS: I only influence their decision. What goes through their shaggin' minds, I'll never know.

TOMÁS: Five years ago you knew. You predicted I'd be elected to Dail Eireann at my first attempt. It was you who put me forward at the Party Convention. You were bang on. I eased in at the first count. Amazing. The biggest poll topper in the constituency for over half a century. How did you know that?

DENIS: I never expected the size of that win. Never in my years have I seen such a comprehensive margin. I couldn't have predicted that, but I knew you'd win.

TOMÁS: What made you so sure?

DENIS: Instinct.

TOMÁS: In politics there is no such thing. Only certainty and uncertainty.

DENIS: Last time you were a certainty.

TOMÁS: And this time?

DENIS: Soon enough we'll know for sure. *(There is an uneasy silence.)* Is herself coming in?

TOMÁS: I told her to stay at home until the last minute. No point in her waiting around for hours like the rest of us.

DENIS: True for you, boy. The wait for the final count is always the longest.

TOMÁS: Tis the cruelest of waits. We don't need those out there to confirm it for us. All those amateur mathematicians with their scraps of paper. Thank God this is the last election with manual counting. Dempsey is in. I can't catch her.

DENIS: Why don't we wait and see.

TOMÁS: There's no point in clinging to a miracle.

DENIS: I thought you'd at least wait for the result before you began your lament.

TOMÁS: So you agree. It's over.

DENIS: I never said that.

TOMÁS: But?

DENIS: I wouldn't be betting the mortgage on you.

TOMÁS: I wouldn't bet your mortgage on me. *(They laugh.)*

DENIS: Hold your head up, son. That's all you can do now.

TOMÁS: Yeah!

DENIS: Are you hungry? I can send out for a sandwich.

TOMÁS: No thanks. I have no mind for food.

DENIS: Jesus, things must be bad if you're refusing a bite. Is there anything I can do?

TOMÁS: Answer me one more question.

DENIS: That's not what I meant.

TOMÁS: I've always trusted you, valued your opinion. I need to know one thing.

DENIS: Ask your question.

TOMÁS: Did you know I'd lose?

DENIS: Yes.

TOMÁS: When did you know?

DENIS: That's two questions.

TOMÁS: When?

DENIS: I suspected it for some time but I suppose I knew for sure about three weeks ago. Around the time the campaign stepped up a gear. You didn't stand a chance with her. She was the darling of the media. Housewife stands after death of daughter. That's a tricky opponent to have.

TOMÁS: Why didn't you tell me?

DENIS: And what would that have achieved. Tell me. A defeatist look in photographs. You don't back a boxer who has thrown in the towel before the bell rings. I've run a few of these in my time. The golden rule is to behave like you're going to win. Politics is persuasion. If you don't believe you can win it, how am I supposed to convince that crowd out there you can?

TOMÁS: You had no doubt?

DENIS: No.

TOMÁS: Did I even have the slimmest of chances?

DENIS: Come on, this is getting us nowhere.

TOMÁS: How come you were so certain?

DENIS: Instinct. It does exist in this world of ours, despite what you may think.

TOMÁS: Where did I go wrong?

DENIS: Dwelling on the past. You have a conscience, plus you're too honest.

TOMÁS: What is so wrong with being honest? People surely appreciate an honest view.

DENIS: No place for that in politics. More fool you for thinking so.

TOMÁS: I disagree. People like an honest politician.

DENIS: They might elect them but do they get value from them. Ask yourself this, Who would you prefer to have representing you? Mister straight, honest, clean as a whistle politician? Or Mister pull a fast one to get a grant for the local swimming pool? I always said you were too straight but no, you wouldn't bend.

TOMÁS: I'm not the cleanest, we both know that.

DENIS: You're a choirboy in comparison to some of those fellas in Leinster House. Christ, tis like a Godfather film up there at times.

TOMÁS: But why do politicians have to bend the rules? God knows I do it myself at every clinic. Mammies trying to get their sons into the guards. Looking for medical cards, grants, planning permission. It goes on and on. God knows, I've pulled a stroke or two.

DENIS: 'Tis your job to do so.

TOMÁS: I don't need this now.

DENIS: Would you prefer a whiskey?

TOMÁS: Your job is to support me.

DENIS: Don't play that card with me. I was always there for you. Manys a night when the media were hounding you, who did you run to for advice? There was a time you even listened. When you were new to all this. Once you got your square foot of leather things changed. It was all about new blood. Get in touch with the youth. Make an appearance in this nightclub or bar, where the youngsters hang out. Half those apes you surrounded yourself with couldn't run to the jacks, let alone run a campaign.

TOMÁS: We had a good team. Diverse. People ranging in age and expertise.

DENIS: Save the press release for the media. I had to work alongside your diverse team, remember? There was no need for half of them. Did we need them the last time round?

TOMÁS: We needed to broaden our appeal.

DENIS: By employing the likes of Henry, 'the Fox'?

TOMÁS: Henry has his merits.

DENIS: He's a know-all who knows nothing, like most know-alls. He won a student election once and he thinks he's Henry… Kissinger.

TOMÁS: He's a hard worker.

DENIS: So was Florry.

TOMÁS: Who's Florry?

DENIS: My father's mule. Never let us down. A great worker but that's where it stopped. Florry didn't run the farm, my father did that, while Florry stuck to his patch of field. Henry should have stuck to his. He should never have been allowed to make decisions.

TOMÁS: Name one decision of his that went wrong.

DENIS: The 'Grab a Granny' campaign.

TOMÁS: Elderly people need to be ferried to the polling booths.

DENIS: According to Henry anyone over fifty was elderly. Which in effect means half of Dáil Éireann is.

TOMÁS: He's a bright lad.

DENIS: He's an eejit. If he was around the time of the Easter Rising, he'd have complained it was held on a Bank Holiday Monday.

TOMÁS: His hard work deserved to be rewarded by giving him more responsibility.

DENIS: This is not a charity. You put him in charge of the advertising budget.

TOMÁS: He studied accountancy.

DENIS: So did Charlie Haughey. I'm always telling you... *(Phone rings)* Go on! Yeah, his phone is switched off. Not too good. I'll get him to call you as soon as we know. We're still in there fighting. All the best.

TOMÁS: The wife?

DENIS: She's watching on telly. Wondering why she hasn't seen you.

TOMÁS: If she'd wanted a TV star she should have married Marty Whelan.

DENIS: She's worried for you. So am I.

TOMÁS: Sure I'll be fine. *(Pause)* Now, what do you suggest we do?

DENIS: Let's stop arguing about past mistakes for a start.

TOMÁS: Hear hear!

DENIS: Let's get our arses in gear and make an appearance downstairs.

TOMÁS: Easy for you to face them.

DENIS: Oh, you're not the only loser here. This campaign has been my whole life for the past six months. I knocked on doors in the arse end of nowhere when I could have been at home with the wife.

TOMÁS: Isn't that why you were so enthusiastic about knocking on those doors?

They laugh

DENIS: True. Twas a blessing in disguise. I'll miss my nightly trips around the county.

TOMÁS: *(Getting another drink)* One thing you must never doubt, Denis, is my appreciation for all you've done.

DENIS: Good to hear. We may be down but we're not out. We have to plan your future.

TOMÁS: I told you. I'm not sure I want one.

DENIS: Arrah molléir. You want one. It might not be clear to you now but trust me, you want it.

TOMÁS: How do you know?

DENIS: Instinct.

There is a knock at the door. HENRY enters enthusiastically. He is in his late twenties, his dress sense is old-fashioned and loud.

HENRY: So this is where the elite hang out?

DENIS: Well, if it isn't the hurler in the ditch.

HENRY: There's a room full of constituents down there trying to figure out where their man is.

TOMÁS: I was wondering when you'd find us.

HENRY: It looks bad that you're not there amongst them, Deputy. Anyone would think you've given up.

TOMÁS: How did you know where to find us?

HENRY: You know me, boss. Always keeping up with the action. In college, I was known as the Fox. Never missed a trick.

DENIS: Student politics. Huh! I bet you were the life and soul of Rag Week. What's happening below?

HENRY: You should see Dempsey, she's in the middle of it, smiling for the cameras. If there's a flash, she's in front of it.

TOMÁS: If she were good looking we'd be fucked.

DENIS: Stop the lights. You wouldn't take her if you got a present of her.

TOMÁS: What's the mood like downstairs, Henry?

HENRY: The Grinder Quinn is holding fort. They tell me it's his eleventh general election as head tallyman for the Party. The man is like a walking computer. He's rattling off the statistics.

DENIS: Best Tallyman in the history of Fine Gael.

HENRY: He's the best from any Party. Fianna Fáil have a new guy. He's wearing headphones, punching numbers on his calculator. Looks every inch the part but he hasn't made an accurate call all day. I'm not sure he even understands proportional representation.

TOMÁS: What does Grinder say?

HENRY: Too close to call. Even for Grinder. They're eliminating the final three. Dempsey should pick up preferences across the board being non-party but we're still in with a shout. She's done well from Gleeson but we've pulled a few back from Hannon. It's going to come down to O'Mahoney's.

TOMÁS: Fianna Fáil. A bad day if we're depending on Fianna Fáil.

HENRY: Yes, but he's from our side of the county. Plus his grandfather on his mother's side kicked with our foot. Fought alongside Collins. People don't forget that. I estimate if we can pick up a third of his transfers, we're heading back to Dublin, boss.

TOMÁS: The only reason for me to head back to Dublin is if Kerry make it to the All-Ireland. Even that is no longer guaranteed, Henry. There's no need to colour it. I know.

HENRY: You do.

DENIS: I informed him.

TOMÁS: We may as well face facts, lads. It's over.

HENRY: There is still a chance.

TOMÁS: A glimmer.

HENRY: A chance nonetheless. Elections are never over until every vote is counted. Tallies can be wrong. In college we ran a guy for Entertainments Officer of the Union and it all came down…

TOMÁS: I appreciate your optimism. I truly do. But at this very moment, it's misplaced.

HENRY: Are you conceding, boss?

TOMÁS: I can't concede. I have to wait. This is the worst of it. I may not like what's been said but the people have spoken.

HENRY: With respect, they've spoken but do we know for sure what they've said? The Grinder says it's all to play for.

TOMÁS: The Grinder loves the thrill of the count. This is what he lives for. He'll stay here all night if he can. Doing the maths. Working out every possible scenario, will this part of the constituency transfer to Dempsey or us? Whatever way he paints it, the figures no longer add up.

DENIS: We know the outcome.

HENRY: How can you be sure?

TOMÁS & DENIS: Instinct.

HENRY: In politics there is…

TOMÁS: Always a winner and always a loser. Now, if the debate on the outcome is over, I'd love another drink.

DENIS: Let's wait for the result, get through the speeches and then I'll join you.

We'll make a night of it.

TOMÁS: Sounds good. Henry you can play as well. We'll show you a thing or two about partying.

DENIS: It'll make your student days look like an I.C.A. cake sale.

HENRY: I can't believe you both are speaking this way. There are hundreds of people down there in that hall, sweating like their lives depended on it] and here you are, the man of the moment, giving up.

TOMÁS: Welcome to the sad, morose, self-pitying world of politics.

DENIS: You left out self-indulgent.

TOMÁS: That goes without saying.

HENRY: I never thought you'd give in like this.

TOMÁS: And I never thought this night would come. Nothing prepares you for this when you're out there on the campaign trail. Shaking hands, smiling for photos, visiting hospitals. Weeks of hard work and for what. One night in a hall full of 'experts' working their brains overtime on my behalf. Wondering if my seat is safe or am I going back to the classroom.

HENRY: Everyone is stunned that you're in a fight for your political life, it's true, but they all say you're a battler.

TOMÁS: I'm glad my plight is keeping them entertained. I'm just sorry I have no more surprises for them. Do you realise I was only twenty-nine when I was elected?

DENIS: The youngest TD this constituency had in over fifty years.

TOMÁS: Never thought I'd lose the seat this soon.

DENIS: Michael Pat Dolan was twenty-six when he was elected in 1942. As cute a whore that ever walked. Held the seat until 1969. I remember it well because it was my first campaign. We unseated Dolan at the first attempt. Replaced him with Batt Logan. Batt the bore. He had the demeanour of a funeral cortége. In twenty-eight years he spoke only once in the Dáil and that speech lasted two and half hours.

HENRY: What was it about?

DENIS: The price of postage stamps. Batt was passionate about postage stamps.

TOMÁS: He worked well for his constituents.

DENIS: True, still we were delighted when he retired. We needed young blood and you were our man, Tomás. It was time for a change.

TOMÁS: Is that what this is?

DENIS: Sure you were only there five years. Hardly time to warm the seat, boy.

TOMÁS: By all accounts it was warm enough after Batt. He never got off his arse.

They laugh.

HENRY: Is it because we came up against a woman?

DENIS: There are several reasons why we lost and it has nothing to do with coming up against a woman. The days when women were a novelty in politics are long gone. This is not 1990.

HENRY: What happened in 1990?

DENIS: See what I mean. He's just a kid.

TOMÁS: We lost because of that night. Three years and it still hangs over. Some mistakes are unforgivable.

DENIS: Every mistake is forgivable. Ask Clinton.

TOMÁS: My main regret is not coming clean.

DENIS: Fair enough. But live with the consequences.

TOMÁS: I have done ever since that night. How much longer do I have to?

DENIS: It will always prey on you. What you must do is not let it show. Especially in front of the press.

HENRY: That's the very reason I came looking for you. You're wanted for another interview. Someone from the Radio Kerry.

DENIS: Probably Fitzgerald. Killarney's answer to Bob Woodward.

TOMÁS: I'm giving no interviews for the time being.

HENRY: I can speak to him if you like.

TOMÁS: Would you, Henry? I'd appreciate it.

DENIS: I'd have to advise against that.

TOMÁS: Let him go. You know what to say, Henry?

HENRY: No problem, boss. I can tell them I don't have the figures yet but we're still optimistic and have full confidence in the Irish electorate to deliver the right result.

TOMÁS: Fine. Just avoid the college stories.

HENRY: I won't let you down. *(To DENIS)* I'll phone as soon as I get another tally.

DENIS: Good man, Henry.

HENRY exits.

TOMÁS: Jesus Christ. I think he's going to be more upset than any of us. Can't he tell a loser when he sees one?

DENIS: Let's have that drink before you bring out the violins.

TOMÁS: You've changed your tune.

DENIS: You're cróanáining is driving me to it.

TOMÁS: Come on. You wouldn't begrudge me some self-pity.

DENIS: I wouldn't, except you're so bloody good at it. Same again.

TOMÁS: If you insist. *(Pause)* Do you really feel it would have hurt to have admitted my involvement?

DENIS: Most definitely. *(Hands him a drink.)*

TOMÁS: Thanks.

DENIS: I don't condone what you did. I think you were stupid, but keep it to yourself, man. The day you were elected, you stopped being a regular person and became public property. No room for dirty laundry in the public eye.

TOMÁS: I should set an example.

DENIS: Christ, man, if that was the way it worked there'd be nobody left in Dáil Éireann. Sometimes I wonder about you. I suppose that is why you are up front, on show, and people like me are behind, pulling the strings.

TOMÁS: You make me sound like a puppet. Is that all I am?

DENIS: Your words.

TOMÁS: Your ideas.

DENIS: Here you are about to lose your seat.

TOMÁS: Tis only a seat.

DENIS: We both know you don't see it like that.

TOMÁS: Maybe I don't, but I feel better for saying it.

DENIS: Sure I know, but remember it's not all bad.

TOMÁS: Isn't it?

DENIS: Will you whist. You've a lot going for you. A wife, a young child. Think of them, before you decide to pack all this in.

TOMÁS: My family is separate to all of this. To them I'm a husband, a father. Not a TD.

DENIS: That's the greatest load of horseshit I've ever heard. Eileen has made sacrifices to get you where you are. This is not just about you. There are other political avenues to pursue.

TOMÁS: Are you suggesting the Senate?

DENIS: Better than a dingy classroom full of spotty teenagers.

TOMÁS: I don't know about that.

DENIS: It's an option you should consider.

TOMÁS: I'm too young.

DENIS: Nonsense. Look at Healy in Cork.

TOMÁS: It's a retirement home.

DENIS: It could be a means to an end.

TOMÁS: More likely an end.

DENIS: Listen. The Party is in tatters. Two election defeats in a row. Those bastards could last another five years. After that who knows? Tis very hard to be returned to Government three times in a row. Our time will come. Next election you'll walk in. There may be a Ministry or two up for grabs. At worst a Junior one. One day, if you play your cards right, the top job might come up.

TOMÁS: Climb off me, will you! Now you're the one talking horseshit.

DENIS: Am I? We stand to lose a lot of seats tonight. All over the country. A lot of experienced politicians are being forced into early retirement. Why is that? Because they're past it. Their time is up, but not you, boyo. Oh no. You hang in there for the long haul.

TOMÁS: What makes you so certain I could get re-elected.

DENIS: She's an Independent. A single-issue politician. The worst kind. The Dáil will be littered with them this time. She'll be hard pressed to find her way to Dublin, let alone Dáil Éireann. Trust me, she has one term and it might not even last five years.

TOMÁS: It was good enough to get her through this time.

DENIS: This time, yeah. People will tire of her and her anti-drink driving slogans. They've heard it all before. Where does she stand on housing? The hospitals. Education. She wouldn't know the first thing about taxation.

TOMÁS: Where do I stand on those issues?

DENIS: Where we tell you, boy. You have us to look after you. She's alone. She'll be back down from Dublin with her tail between her legs before you can say Budget Deficit.

TOMÁS: Ah stop! You're an awful man.

DENIS: I'm glad you think so.

TOMÁS: I know so.

HENRY re-enters.

DENIS: That was quick. You must have given them your life story.

HENRY: They didn't want to speak to me.

DENIS: Go on! I would have thought the biggest names in Irish media would have been queuing up to get an interview with you.

TOMÁS: Leave him alone, Denis.

HENRY: No reflection on myself. They just want the main man. Can't blame them for that.

TOMÁS: They all want to be the first to interview the loser.

HENRY: Now, now. We'll have none of that talk. It's not all over until the fat lady sings.

TOMÁS: By now she's well into her final verse.

HENRY: With respect, there's always hope. Remember Spring? The time he almost lost his seat back in the eighties. They thought he was gone but he scraped through. The rest is political history.

DENIS: Remember much about the eighties, eh Henry?

HENRY: I've read books.

DENIS: He's read books. Why didn't you say? If we'd known you'd read books we could have promoted you to Director of Elections.

HENRY: What is your problem with me? Spit it out. Every time I open my mouth…

DENIS: You say the wrong thing. Always putting your foot in it.

HENRY: That's not true.

DENIS: Oh, but it is. There was the time you went on local radio to defend some of Tomás's more unorthodox planning decisions. What was it you said? Oh yes, the deputy is not guilty of any discrepancies. His only crime was to look after his friends. Brilliant. You were quoted in every national newspaper the following day. You could have ended the campaign with one sentence.

HENRY: I got us in the news. No such thing as bad publicity.

DENIS: It's just one cliché after another with this fella.

TOMÁS: Can both of you calm down, please? It was a messy campaign.

HENRY: Is there any other kind of campaign?

DENIS: How would you know if there was? You've somehow managed to be involved in only the one. What possible comparisons can you make?

HENRY: Don't get mad when I say this, but I have read books on previous elections.

DENIS: Tomás, when you analyse what went wrong here over the last few weeks, look no further than the bookworm here.

TOMÁS: The damage was done before the campaign. That surely is something we can all agree on. I'm tired of arguing. This backbiting is pointless.

DENIS: This is the time to do it. Soon we'll have to smile for the cameras.

TOMÁS: I was always good in front of the cameras. Tonight I'll probably get an Oscar.

DENIS: Stand proud and suffer defeat graciously, boy.

HENRY: It could be worse. You could be a Green, like Kissane. Eliminated first count. It will be a long time before we hear from that eco warrior again.

TOMÁS: He isn't an eco warrior. He's a barrister and at least he believed in the issues he fought for.

HENRY: Exactly. Look where it got him. Four hundred and forty-two first preference votes. I wouldn't like to be in his shoes tonight.

TOMÁS: Same place as myself. A loser.

DENIS: You're not a loser. You just didn't win.

TOMÁS: Thanks, Denis. Remind me to enter that for political quote of the year.

HENRY: If it's any consolation, the place is in shock down there. The fact that it's an unknown housewife who's battling for the seat makes it even more amazing.

DENIS: Good man, Henry. Keep going. There's still a nail not fully belted in.

HENRY: I'm only stating fact.

TOMÁS: She fought a good campaign. I'll give her that.

HENRY: On little resources too. Big achievement.

DENIS: Whose side are you on? I'm beginning to think he's enjoying all this.

HENRY: I'm just giving credit where it's due. She would have to have fought a good campaign to beat us.

TOMÁS: We were very beatable. We had more negatives than a one-hour photo booth.

HENRY: Yes, but more positives than a… than a…

DENIS: Than a what?

HENRY: I can't think of an amusing metaphor.

DENIS: There isn't one.

TOMÁS: We lost because we were weighed down with negatives. There was the planning scandal. That hit us. Then the controversy over the proposed dump.

DENIS: I think we managed to come out the good side of that.

TOMÁS: Just about. Then there was that night and my role in those events.

DENIS: We… You dealt with that as any decent politician would.

TOMÁS: That was my mistake. I dealt with it as a politician, not as a person.

DENIS: Never show them too much of yourself.

TOMÁS: Stop talking to me like you own me.

DENIS: I'm only trying to protect you.

TOMÁS: You protect your precious Party. Serving your own interests is all you're good for.

DENIS: For sure that's what I do. But I've always served yours as well. That you can't deny.

TOMÁS: I know. I appreciate that.

HENRY: With respect, what do you mean by your role in those events?

DENIS: Let's have another drink. Henry, will you join us?

HENRY: I really should get back downstairs. We have to keep up a presence there. The returning officer is due in the next half hour.

TOMÁS: Another five minutes won't matter. You've been flying the flag all day.

HENRY: If you say so, boss. I'll have a Diet Coke.

DENIS: You will not. All that is on offer is whiskey.

HENRY: But I don't drink…

DENIS: You do now.

HENRY: They expect to have O'Mahoney's counted shortly. The Grinder feels we may have pulled a few back.

TOMÁS: How many is a few? *(He distributes drinks)*

DENIS: Slainte. *(They drink)* Did that hit the spot?

HENRY: Ooh yeah!

TOMÁS: How many is a few, Henry?

HENRY: A respectable return.

TOMÁS: A respectable return. He's learning the lingo. Political speak for not enough. I'm fucked. Back to the classroom boy. *(There is an uneasy silence.)*

DENIS: Do you remember the time we were at the Ard Fheis and we went drinking with Weeshie Sullivan, the Senator from Galway.

TOMÁS: The all-nighter. Jesus, we got blotto!

DENIS: The residents' bar closes and Weeshie announces, 'Do you know what, I have a bar in my room, do you chaps have one of those?'

TOMÁS: No, says Denis, mar dhea. You must have paid more for your room to have a complimentary bar in it.

DENIS: So he invites about four of us up, delighted with himself and we drink his mini-bar dry. He had no idea he had to pay for it.

TOMÁS: How drunk did we get that night?

DENIS: Yeltsin drunk!

TOMÁS: I'd have given anything to see his face next morning when he saw the bill.

DENIS: I'd have given anything to be able to see next morning.

TOMÁS: Weeshie was some gobshite.

HENRY: If he was such a gobshite how did he get elected to the Senate? (*TOMÁS and DENIS look at one another, and break down laughing*.) Did I say something funny?

DENIS: Young fella, you have no idea.

TOMÁS: I want to propose a toast, to the losing team.

DENIS: To five years' time.

TOMÁS: The Party might not run me.

DENIS: Of course they will. Sure who else have they?

TOMÁS: Thanks.

DENIS: You know what I mean. Despite this result no one has the same pedigree as you.

HENRY: I'm not used to drinking.

TOMÁS: That's another of my qualities. I can drink. Vote Cahill, hard working, hard drinking. He can make a difference.

DENIS: Are we back to self-pity? Cnáimsháiling like an ould one.

TOMÁS: (*He holds up glass*) The root of all my problems. Henry, if you ever want to know why I lost my seat, look no further than that bottle. Forget the planning scandals, controversies over proposed dumpsites, the real reason is drink.

DENIS: You can't blame it on drink.

TOMÁS: Correct. Once again, Denis, you are correct. Alcohol was merely the ignition. The reason Tomás Cahill won't be back on his square foot of leather when Dail Eireann resumes is because of Tomás Cahill.

DENIS: How many times do we need to go over this?

TOMÁS: As long as it takes. Besides Henry here has never heard the true version of events.

DENIS: For very good reason. Henry hears only what Henry needs to hear.

TOMÁS: Well he needs to hear this. He's walking around thinking I'm Nelson Mandela. There is nothing he won't say or do to protect me. Have you any idea the type of man you've been protecting, Henry?

DENIS: It's been a long day. Let's not say things we might regret later.

TOMÁS: Regret! If only you had let me tell the truth.

DENIS: You would have stood no chance. At least you gave her a run for her money.

TOMÁS: Is that what this is about? Giving her a run for her money? I should never have stood. I caused Dempsey and her family great pain and she has paid me back in the best way possible. By taking my seat. I think they call that poetic justice.

HENRY: The drink-driving thing. Sure that had nothing to do with you, everyone knows that. The driver was your friend. Nothing wrong with knowing a man, no matter what crime he has committed.

TOMÁS: The night Maura Dempsey's daughter was killed I was close by.

DENIS: For the record, I think this is a bad idea.

TOMÁS: Noted. Let the record show that Denis Grimes once more would like to shut me up.

DENIS: He knows what happened. It's been well publicised throughout Dempsey's campaign.

HENRY: You lobbied on behalf of your friend. His sentence was reduced. Any one would have come to the help of a friend.

TOMÁS: I had good reason. It was my fault.

HENRY: But you weren't there.

TOMÁS: I might as well have been. I was five miles away in my friend's house. Eileen and I were having dinner with the Falvey's, Eamonn and Julia. A reunion of old friends. We all knew nights like this were rare. After dinner we drank brandy, told stories. There was plenty of this stuff but we were running low on Brandy. I had a rare bottle of cognac at home. So, being the big man, I insisted we get it. I know all I was doing was showing off. Drinking it didn't matter. I just wanted them to know I had it. Who would drive back to get it? No one wanted to, we'd all been drinking, but I persisted. Eamonn was in the best condition. His wife opposed this motion but my years in Dáil Éireann stood to me and I got my way. I even mapped out his route. Down back roads so as to avoid detection from the Gardaí. It wasn't his fault, he was only following my orders. *(Pause)* He didn't see her until it was too late. She was eighteen.

DENIS: It was an accident.

TOMÁS: I caused it and then I had the callousness to cover up my involvement. When Eamonn was released early, Maura Dempsey came to me for help, unaware of my part in it. I said I could do nothing. Her own TD refused her help. I'm a great man when you need a grant or planning permission, but when you really need my help, forget it. Her only option was to run against me so this kind of thing could stop.

HENRY: If this ever got out you'd be ruined.

DENIS: The most sensible thing you've said all night. Now, if the Angel Gabriel is finished cleansing his soul.

HENRY: Who else knows about this?

TOMÁS: Eamonn and Julia Falvey, my wife and us.

DENIS: The Falveys know the value of keeping their silence.

HENRY: This is unbelievable.

DENIS: A long way from student politics.

HENRY: Light years. If I had known this…

DENIS: You would never have got involved in the campaign.

HENRY: I wasn't going to say that.

TOMÁS: Now you know what I'm like I take it you won't feel like speaking on my behalf.

HENRY: Was winning the Election more important than admitting your involvement?

DENIS: Oh yes.

HENRY: I wasn't talking to you.

DENIS: You were talking to my man. Same thing.

HENRY: This is just a game to you.

DENIS: Right you are. Now you're getting the hang of it. I've worked on ten general elections and my appetite is stronger than ever before.

HENRY: I looked up to you two.

TOMÁS: I'm sorry. You had a right to know.

HENRY: You have a reputation as the honest politician.

DENIS: There's a nice play on words.

HENRY: I never imagined it like this.

TOMÁS: Don't let this put you off politics. There's a lot of good gets done too. The problem is the good is easily forgotten.

HENRY: What are you going to do now?

TOMÁS: I'm going to go down to that hall. Shake hands with as many of those election fanatics as is humanly possible, make a speech, graciously accepting defeat, then walk out the door, leaving politics behind.

DENIS: Now listen here…

TOMÁS: Please, Denis. It's not just talk, or the night that's in it, or whatever. I'm leaving all this behind.

HENRY: Who'll take your place in the next campaign?

TOMÁS: Not my problem. Perhaps one of you could.

DENIS and HENRY look at one another.

HENRY: Now you're having a laugh.

TOMÁS: Why not? Henry, you have youth, enthusiasm, commitment. You may never have the exact figures but you're easily the most optimistic canvasser I've ever known. Denis, you have the experience. Nobody knows more about winning an election campaign than you.

DENIS: Or how to lose one.

TOMÁS: Now who's feeling sorry for themselves?

DENIS: I'm a long way past feeling sorry. There is a reason why I work behind the scenes. I'm good at it. That is why I intend to stay behind the scenes in the future. There is another campaign in five years to win. The name on the ballot paper doesn't matter. My job stays the same. Get that person elected. I'll not let one defeat deter me.

TOMÁS: Easily said when it's not your defeat. Your name isn't on every poster, every newspaper headline. Tisn't dancing across every lip in that hall down there.

HENRY: Why don't you both calm down?

TOMÁS: Shut up, Henry. When we need you to contribute, we'll ask.

HENRY: You never asked before.

TOMÁS: I didn't need to. You were working for me.

HENRY: I still am.

TOMÁS: Despite what I've just told you.

HENRY: You did what you had to do. If that's the way politics has to be, so be it. I'm either in or out. I slogged too hard to get a foot in the door to walk now.

DENIS: Good man yourself, Henry. We might keep you yet.

HENRY: Was that a compliment?

DENIS: No, a statement of fact.

TOMÁS: What do you mean we?

DENIS: You're just the pawn. We're the Party. You are about to walk out. Free. The first sign of trouble and you're gone. We'll still be here.

TOMÁS: Why do you do it?

DENIS: Because I love it. I love the Party. My Father helped to establish it. It's in my blood. I love the campaign. I love the Election night. Tomorrow, I'm a pharmacist once again, Henry has his career. The Grinder… well, nobody knows exactly what the Grinder does. But tonight, we're something else altogether. We're important. We have a say in the next Government. Not many people in many countries can do that. Get this close to the action. I love being involved. The greatest irony is that the candidate doesn't share my passion. You have no idea what you've lost. You had what I could only dream of having.

TOMÁS: You could have run when you were younger.

DENIS: Could I? If you were at those conventions you would know I was never going to be allowed run. Too valuable behind the scenes. Pulling the strings. (*DENIS's phone rings.*)

HENRY: Jesus, that was some speech.

DENIS: (*On the phone*) Go on. No. How sure are you? All right. Thanks, Mossie. (*He hangs up.*)

HENRY: Who's Mossie?

TOMÁS: The Grinder.

HENRY: What's he say?

DENIS: I thought I'd been through it all before, but tonight beats all. *(Pause)* We lost.

TOMÁS: No surprise there.

HENRY: Shite!

DENIS: Don't you want to know by what?

TOMÁS: It hardly matters. I need another one. (*He goes for whiskey*.)

DENIS: Twelve votes.

TOMÁS: What?

HENRY: Only twelve?

DENIS: You know what that means.

HENRY: We have to call a recount.

TOMÁS: Twelve lousy votes.

HENRY: We must recount. It's too close.

DENIS: It's the Deputy's call.

TOMÁS: Twelve! What should I do?

DENIS: There are a lot of people depending on you.

TOMÁS: Jesus, Mary and Joseph!

DENIS: Them as well. Come on, Tomás. We can turn around twelve votes. It's too close to concede.

TOMÁS: How?

DENIS: O'Mahoney came through for us.

TOMÁS: Jesus, Fianna Fáil!

HENRY: It's a funny old game this.

DENIS: It certainly is, Henry, it certainly is.

DENIS hugs HENRY.

TOMÁS: We're still in there fighting.

DENIS: We surely are.

TOMÁS: We'd better call the recount then.

DENIS: Right you are, boss! This night's a long way from over.

HENRY: We'd better go down for the official result.

DENIS: Lead the way, Henry.

TOMÁS: I thought we were dead and buried.

DENIS: I told you to hold off on making your retirement speech.

TOMÁS: How well you knew.

DENIS: Instinct!

They exit. Lights down.

THE END

PHOTO BY KELLY CAMPBELL

So Long, Sleeping Beauty
By Isobel Mahon

So Long, Sleeping Beauty was first produced in September 2003.

Director: Michael James Ford
Cast: Philip Judge and Bernadette McKenna
Design: Bianca Moore
Lighting: Moyra D'Arcy

Author's Note:

So Long, Sleeping Beauty was developed from a one-woman piece for radio narrated by Glynis. The challenge I was faced with was in developing the characters of Neville and Glynis. I'd like to acknowledge Mark O'Halloran and Michael James Ford for their great help and support in this process.
When we finally came to the rehearsal period, the script was pretty complete and we made very few changes apart from the last page. It was decided that despite the sympathy between them, too much water had passed under the bridge for Glynis and Neville to remain friends. I still wonder about that. Of course, in America, where everybody loves happy endings, people kept saying to the actress 'Are you crazy, go to Italy with him, he's gorgeous!'

—Isobel Mahon

GLYNIS sits on a park bench. She's a woman in her early fifties who has clearly been pretty and still holds vestiges of her girlish charm. Her clothes are neat but unremarkable, her shoes sensible. There is an air of apprehension around her. She glances around, then takes a novel out of her bag, thinks better of it and puts it back. Time passes.

Enter NEVILLE. He is a small, dapper man, somewhat younger than Glynis. His demeanour on this occasion is tentative but we see that he is probably a 'Character' under other circumstances. He is a natty dresser, wears a good overcoat and silk scarf.

NEVILLE draws in a breath as though to speak, then thinks better of it, exhales and sits down. He glances at GLYNIS out of the corner of his eye. She is feeling awkward.

NEVILLE: Eh…

GLYNIS: Mmm?

NEVILLE: Nice evening.

GLYNIS: Oh… Yes.

NEVILLE: *(Pause. Almost to himself.)* Pleasant.

GLYNIS: Mmmm.

NEVILLE: Do you…?

GLYNIS: Not often

NEVILLE: I see… Nice spot… Verdant.

GLYNIS: Pardon?… Oh yes…

NEVILLE: *(Pause.)* Am I right…?

GLYNIS: Yes.

NEVILLE: In…?

GLYNIS: Yes

NEVILLE: Ah. *(Pause.)* Neville…

GLYNIS: Yes…

NEVILLE: Yes… Thank you for coming.

GLYNIS: That's all right… We…

NEVILLE: Hmmm?

GLYNIS: I… live near here… quite… near here…

NEVILLE: Yes… I know…

GLYNIS: Sorry?

NEVILLE: No… I mean, good. Nice area.

GLYNIS: Yes, yes it is, actually.

NEVILLE: Lovely gardens. Are you a gardener, Glynis, by any chance?

GLYNIS: I am, actually. I was just noticing. *(Pointing to a tree ahead of them.)* That's an Acer.

NEVILLE: Excuse my ignorance… but…

GLYNIS: Maple… Variegated… from the East probably. Lovely foliage.

NEVILLE: Yes…

GLYNIS: Why do you ask? Don't tell me… You noticed my hands…

NEVILLE: Not at…

GLYNIS: I need gloves… my hands are ruined. Ava… the lady who does for us… well… did… Kept saying to me. Look at the state of your hands, missis, you're a disgrace. You'll arrive at the Pearly Gates with muck under your fingernails…

NEVILLE: She doesn't any more?

GLYNIS: No need. I can do for myself now.

NEVILLE: I see…

GLYNIS: *(Pause.)* And yet it never looks clean… And you would think… I mean who is there to cause a mess?

NEVILLE: The?

GLYNIS: No matter how often I clean the windows... it... still seems... dingy... Are you a gardener, Neville?

NEVILLE: Me? Oh heavens, no, I just manage to kill things...

GLYNIS: Yes...

NEVILLE: He liked it here...

GLYNIS: *(A shock runs through GLYNIS.)* Really? I didn't know...

NEVILLE: Only the odd time.

GLYNIS: I see. *(Pause.)* Of course, he knew nothing about gardens. As Ava says... Missis, if it wasn't for you we wouldn't get out the gate for weeds.

NEVILLE: Your garden always looked very nice...

GLYNIS: You've...?

NEVILLE: Only on the way to rehearsal.

GLYNIS: Rehearsal?

NEVILLE: Yes, I'm a singer.

GLYNIS: *(Impressed)* Really?... Professional?

NEVILLE: Well, I work elsewhere. 'Manjare' – to eat, Glynis... as we all must

GLYNIS: Quite.

NEVILLE: But I prefer to say that I follow the grand tradition of the 'Amateur' or 'He who Loves.' 'He who serves his Art without thought o remuneration.'

GLYNIS: I see... So you don't get paid?

NEVILLE: No.

GLYNIS: And where do you...?

NEVILLE: Mountbank Musical Society. And before you ask, nothing at the moment. But we did *Carousel*, end of last year. Three nights. Cracking show. Brought the house down.

GLYNIS: Really? And what part did you play?

NEVILLE: Me? No. No. Chorus. The backbone. Centre of the back row, Neville, that's where we need you, Trevor says to me. Director, you know. You hold the whole bunch together. I don't mind telling you, Glynis, some of the chorus are... well, put it this way: 'tuneless' would be... polite.

GLYNIS: Oh dear.

NEVILLE: People say to me, Neville, why does a good singer... and I don't mind telling you that I am a little useful... Why does a good singer like you not mind being in the chorus? But as I tell them, my wish is to serve... I'll go where I'm needed. And it's true...

GLYNIS: I do quite enjoy the opera. A couple of years after we were married, Maurice and I went on one of his business trips to London. We saw *La Traviata* at Covent Garden. Magnificent. I don't believe I've seen anything quite like it since.

NEVILLE: *(Slightly unnerved by the comparison.)* Lovely. Of course, the music is only part of it. You wouldn't believe the work that goes into a show like that. I mean... the actors can't sing in the dark... can they? They can't stand stock still, can they?... *(Looks expectantly at GLYNIS.)*

GLYNIS: *(Shaking her head dutifully.)* No, I suppose not.

NEVILLE: Dance is my thing. Whip them round the back and lash them through their old one twos, says Trevor. And that's where I come in. Ballroom training.

GLYNIS: Lovely.

NEVILLE: And Tap. You know... step, turn step, ball change, step, turn, step, ball change. Half of them you have to start off teaching them their left from their right. Then, Jesus. It's getting them to start all facing the same direction so they don't end up waving at the scenery... I don't know why I bother, sometimes.

GLYNIS: You make it all sound so easy. I can't imagine getting up there on stage, I wouldn't be able to remember a line!

NEVILLE: Nonsense! But it's hitting that first note, Glynis, that's the tricky part. You might say to me, that's the most obvious thing in the world. But believe me. When you're out in front of that crowd and the lights are shining in your eyes and you can hear those programmes rattling... and the orchestra strikes up your intro and you can feel your heart pounding... It's hitting that note... clear as a bell. Perfect pitch, Glynis, that's the ticket.

GLYNIS: The only time I can remember being on stage was as the angel in the Nativity play in Senior Infants!

NEVILLE: Delightful.

GLYNIS: Not really. It was a disaster... I saw my mother in the audience and tried to climb offstage.

NEVILLE: Puts me in mind of Wexford two years ago…

GLYNIS: Oh?

NEVILLE: Figaro… Marriage of… I'm Basilio.

GLYNIS: *(Clearly mystified.)* I see…

NEVILLE: My big moment. Act Four, right? And I'm in the garden with Figaro and he's got his big number… So his intro starts… the first bar… and it's dreadful. *(Sings a phrase by way of illustration.)* Now this guy, Ray, is a good singer. And we can't believe our ears. And I'm looking at the footman and he's looking at me and we're both nearly pissing ourselves, if you'll pardon the expression. Anyhow, he struggles through to the end and there's dead silence! The audience are stunned. Can you imagine? So we're in the bar afterwards and between us we work out that he's accidentally taken his note from the brakes of a passing bus! Well, we're on the floor! And yours truly is being a bit naughty and taking him off, so Mouse shouts…

GLYNIS: Mouse?

NEVILLE: *(Taken aback)* Maurice…

GLYNIS: Maurice was there?

NEVILLE: Oh…

GLYNIS: When, exactly… October, was it…?

NEVILLE: Yes…

GLYNIS: I see…

NEVILLE: I'm sorry…

GLYNIS: So… did he enjoy himself?

NEVILLE: Yes… I believe he did.

GLYNIS: Well… that's… something. *(Pause.)* I feel terribly stupid.

NEVILLE: Don't.

GLYNIS: No, really. I do. I can't help feeling it's my fault. Does that sound silly? Ever since… I've been thinking, where did I go wrong? *(Turns to face NEVILLE.)* Where did I go wrong?

NEVILLE: You didn't.

GLYNIS: *(Indicating her bag.)* I have them here. It didn't seem right to keep them. They belong to you.

NEVILLE: My letters?

GLYNIS opens her shopping bag and takes out bunches of old letters on mauve paper, held together by elastic bands, she places them on the seat beside her. NEVILLE looks at them. He is silent for a while.

NEVILLE: Oh. *(Pause, touches the letters, holds them.)* So many. I didn't realise… I'd written so many… *(Moved.)* Oh, I remember this one… French post mark. First time I'd been away… sorry… thank you. *(Sits holding them on his lap.)*

GLYNIS: Yes.

NEVILLE: Where…? How did you…?

GLYNIS: The night after I arrived back from the hospital.

NEVILLE: Oh.

GLYNIS: That night was the first time I'd ever opened the bureau. The key, you see was on the bunch. His last effects. Just a sodden wallet and the keys. I felt so guilty. Like a snooping child. Kept waiting to hear his voice behind me… The top drawer was all the usual stuff. Bills, receipts, insurance, marriage certificate. The second drawer had his lodge business, sash and medals. And the bottom drawer. I remember the key turned so easily… and there it was. A big oblong chocolate box with two fluffy white kittens in pink bows on the lid… The moment I saw it… I knew.

NEVILLE: Oh.

GLYNIS: I couldn't touch it. Isn't that stupid? Couldn't look at it. There was a blue and white striped shirt I'd been mending when the… doorbell rang. And it was still lying over the arm of the sofa where I'd left it and I thought, not much point in finishing that. But I picked it up and started sewing anyway. I was a wife when I started… when I finished I was a widow. Funny. Everything changed and yet nothing… You know the way when ordinary things are still the same so you could nearly forget that anything had happened at all?

NEVILLE: Yes.

GLYNIS: I finished the button… and bit off the thread… and went over to the box and turned it out on the floor. And… I couldn't believe it… All those letters, cards, menus…

NEVILLE: I'm sorry. I didn't know…

GLYNIS: I sat up all night reading them and rereading them. This secret world of two strangers. One of them my husband. And I didn't recognise him. Can you believe that? He sounded like… like a completely different person… like somebody I wouldn't know. I never thought he could be so… *(Pause. Quietly.)* We weren't like that.

NEVILLE: I don't know what to say to you.

GLYNIS: I kept thinking about it… whether to contact you. Every day for the past three months. What would I say to you? I should feel angry. If anybody knew. What would they think? His firm. The bridge club. The bowls club.

NEVILLE: I've waited every day since the accident for that phone to ring. You're the only one… *(Pause.)* You're all I have left of him.

GLYNIS: I see. *(Pause.)* Neville… Did Maurice ever talk about me?

NEVILLE: No… not really. Hardly at all, in fact.

GLYNIS: I see. *(Not sure how to take this.)* Well… probably for the best.

NEVILLE: Yes. *(Silence.)* I used to wonder about you…

GLYNIS: You never.

NEVILLE: No, really, I did.

GLYNIS: The other woman?

NEVILLE: *(Laughs in spite of himself.)* I suppose.

GLYNIS: And… how did you imagine me? Or dare I ask?

NEVILLE: Well… not as pretty… definitely.

GLYNIS: Really?… Oh, go away! Pretty!

NEVILLE: No, I'm serious. Surely Maurice must have told you that?

GLYNIS: Not really. Oh, he might say something like, You look well in that dress, dear. But somehow that's not the same. He never said to me, Glynis, you're a beautiful woman, like they do in the films. But then I don't know if that ever happens in real life… does it? I mean between husbands and wives? I mean… half the time husbands don't notice what their wives wear at all. There were times when I'd a good mind to go out wearing nothing at all, just to see if he'd notice!

NEVILLE: I dare say he'd have noticed!

GLYNIS: I wonder…

NEVILLE: Glynis, may I be honest with you?

GLYNIS: *(Looks a bit nervous.)* Yes.

NEVILLE: Now, don't take this the wrong way... I say this as a professional...
Those clothes don't do you justice.

GLYNIS: Oh.

NEVILLE: I'm in the rag trade, as they say. Gents outfitters. But I've an eye. You've
the figure, you see. You could wear anything. Nice little Chanel-type
thing, spring shades... neat bob... smashing.

GLYNIS: *(Suddenly feeling self-concious.)* Yes... well I do... I try to get at least two
years out of a coat. But I'm good like that. Domestic Economy was always
my thing at school... One year for our summer test we had to turn an
old garment into something new... and I... managed to turn my aunt's
bedspread into *(indicates)* this sweet little dress and jacket... with
matching bag and shoes. Everyone was amazed! I'm handy like that... I
can make do. Slip in a pair of shoulder pads, and...

NEVILLE: Voila!

GLYNIS: Of course Maurice had... views... about wasting money on clothes...
well... my clothes... He always went shopping alone... I never really
knew what he... *(Trails off as the truth begins to dawn.)*

NEVILLE: Plenty.

GLYNIS: I see. It seems there's so much I didn't know about my husband. Do you
know how long we were married? Thirty years. Thirty years of washing
his socks, thirty years of cooking his dinner, thirty years of having his
mother to lunch every bloody Sunday... Excuse me.

NEVILLE: You could sing that, if you had an air to it... Sorry.

GLYNIS: No. Go on. You might as well. I didn't even know Maurice liked musicals.
I used to love musicals. I remember when I was ten being brought to
Calamity Jane in the old cinema in Rathmines... Doris Day. I used to idolise
Doris Day, all I wanted was to be like her... wear a stetsun and
sixshooters... Can you imagine?

NEVILLE: I think that was *Annie Get your Gun*.

GLYNIS: Was it?

NEVILLE: In *Calamity Jane* she wore...

NEVILLE & GLYNIS: That suede outfit! 'Oh the Deadwood stage...'

GLYNIS: *(Animated)* That's right. She was afraid of nothing. Climbing out of the
stage coach window and shooting at the poor Indians... Of course, I
thought this was fantastic! Remember at the end when she gets reformed

and starts wearing a dress? And you were supposed to be glad? Well, I wasn't. I was disappointed.

NEVILLE: Of course. *Calamity Jane* is all… code.

GLYNIS: Code for what?

NEVILLE: Oh, come on…

GLYNIS: No, really.

NEVILLE: Well… The two girls. The pretty one and the…

GLYNIS: Ah, no… no! Doris Day was just a tomboy… sure didn't she fall for Howard Keel in the end… or was it the other fellow?

NEVILLE: 'Once I had a secret love…'?

GLYNIS: But that was about… *(Pause.)* Do you think so?

NEVILLE: Looked like it from where I was sitting.

GLYNIS: … My Aunt brought me to that. If she'd only known…

NEVILLE: Maybe she did…

GLYNIS: Oh, that's wicked.

NEVILLE: I'm telling you…

GLYNIS: *(Wistful.)* I used to love her in those films with Rock Hudson. The first time I met Maurice, that's who he reminded me of. So tall and… hunky.

NEVILLE: Tell me about it.

GLYNIS: But that was when he was young. You didn't know him then. Doris Day always looks so… happy in the old films. And so glamorous. And Rock adores her, even though they fight. I saw one recently… very late at night and I couldn't help thinking, What happened to me? What happened to the girl who wanted to be Doris Day, with her lovely shining smile and her lovely shining life? How did I end up like this? I read about Rock Hudson in *Woman's Own*… or was it *Woman's Way*. That he was…

NEVILLE: Yes.

GLYNIS: I miss the world I thought I knew. *(Pause.)* Is it just me? Was it that obvious? Was everybody laughing up their sleeves, thinking poor Glynis?

NEVILLE: It wasn't obvious.

GLYNIS: Then how did you know?

NEVILLE: Because he was sitting on a barstool in Bartley Dunnes and offered to
buy me a drink.

GLYNIS: I see. *(Upset.)* I see.

NEVILLE: Sorry.

GLYNIS: No, I think it must have been me.

NEVILLE: It wasn't you.

GLYNIS: Oh, I don't know. I can be very dull sometimes. I don't get out much…
I don't dress very… but I did… I mean when I met Maurice I did… I used
to wear a mini-skirt and a beret. After *Bonnie and Clyde*. I was the new
young thing when I came to work in Maurice's firm. I was 'It.'

NEVILLE: I can imagine.

GLYNIS: Can you? I can't. Hardly. Any more. Myself and my friend Pam used to
go for drinks with the boys on Friday nights after work. We'd drink
Cinzano Bianco and white lemonade and the barman would wink and
give us a swizzle stick. Oh, we thought we were the business.

NEVILLE: So, how did you end up with Maurice?

GLYNIS: I was packing up my typewriter one Thursday evening when he came
over to me. Maurice was one of the partners, of course, and I was just
the new typist in the typing pool. I was terrified. He said to me, 'Have
you got commitments for tomorrow evening?'

NEVILLE: Commitments!

GLYNIS: I… well I didn't exactly have commitments so…

NEVILLE: You didn't have a family funeral?

GLYNIS: No, exactly.

NEVILLE: So you went?

GLYNIS: To a Law Society dinner. In my false eyelashes and mini… I felt a fool.
And he knew everybody.

NEVILLE: Oh, Mouse had a way of getting what he wanted…

GLYNIS: Now I come to think of it, I married him for the same reason. One
Sunday afternoon we were watching polo in the Phoenix Park… and
Maurice was unscrewing the flask of tea and he said to me, So, shall we
book for June?'

NEVILLE: And you couldn't think of a good enough reason?

GLYNIS: Exactly. I couldn't think of a good enough reason not to marry him. So I did. (*NEVILLE is obiviously amused.*) I don't think it's particularly funny.

NEVILLE: Sorry. You know what he said to me that day in Bartley's?

GLYNIS: What?

NEVILLE: Well, I was a young fellow at the time and I said, 'I'll have a pint.' Do you know what he says? (*GLYNIS shakes her head.*) Have a sherry, we won't be here long!

GLYNIS: Have a sherry! What a bully!

NEVILLE: And do you know the worst part of it? I did! And I don't even like bloody sherry!

GLYNIS: (*Pause.*) Where did you go?

NEVILLE: Sorry?

GLYNIS: He said you wouldn't be there long. So, where did you go?

NEVILLE: (*Shrugs, clearly awkward.*) Just out.

GLYNIS: I see. (*Pause.*) On a weekend afternoon. When all the chores are done, sometimes I go places we used to… and just sit.

NEVILLE: Look… it wasn't…

GLYNIS: I read the letters, Neville. I may be many things, but I'm not a fool. (*Pause.*) He loved you.

NEVILLE: (*Pause.*) Starting to get chilly.

GLYNIS: East wind. I think I'd better get going, it's half past four.

NEVILLE: No, wait.

GLYNIS: No, really, I have to get back. I have to…

NEVILLE: What?

GLYNIS: I was going to say I have to get Maurice's tea. Old habits.

NEVILLE: I know.

GLYNIS: Old routines. I find myself doing things before I even notice. Making two cups of coffee. Buying two lamb chops. Silly. I have to keep reminding myself…

NEVILLE: I know.

GLYNIS: My doctor said to me, Just keep yourself going. All too often ladies in your position let themselves go at a time like this… Go where, I thought? Where would I go if I let myself? And the truth is… I don't know.

NEVILLE: Maybe you will.

GLYNIS: When I read those letters… I didn't feel angry or like I wanted revenge like you hear people on television. I just felt… what a waste! That there was love like that in the world. Right under my nose. And all the time I'd been living in this twilight world. And it was me. I did it. I cheated myself. Not you. Not Maurice. And that makes me angry. That I chose to stay asleep because… being asleep seemed… safer… but it wasn't. It wasn't safer at all. Those letters felt like a bucket of cold water. I woke up and saw that my life had been going on around me… without me… and I'd let it. Can I tell you something?

NEVILLE: What?

GLYNIS: I wasn't surprised.

NEVILLE: Sorry?

GLYNIS: Oh, shocked, yes. But not… surprised. Oh, don't get me wrong. There was never any hint of… impropriety. Quite the opposite. Maurice was always a perfect gentleman. No… more like a… feeling. Sometimes, in an idle moment, I'd be looking out the window or… And this… feeling would creep over me… and I'd talk myself out of it. But somewhere deep down I've always known. Always known I never had all of Maurice. Do you believe in premonitions?

NEVILLE: I'm not sure. Don't think I've ever had one.

GLYNIS: I have. Before… it happened… I started having this strange dream. I had it about three times. I'm on this train, very plush and genteel like… The Orient Express. And I look out the window and there's this beautiful view of sky and sea, but it's very far away… far below, and I realise we must be going along a high cliff… I look around and there's Maurice sitting across the aisle but he doesn't seem to notice me and then I see… he has this big purple bird sitting in the seat beside him. It's mad, I know. And I say, Maurice… I thought you were at work… but he doesn't answer, just keeps looking straight ahead. And Ava is bustling up the aisle selling tickets, but they're really brown bread and I say to her, there shouldn't be a bird on the train, but she shakes her head and says, Oh, no, it booked… And the bird looks at me with this funny eye and winks and says, Hello, Glynis, we've been in Courtown. Then the train lurches and the driver shouts, Hold on! And I realise it's my father. And then were we're falling, falling over the cliff... me the bus and the bird... and Maurice. And I wake with a jolt. And all the day after I have this feeling of dread.

NEVILLE: Purple bird, hmm? I don't think I had a premonition exactly. I... He didn't phone that day. And that wasn't like Maurice... I couldn't phone him... we... he... had this rule. So, naturally, as the day went on I thought something must be wrong. I was driving home that evening and it came on the radio: The driver of the car taken from the water at... Sir John Rogerson's Quay has been named... And... I... I don't remember exactly. I must have pulled in somehow... at some roundabout in the middle of nowhere. I remember holding onto the steering wheel and... screaming. And then just sat there still holding the steering wheel as it grew dark...

GLYNIS: Oh, Neville... I wish I'd known.

NEVILLE: How could you have? Nobody knew. We'd spent our life that way. All the time making sure nobody could notice anything... queer. Bar men, car park attendants. It's not like that any more, of course. Now it's all, so what?... all out in the open... At that moment I'd have given anything for somebody to have known...

GLYNIS: I'm sorry... I wish I'd known.

NEVILLE: What would you have done?

GLYNIS: I don't know. Just to have known there was somebody else in the world feeling the same... (*Pause.*) What do you remember most about him? No, don't answer that.

NEVILLE: Why?

GLYNIS: Because I'm afraid of what you might say.

NEVILLE: I wanted him to come away with me.

GLYNIS: What?

NEVILLE: To Sicily, a little place I know near Palermo.

GLYNIS: For good?

NEVILLE: Oh, not for good. Maurice would never have done that. No, just for a while.

GLYNIS: Maurice wouldn't have gone for good?

NEVILLE: No, Maurice was a homebody. He...

GLYNIS: Needed me?

NEVILLE: I wasn't going to say that…

GLYNIS: But I need to know…

NEVILLE: What?

GLYNIS: Did he love me?

NEVILLE: He must have.

GLYNIS: Crazy, isn't it? After all these years… it's you I have to ask. I'm sorry.

NEVILLE: There's nothing to be sorry for.

GLYNIS: It's all the things that never got said… Suddenly, time's up, and you're just left with…

NEVILLE: I know…

GLYNIS: A whole lot of unsaid things just stored inside… Can I tell you about something… something I've never told anybody?

NEVILLE: Sure.

GLYNIS: I don't know why I'm telling you this… but… Anyway… It was our honeymoon… We took the mailboat from Dun Laoghaire. We were doing a driving tour of Wales, you see. *(NEVILLE nods.)* Anyhow we were spending the… first night in a very nice hotel in Holyhead. I thought this was marvellous, very exciting. I had a little pink suit on with a pillbox hat and matching slingbacks with kitten heels, I remember and for my trusseau I had this slinky… when I think of it now, this cream satin nightie with swansdown in… *(Indicates)* front.

NEVILLE: … Sounds fab.

GLYNIS: Neville, would you have found me attractive in that?

NEVILLE: What? I don't know… I suppose…

GLYNIS: Sorry. Silly question. Anyhow, *(nervous, remembering)* that night we had dinner in a smart restaurant. Maurice was so attentive, he was such a… man. The way he ordered the wine and dealt with the waiter and asked for the bill. Then we retired to our room… Our room. I was so nervous. But excited too. I was ready first and got into what seemed like this… enormous bed… and waited… But he was in the en suite for… it must have been three quarters of an hour.

NEVILLE: Three quarters of an hour!

GLYNIS: My heart was pounding. I can still remember the swirly pattern of that wallpaper. At last the bathroom door opened and he emerged, in his paisley dressing gown. Belted up.

NEVILLE: Oh oh.

GLYNIS: And he hardly looked at me. Just took it off and folded it very carefully on the back of a chair. Yellow pyjamas.

NEVILLE: *(Quietly, with an air of wonderment.)* Yellow pyjamas.

GLYNIS: Then he climbed in the other side. Leaned over, switched off the light, and said, Long day tomorrow, old girl, and turned over. What was I to do?... I mean, I didn't know... anything. I just lay there like a statue... in my silk nightie, feeling like a fool. I lay there for what seemed like ages... Then, from the other side of the wall, this noise began... a... couple... you know... passionately. All night. And I just lay there. I never felt so alone in all my life. I can't help wondering... even now... If I'd only done something at that moment. Leaned over and touched him, done... something... would it have changed anything?... would it have changed our marriage? *(Turns to NEVILLE.)* I mean we did... later... but never like that.

NEVILLE: It wasn't your fault.

GLYNIS: *(Pause.)* And we never mentioned it. Even though he must have heard it too. Maybe that's when it all began. Of us not being able to say things... Where did I go wrong?

NEVILLE: Maurice was gay. There wasn't anything going to change that.

GLYNIS: Yes.

NEVILLE: What we do to ourselves...

GLYNIS: What a waste... What a waste of my life. All my marriage I've felt invisible. That's the truth. I'd say something like, Would you like a cup of coffee, Maurice? And he'd turn to me with a look. Of surprise. As if he'd completely forgotten I was there. As if he needed reminding... I think that's what hurt most about those letters. It was so obvious that you saw each other. Every detail. That's loving someone.

NEVILLE: *(Pause.)* I feel bad.

GLYNIS: Why should you feel bad? It was me that stayed. No, Neville, the truth is, you took nothing from me that was mine in the first place. You had one part of him, I had another. That's how it was.

NEVILLE: Would it have been worse if I'd been a woman?

GLYNIS: *(Pause.)* Yes. Actually, it would.

NEVILLE: That reminds me. The past. Of a disco… or a dance as it was then… way back early 70s. In the town where I grew up, the boys all wore cords and tank tops their Mammies had knitted them… and I felt like an alien…

GLYNIS: Did you know you were…?

NEVILLE: From the age of eight. Sooo, I was hanging out with a gang of lads. Course in those days… forget it. You had to hide no matter what. So I was killing myself fitting in, making sure they didn't catch me reading Sartre or wearing suede shoes, I kid you not! Course there were plenty more. I could see it before they did. Anyhow, this night we went to the local hop, a hornet's nest of testosterone and frustrated libido, all of which got channelled into drinking ten pints and playing air guitar to the Rolling Stones. By some freak of nature, don't ask me how, we hooked up with a group of corresponding females and headed off. I won't go into the sordid details, save to say that my friend, Mervyn and I got separated from the pack after a fracas outside the wimpy bar.

GLYNIS: Lord.

NEVILLE: I can remember it to this day, Mervyn had Nancy and I had Noleen, a fine girl, but a bit broad around the withers for my taste.

GLYNIS: Neville!

NEVILLE: Sorry. But put yourself in my position. What was I to do with this more-than-amply endowed girl in… gingham… and all I can think of is Mervyn… you should have seen him… his mother was English and he had this lovely sallow skin…

GLYNIS: Go on!

NEVILLE: Anyhow… we're sitting on a bench by the canal and Mervyn and Nancy are out of sight somewhere behind us. And Noleen says to me, *(Strong Cavan accent)* Neville, you're gorgeous, I love your aftershave! Soo, we managed some kissing and that was OK.

GLYNIS: I see.

NEVILLE: Then, just as I'm trying to light a smoke, you know, for some distraction… she lunges at me. Neville, she says, you're the first.

GLYNIS: No!

NEVILLE: And starts unbuttoning the tablecloth.

GLYNIS: That's so… fast!

NEVILLE: My feelings, exactly! So, we're down to the brassiere.

GLYNIS: Brassiere! Even I never called it that!

NEVILLE: *(Warming to his description.)* It's vast and it's straining under the weight… of holding up these things… and I'm looking at it… and I'm starting to feel sorry for it… and that's not a good sign.

GLYNIS: No…

NEVILLE: And then… some primitive survival must have kicked in… because…

GLYNIS: You… ran…?

NEVILLE: I fainted… And I vaguely recall this blood-curdling scream, Nancy, I'm after killin him!… because I came to with the three of them standing over me, fanning me with Nancy's clutchbag.

GLYNIS: Desperate.

NEVILLE: And do you know the best part of it?

GLYNIS: What?

NEVILLE: About two years later, when I'd finally copped onto myself and moved up to the Big Smoke, who did I run into one night in the Incognito Club?

GLYNIS: Mervyn?

NEVILLE: Yep.

GLYNIS: No! So all along…

NEVILLE: All along… We just hugged and hung onto the bar laughing… we saw each other for a while after that… but then… aaah…

GLYNIS: First love…?

NEVILLE: *(Sadly.)* I suppose…

GLYNIS: What happened?

NEVILLE: He… Oh, it's a long story.

GLYNIS: No, tell me. It sounds 'Happy Ever After.'

NEVILLE: No. It didn't end happily.

GLYNIS: Why not?

NEVILLE: Mervyn… couldn't accept who… he was. And… he… hated me for showing him… *(A lot more is left unsaid.)*

GLYNIS: Where is he now?

NEVILLE: Oh, he's married somewhere.

GLYNIS: Married?

NEVILLE: Yes. *(Pause.)* So, what about you?

GLYNIS: Me…?

NEVILLE: Was Maurice your first love… or was there somebody else?

GLYNIS: How did we get onto this?

NEVILLE: I don't know, you started it.

GLYNIS: No, I didn't.

NEVILLE: Yes, you did.

GLYNIS: How did I?

NEVILLE: Anyhow, I told, so you have to.

GLYNIS: Well, there was this boy… when I was in Brigade.

NEVILLE: Brigade?

GLYNIS: Girls' Brigade.

NEVILLE: He was in Girls' Brigade?

GLYNIS: No! He was there to shift scenery. It was the display. I'd won first in Hoop and Ball.

NEVILLE: What in hell is 'Hoop and Ball?'

GLYNIS: Well, you have a ball…

NEVILLE: Or a hoop.

GLYNIS: Obviously. And you perform exercises… to demonstrate… *(Demonstrates)* grace and rhythm

NEVILLE: And how old were you?

GLYNIS: Eighteen.

NEVILLE: Eighteen!

GLYNIS: Well… they had a senior section…

NEVILLE: Evidently…

GLYNIS: Tch! Anyhow… I caught Martin's eye in my shortie tunic…

NEVILLE: Cor!

GLYNIS: And after the prizes had been given out… and everyone retired to the vestibule for refreshments… I stayed behind to 'help.'

NEVILLE: This is so romantic.

GLYNIS: And to cut a long story short we… ended up kissing in the craft cupboard. And Martin got so carried away… he put his elbow right through a tambourine!

NEVILLE: Wild!

GLYNIS: Well, it was at the time.

NEVILLE: Glynis, you really are a good woman.

GLYNIS: Why does that not make me feel good?

NEVILLE: Doesn't it?

GLYNIS: It's just that… that's exactly what Maurice used to say to me. He'd mean it as a compliment. But it wasn't… isn't. It's a prison. I'm sick of it. Sick of being a 'Good Woman.' Do you know something? I was always told that if you were a 'Good Girl,' and kept all the rules, that you'd get your reward, that everything would work out. But that's not true, is it? I've tried so hard to be everybody's idea of what I should be… but that's all it was. An idea, not me.

NEVILLE: No.

GLYNIS: I kept all the rules. Married on sound advice…. From my mother, he's a fine man, Glynis, you'll have a good life with him… It was her feelings I was following… not my own. I didn't even know what mine were. Still don't. My life feels like a collection of fragments that don't quite add up, like I'm floating among the debris of some shipwreck. Clinging on for dear life.

NEVILLE: *(Pause.)* What will you do now?

GLYNIS: I don't know.

NEVILLE: Come to Sicily.

GLYNIS: What?

NEVILLE: I told you. It's a little town I know, just outside Palermo. Very quiet out of season. We were planning to go there.

GLYNIS: You and...?

NEVILLE: Yes... but we could go. There's the square made of crumbling pink stone with two little cafés. One gets the sun in the morning and we could sit there as the cobblestones warm up, drinking coffee and eating freshly baked bread rolls.

GLYNIS: Neville...

NEVILLE: And you could wear white linen and sunglasses. Very *La Dolce Vita*... And in the evening we could sip an aperitif in the other café, served by Señor Jack, who has a passion for the Wild West and was an extra in the old spaghetti westerns. Then we could stroll down to the harbour where the fishermen unload the sardine nets onto the quay and we could smoke a cigarette and watch the sun set.

GLYNIS: Neville, I'm not Maurice.

NEVILLE: No.

GLYNIS: Why don't you go?

NEVILLE: Me? What would I do in Italy? An ageing queen with a great future behind him and a head full of memories.

GLYNIS: Do you know something strange? I feel like I have no shape. It's as if the only shape I had was around Maurice.

NEVILLE: I keep waiting for the phone to ring. *(Pause.)* He used to phone me every day at four o'clock. His tea break.

GLYNIS: I see. He used phone me very morning at eleven. His coffee.

NEVILLE: *(Pause.)* I see. When you phoned me yesterday... it was as though... *(Breaks down.)* Sorry. It was as though I'd some hope of getting a part of him back.
GLYNIS: I know...

NEVILLE: I just want to be able to talk to him one more time. Say, I miss you.

GLYNIS: I know... I want to be able to tell him... that the pink azeleas are in.

NEVILLE: Sold two suits today to a gent in advertising.

GLYNIS: ... The cat is fine... Is this really what makes up our lives? These mundane moments?

NEVILLE: They only seem mundane when we think that life lasts forever. But looking back each detail becomes infinitely precious. That last evening we spent together… I remember every word… I keep re-running it in my mind…

GLYNIS: *(Pause.)* Yes.

NEVILLE: What will you do now?

GLYNIS: You asked me that before. I don't know. Really. You know, inside I'm still nineteen. I still feel the age I did when I sat in the park and Maurice asked me to marry him… It's like part of me fell asleep then… and it's just woken up.

NEVILLE: So, Sleeping Beauty, if you could go back…?

GLYNIS: To that Thursday evening? Would I find some excuse not to go? But the truth is… I wanted to go with him and everything followed on from there. The future is hard to change. How about you?

NEVILLE: Wouldn't change a thing.

GLYNIS: In spite of everything… I did love Maurice. Does that sound… mad?

NEVILLE: No madder than living half your life in secret. *(Pause.)* So, what did Sleeping Beauty do when she woke?

GLYNIS: Married the Prince, of course. No, wait. She slept for a hundred years and a huge hedge of thorns grew up around the castle…

NEVILLE: And the Prince had to hack through them with his sword, poor sod… He must have been knackered by the time he got to her.

GLYNIS: Yes.

NEVILLE: So, she woke all right. But the place was in a hell of a mess. Everybody gone…

GLYNIS: And a load of pruning to do… *(Pause)* It all seems so daunting…

NEVILLE: Pruning?

GLYNIS: Starting my life over…

NEVILLE: Oh, that…

GLYNIS: *(Shivers.)* It's getting chilly

NEVILLE: That wind from the Steppes of Russia. Cuts to the bone.

GLYNIS: I don't know how to be me anymore…

NEVILLE: Oh, I shouldn't try.

GLYNIS: Why not?

NEVILLE: Because it doesn't matter any more. Obeying the rules, keeping the secrets… none of it matters. *(Pause.)* See that tree you were talking about, the thingummy thingummy.

GLYNIS: The *Acer Variagata*.

NEVILLE: That's the one. He's got it sussed.

GLYNIS: Pardon?

NEVILLE: Well, look at it there, just doing its tree thing, winter and summer. Wind rustles it's leaves… carries on. Thunder and lightning… carries on. Doesn't think… Am I growing right?… Is my foliage too ostentatious… Am I a successful tree?

GLYNIS: *(Amused.)* No.

NEVILLE: Just keeps on growing

GLYNIS: Did you know that certain species will only grow beside other species… For instance… an ash will grow beside a Larch because they're complimentary, they don't smother each other. I mean, you couldn't have an ash growing beside a spruce… they just wouldn't be happy.

NEVILLE: Really?

GLYNIS: Oh yes… trees are a lot like people…

NEVILLE: I rather like that.

GLYNIS: *(Pause.)* Neville… I have to go…

NEVILLE: Oh?

GLYNIS: It's getting late.

NEVILLE: Maurice's tea?

GLYNIS: *(Laughs ruefully.)* No…

NEVILLE: Could I… tempt you to a drink?

GLYNIS: *(Hesitates.)* I'd love to, but…

NEVILLE: Then do…

GLYNIS: I… can't, Neville.

NEVILLE: … No. I suppose not.

GLYNIS: I… It's been…

NEVILLE: I know.

GLYNIS: *(Pause.)* Maybe we could…

NEVILLE: Yes.

GLYNIS: *(Pause.)* Goodbye, Neville.

NEVILLE: Goodbye, Glynis.

GLYNIS exits.

NEVILLE remains, leaning against the railings, gazing into the distance. He reaches into his pocket and takes out a letter, the one with the French postmark. Smiles to himself. Slowly opens the envelope and pulls out the letter and begins to read.

Lights fade. Music up.

THE END

**HAVE YOUR LUNCH AND SEE A SHOW IN
DUBLIN'S FOREMOST DAYTIME THEATRE VENUE**

BEWLEY'S CAFE THEATRE
PRESENTS

Jimmy Joyced!

James Joyce's
Odyssey
Dublin 1904

A New play by Donal O'Kelly
Directed by Sorcha Fox
Designed by Paula Martin

Previews from Tuesday May 25th
Opens Monday May 31st
For four weeks only! *until saturday June 19th*
At 1.10pm daily (doors open 12.50 pm)
Admission 12 euro (includes soup and sandwich)
Booking information 086 878 4001
Bewley's Cafe Theatre, 2nd floor, Grafton st.

PHOTO FOR FLYER BY KELLY CAMPBELL

Jimmy Joyced!
By Donal O'Kelly

JIMMY JOYCED! WAS FIRST PRODUCED IN JUNE 2004.

DIRECTOR: SORCHA FOX
CAST: DONAL O'KELLY
DESIGN: PAULA MARTIN
LIGHTING: MOYRA D'ARCY

Author's Note:

Michael Ford suggested it. Something for Bewley's connected with the Bloomsday Centenary 2004. I counted. Nine weeks away! There wasn't time to find out if we'd get permission to present something from Ulysses. But what about the real people whom Joyce transposed into the characters and happenings of Ulysses? I spent a few busy but very enjoyable weeks making the imaginary acquaintance of Joyce's father John Stanislaus, Alfred Hunter his main model for Bloom, Oliver St John Gogarty and, of course, Nora Barnacle, tracing Joyce's own odyssey through 1904. I'll never forget Bloomsday 2004 in Bewley's. Three performances, jammed houses, unbearable heat. Sheer bliss. And, more than four years later, we're still Jimmy Joycing! Thanks for the call, Michael Ford and Bewley's Café Theatre. And crucially, thanks for the direction, Sorcha Fox.

—Donal O'Kelly

A blast of loud music. Lights up. JJ Staines, in leathers, with wings, lying face down on an upturned trunk.

Have I been sleeping? Was I dreaming? Have to get my bearings. I'm in my father's stall in Rathmines Market. Antiques, books and bric-a-brac. JJ Staines and Son. I woke up on the Joycebox. I don't like that. The Joycebox is out.

My father's dying words – Don't sell the Joyce stuff. Keep it! It's ours. Okay, I said. But lately, the year that's in it, I fear I have been – interfering with the Joycebox. *(Picks up boater)* He swore it was Joyce's original.

I know. I'm wearing wings. The problem is – I don't remember putting them on. They're ancient. I got them for my 22nd birthday. From Pappie. His idea of a Joycean present. No first editions, no signed copies. Very Pappie. Off you go now! But be careful! Too low and you'll snag on trees and cables! Too high and you're into flight paths and low oxygen.

Is this your idea of a joke, I said.

Sonny, this is deadly serious! Fly! Rescue Jimmy Joyce! He is in the labyrinth! The academics have him! He is one of ours! His parents were married in that church there! They walked on this very bit of ground! Not only them, but Alfred Hunter too! Alfred Hunter who stepped into Jimmy Joyce's mind and bloomed to become his most celebrated – no time! Fly!

And I'm up on top of the Rathmines dome. Across the dip of Anna Liffey, on the north spur a spire points, Saint Peter's Church. Beside the floods of Dalymount!

Front door red-brick parts to reveal bog-oak hallstand, a jumble of crumpled hats, a cane, speckled mirror, Jimmy Joyce, 22nd birthday, 2nd of February 1904. 22nd birthday, the first without Mam. Sad a bit, he sighs, head to the side, then –

He leaves the house in Staint Peter's Terrace in Phibsboro the highest spire in Dublin look the shadow like an arrow Jim dodges and dashes into town with his wide-stride walk a roll of papers sticking out of his pocket around the railings of Trinity prong prong built to last to Kildare Street the National Library up the marble staircase and the golden banister shiny from a million student hands a seat at the top of the stairs outside the reading room Jim doesn't sit but gives the pages to Magee whom he knows and who works there and he's the editor of a literary journal called *Dana* 'named after the Celtic Goddess' shite and onions rabblement anyway Magee reads reads reads flips the page and reads reads reads Jim is on his shoulder like a bird of prey mouthing the words carefully written in his sister Mabel's penny copybook Magee Gee Gee pursed mouth serious hair tweed sleeve pudgy hands he smudges the vellum then turns and says: I can't publish something I find incomprehensible.

Jim takes the manuscript – little Mabel's copybook. Turns. Step steps down the winding staircase. Haughty. Spurned. Marks Magee down as an enemy. For life. Magee is – Joyced!

Jim's gang of student pals all jammed into the one short day of frenetic activity – Cosgrave and Byrne and Curran and Kettle and Skeffington too and Sheehy and Clancy and Gogarty a recent tagger-on oh young men on the make the talk they threw at each other and the notions they blew across each other's bows it must have been – fabulous…

That night, at home in Saint Peter's Terrace:
kitchen table, bleak puddles and crumbs, and a cracked sour jug with its pursed spout sniggers at the genius sitting with his siblings all around, a guttering candle sepias the sagging ceiling and the gaunt faces Rembrandted round the blackened teapot sing his joy –
(*Sings*)

> For he's a jolly good fellow,
> For he's a jolly good fellow,
> For he's a jolly good fellow…

A quick pan around, in chronological order for clarity, place them where you will –
Margaret, next after Jim, known to them all as Poppie, I have no idea why;
Stannie, christened John Stanislaus same as his dad, but changed it himself to Stan, not to be confused, different man;
Charlie, just out after a blip in the seminary, a bit of a mistake on both sides, happily rectified;
A vacant space where George might have been, Georgie, who died of peritonitis two years ago;
Eileen, aged fifteen; May, who was fourteen; Eva, thirteen; Florrie, ten; and Baby Mabel, who was nine, five little girls all sitting in a row. And there would have been Freddie as well, bringing up the rear, but he died when he was a baby.
And of course the biggest absence of all. Mam. May Joyce nee Murray. Who died last August. Less than six months ago.
> (*Sings*) And so say all of –

boot-kick at the dampened base of the door
shudder-open-board-roar, sway, step the thresh, hold,

pause in the hall cane clatters on the hallstand
John Stanislaus the father of the house is home
squinting at the thin line of dim light
the crack beneath the kitchen door –
the girls oh no go eyes-wide, moon-aghast, don't, let him, come in to us, please, God,
pause,
he thumps up the bare boards heaving sighs to Jesus Mary and Holy Saint Christopher
bury the heaving body of loose futility in the slumber-hollow dump
bed-springs groan audible through the ceiling
the bar-warrior lays his body-weapons down, God above,
God above boot-thunder-rumble-once, boot-thunder-rumble-twice,
the girls breathe held hands aquiver
Jim wondereyesies why don't we give him the benefit of my birthday campfire… he
is our father after all…
but the blinking eyes bitten lips a silent chorus of Noh
So. Let the sleeping dog lie
cards they play on Jim's birthday
they quietly party round the flickering table
they whisper-celebrate.
Jim swears to Stannie when the girls have gone to bed
I'm going to expand the Portrait piece Magee rejected
into a novel. Ah the relentless tenacity! Stannie gives the title. *Stephen Hero*.
Yes says Jim. Stephen Dedalus, son of Dedalus the puzzlemaker. The candle flickers
out. Moonlight, dim.

Stannie goes to bed. 'Night. Jim's busy head.
The ceiling sags peacefully, John Stanislaus snores
his long excuses. Once upon a time he angel-sang.
Rathmines Church with its big green dome,
the ring, the I-do-I-dos, the setting up home,
matrimony catapulted John Stanislaus and May
on a merry-go-round of Portobello doorbells
while they waited for his ratesman job and his first pay-day,
only glory be to be shot in the arm with a legacy by God
that cannoned them out to

(JS) Kingstown-for-crying-out loud
a town for kings of sport like me, thwock, John Stanislaus of Cork.
(J) Left eye agoggle rim-fills the monocle
as he muscles his maw on top of May Murray my mother by Gaw
jiggle jiggle bedstead huffa-puffa
(JS) whaw thanks be to the mother of Aw Jee aujeesea
the choir I thought were in excellent voice
(J) moustache wax straighten to the – **(JS)** tip top
(M) May nods once or twice – his own mother –

tried to put her off, hid her in the front room
to let her hear him bawling raw for his dinner
shocking gruff true enough
but she was smitten, love bitten
no point denying and he's dying for a son
since the first one…
oh the eight days
in Ontarioh-no-no-no torment-Terrace
where they lived back then
John they christened him – after his dad,
lies in Glasnevin, the perfect hands he had
joined inside the coffin made of oak,
wet lonely clay up there, weed-burning smoke.

Taking care this time they move to Brighton Square,
among people of substance, the rich and the –
(JS) dare I say it the ruling elite, barristers and doctors,
And the Three Patrons Church choristers –
oh, how we sing, in Palestrina har-mon-y,
through the pregnancy, May and me.

Birth to Clongowes

Thursday the second of February,
eighteen eighty-two,
the Feast of Candlemas,
six bells knell,
a baby boy bawls,
sweet Jee – an aria,
James Augustine,
May smiles,
a star glides,
blue eyes azuria.

Then out to Martello Terrace – overlooking the bay
at back and front attacked by spray,
the Vances next door, in Bray Bray
duets and trios in Bray Bray
oh happ-i-ness, happ-i-ness in Bray
the Vances, the Coffeys, John Stanislaus and May,
the piano tinkles sweetly Jim Agugga-gugga plays
at the feet of the people, they sing, they sway
they sing they sway, they sing they – spray.

Another baba coming means cash stretched thin,

take in fat Dante and noble Uncle Bill,
a household of chat-of-tat, conversation drill,
old Fenian Kelly calls, a nation once a
day and night freedom fight
(JS) sure have a bite baba bawls, wrapped and christened: –
young Stanislaus of Bray hurray, another Joyce boy,
I row stroke in a four-man boat across the bay for joy.

(J) Another boy Charlie then Georgie makes four
boys and Poppie to be heard you have to roar,
(JS) crisp work on a public wage,
never fear, strut the stage,
the boys follow in my choral wake,
with Finnegan's Wake and Houlihans Cake hip-hip hurray,
(J) concerts in the drawingroom, and playing on the beach,
summers of the skylark,
(JS) come-all-ye songs I teach to the son I love in his sailor suit so much – May cries
but she knows I'm right,
I send him away to Clongowes Wood,
the Jesuits, so it's up to you, now Jim, be good.

(J) Half past six he says when he's asked his age,
the smallest boy of the whole bloody lot,
but he does the Clongowes the Jesuits the listening the learning the being good for
the greater glory of Gaw-gaw A M D G piano lessons pandybat cinders-track sick bay
Clongowes, Clongowes, Clong—

The Fall

Parnell defeated when named by O'Shea.
John Stanislaus pensioned, on less than half pay. Uh-oh.
Tic toc tic the Clongowe stopped. A little after nine.
John Stanislaus carts his family in to Carysfort Blackrock,
four more girls makes nine in stock.

Deeds of the properties down by the Lee
seized by Dodd
(JS) bloody Shylock philosophy,
(J) nothing to do but to cross the bridge,
(JS) in dependents awash, I'm under the kosh,
down but not out, the heart it is stout,
(J) ancestor Dan O'Connell looks down as we pass headed for –
(JS) Fitzgibbon Street, God help us, give the nag a lash
while I take Jim on a little detour
my pound of flesh wound in need of a cure,

at Capel Street Bridge I give Jim a closer look at Anna Liffey's charms, chuck him
ankle-dangle down at the swell,
I wouldn't let you fall, Jim, there's no need to yell!

(J) Cold windows, cross door,
ceiling wrinkled, moaning floor,
piano gone, bureau pawned,
emptiness is all around,
the canal is frozen over,
black ice is on the ground.

A bad interlude with Paddy Stink and Micky Mud,
Christian Brothers thunderblood, then chance meeting –
(JS) Jim's accepted in Belvedere, and Stannie to boot, a little bit of cheer
(J) to counterbalance the general air of northside gloom
Sinbad the Sailor –
(JS) the Gaiety panto-boom tomb-a-womb-a-riddle-me-malady
the hero-mariner struggles through a dark and hostile land,
ring-a-ring-a round the downstage off into the wings
he's done for now, poor Sinbad…
here he is again ring-a-ding-a-dee come back to me I'll swing
for you Sinbaaaad…
my pension suspended, Christ, investigation planned,
baby son Freddie dies, May can't stand it any longer
the goading eyes glare at me a scream behind the painted stage façade she drives me
mad Christ almighty who else stalks me,
dagger drawn rant I rave yes who can blame me if I sin I will sin BAD – finish it – I
cry to blazes
fingers on her squealing wind Pipes of Pan the blood is up the chase is on for
reel-ing backwards who the blazes Jim on my back get off his fingers in my eyesockets
blind rage damn the kitchen table upturned a bloody cage
(J) Mam staggers out the door for the shore of next-door-land a bright and blue
tomorrow
(JS) just a minor domestic row, officer, right as rain today,
just back from pinkeen-fishing with the children down the ol Tolkay.

(J) He has to trim his sails in, tack back to town,
to Richmond Street near Summerhill, cul-de-sac brown,
(JS) Jim's taken to saying his rosary on his way to school,
(J) Hail Mary full of mercy-lips in nomine domine madonna-me madonna-me
(JS) some piddling incident reported with our roundy-poundy maid,
(J) Mar-y, piddle in a puddle for me, please…
(JS) the less said the… – best scholar in Belvedere,
first in English in Ireland you hear? Ball of malt, thanks.
He's prefect of studies, the best they ever had,

took off the rector in the play, by dad
he didn't lick the stage talent off the bloody floor
no, by God, he's got the joycepaint roar.

Then the pub basement jacks fiasco, cut his bloody tongue,
Tom Devin got him out of it,
(JS) ank you Hom you haw me hafehy home.
(J) Tom Devin and Mat Kane, Tom Devin and Mat Kane,
poor May they say, the palaroundies wag the finger,
now now, John Stanislaus, heed the warning sign, surly whine,
Tom Devin feels the need to lighten what's becoming a difficult scene,
wonders will he perform – his clucking hen routine.
Plahp-plup-pluph, the whole house laughs,
(JS) all ih onth again therene.
(J) Finished school, start college,
now attending the Sheehys' dos
(JS) if you please, the MPs,
doesn't ask me to go along as well,
but invites May, the piano to play…
perhaps he imagines I'd get in his way…
in college Jim whipped Hugh Kennedy red
with his paper on Ibsen, left him for dead
oops the Boer War erupts,
(J) boom he faces the fact of another forced evacuation,
done without loss, as there's nothing to lose,
he runs a ruse with the upstairs Hughes
they write each other's landlord's references,
romantic fiction for pounds and pences,
(JS) shake hands on an ordered retreat,
to Richmond Avenue just up the street
(J) where, believe it or believe it not,
a piano graces the vacant lot, upright on bare boards,
proud stout body, like a shimmering mirage,
an Arabeean wadi.
The air fills with the Joyces' voices,
(Sings)

> Oft in the stilly night ere slumbers chains has bound me,
> Fond mem'ry bring the light of other days around me,
> The smiles, the tears of boyhood's years,
> The words of love are spoken,
> The eyes that shone, now dimm'd and gone,
> The cheerful hearts now broken.

We vesper our travel-songs across Fairview
when my Ibsen piece is published in the *Fortnightly Review,*

(JS) he's brandishing his weapons see, swinging them around,
soon he'll – strike oil, Christ, Jim, my metaphors abound,
(J) not only that, but Ibsen sends a letter,
(JS) Jim reads it on the tree-swing, things could not be better,
we take a trip to London on the twelve guinea fee, Jim and me,
we pass our time in good companee,
he's like my second skin, is Jim to me…

(J) Finish college, try medicine, not for me,
I go away to gai Paris, where I moan with Synge, deride his *Riders To The Sea* they're
all gone now John Millington
mainly because I'm so bloody hungry, wrote home for money to mam who sent the
postal orders late but better than never for her eldest son Jim she doesn't understand
the artist in me Notre Dame, the Seine, the bells, the bells, Joyce, Synge, Joyce Synge,
Joyce… what? Telegram!?

NOTHER DYING COME HOME FATHER

He couldn't even spell the word. Couldn't put his lips together long enough for M.
Not Mother. Nother. Nother dying. He'd tortured the woman slowly for more than
twenty years. Oh yes, he made her laugh when he was in a good mood, singing
to her, serenading, showing off his voice, oh yes, John Stanislaus, the Flower that
Bloometh Mary Jane and he'd smile mistily into her eyes and he'd melt her resistance
and she'd think that maybe there was a chance that deep down he really loved her
yes, she remembered the letters he'd sent, oh lovey dovey, way back then in the
happy Clanbrassil wooing days when he was on his best, and the nights up high in
the balcony singing in the choir of the Three Patrons, my God they were half way to
heaven, and the glorious voice he seemed to smile to get the high notes as if it was
easy up there, and with the Vances and Coffeys, ah the happy days in Bray –

NOTHER DYING COME HOME FATHER

It's because he was Cork. The compression in Cork so absolute it fires out its miscreants
like – a cork from a fire-bottle thwock and they bounce off the walls of wherever
they're sent driving the rest of us crazy, in Dublin for example it's tight and narrow
and Cork squeezes the doubts out of people and High certainty bloody emperor John
Stanislaus Joyce is the worst that ever came out of it. With his mammy wouldn't you
know chugga chugga on the train moustache tip a stiletto gashing all around him
maybe there's a way of blaming everything on Cork –

NOTHER DYING COME HOME FATHER

Five words to save cash for a half a ball of malt. Dapper monocle and spats Bejasus in
a constant state of could you believe what people will stoop to to thwart and cripple
their fellow man God help us so sorry for himself he put the pennies on Georgie's eyes
the quack he got cheap to tend the typhoid ordered a feed of mutton chops missus for

Georgie now to build him up oh Mam gave it to him in loving spoonfuls yummy yum but terrible wrong terrible intestine not able to… to Glasnevin the smoky weedbin and now the wife is sickly and the drain on resources if not already bad enough but what now with the sick bill and doctor's fees and her not able to get out of the bed and the moananoaning on the moananoaning on –

NOTHER DYING COME HOME FATHER nother dying just a nother

And when Jim gets there, she doesn't die. The way it goes. She lies there with the bile bowl beside her cyrrhosis of the liver God's cruel joke from Easter til –
then another Sinbad rollick, John Stanislaus roaring drunk on a large bottle of self-pity just go and die and have done with it Jim locks him in the boxroom but he climbs out the window dangles down a pipe and in the door again. Like a devil. Whuh!
And Jim won't kneel for May on her deathbed, won't take communion he stands on truth he stands staunch in the face of – her gentle entreaties please Jim please.
Glasnevin again, wet clay, oak, smell of smoke from the weed-burning barrel.
(Sings)

> I am stretched on your grave.
> And will lie there forever.
> If your hand were in mine.
> I'd be sure we'd not sever.

Feis

Birthday boy slouches into March. Writing *Stephen Hero* now when not in bed, Pappie roaring blue about it in between getting tanked four nights of the week. The girls keep going, coping with the situation. Then there's talk of the Feis. Ah-hah the Feis.
McCormack won it in 1903, took the prize of a year's scholarship in Italy, and came back able to sing high B.
Joyce, he said, you too can B, you too can B, you too can B a tenor like ME.
You have it all, McCormack says, you just need to train it so it happens every time and you can soar like Icarus on wings of *panis angelicus*
It wouldn't be my choice, said Joyce, but the idea's good, and I think I would, like to sing high B after studying a year in Italy.
Then to Palmieri, he taught me, fly to Palmieri expensive Palmieri cashdrain Palmi-borrow it from Gogarty and Curran and any other well-kept sons Jim is staying up at night keyboard a-plinky-planky all the family hear his song…

Then one day he melodies home-ee-oo to St Peter's Terrace, door ajar, 'No Chastening' he's singing he's coming to the B
into the sitting room to play the note and see
if he's doing it for real but – the piano isn't there, where? The piano isn't there just a couple of cobwebs stringin off the wall,
a big conspicuous absence roars m'Appari in a bar down town,
Come To Me…Jim can hear it, steely frown,

the piano has been drunk, by the father who has sunk
so low that he's sold his soul for a bottle of Faustian Powers Gold.
Gone. Father, you have drunk the piano! Jim flaps his angry wings and hate-filled
flies southeast to Beggar's Bush appropriate enough. Sweeney-like he alights on the
McKernans' step, bootscrape,
oh they think he's great, vegetarian Bohemian Theosophists alright they say, there's a
room up above, but put a limit on your stay, and there's a token rent to pay.
Tortured, nonchalant, the genius breezes in.
A piano ordered from Piggotts, paid for by Curran on tick, practice recommences, the
food makes him sick.
Plinky-planky plink to

May the sixteenth, the Feis night arrives. All his cronies, his brothers, his sisters, the
Murray cousins and Aunt Josephine flock to the Antient Concert Rooms. No John
Stanislaus. He stays away, huffed, puffed, wounded, unloved. The spurned spurns.

The adjudicator: Luigi Denza, the Funiculi Funicula man. Applause!
All the competitors sing on sing on same song same song …
everybody judges Jim's away ahead, he's singing like an angel, Denza's uplit face
aglow with admiration
bellissimo bellissimo the Latin lips go.
And now! The sight-reading round! A mere formality. The others just making up
the numbers now. Jim takes the pages. Glances. Quavers, semi-quavers, demi-semi
mixed with triplets,
truncated piano lessons Clongowes coming back to haunt,
he – drops the manuscript. This is not art.
He strides offstage.
Denza taken aback a bit, but, still wants to give the gold to Signor Joyce.
But rules are rules the committee men say.
Listen, gentlemen, he's the best by far,
Maybe so, but the rules you can't ignore,
he didn't do what he was told,
and so he won't be getting gold,
the committee men unite, Denza's situation's tight.

Then the silver man is disqualified – for what?
I don't know, cursing in the corridor making lewd remarks taking opium having a
wank in the wings
so Denza insists that the bronze medal go to Signor Joyce – hurray!
Palmieri – has offered – free lessons – to James Joyce – in return – for a cut of his
earnings for the next ten years! Flah blah, Feis hysteria!

Bronze. On the way home, Joyce DOESN'T throw his medal in the Liffey. He tosses
it instead into the basement area of Auntie Josephine's on the North Strand. Oh the
careful iconoclast. And down she goes, ah Jim, you're a terrible ma – and retrieves
it for him, you're your own worst, there's one who's worse he thinks as he grips the

railings staring at the moon, and up she comes and back to him she gives it in case he'd like it as a keepsake. And he does. Flip. Flop. The bronze feis medal of 1904. Pappie didn't come. He sulks behind his Cabra ramparts, his fearful minions mince around their testamental prince, God's curse on you bastards and bitches, he whips. John Stanislaus. Trapped, corked in haughty hostility. Harumph.

June

The McKernans nice but fed up now. The piano repossessed by Piggotts, oh scarlet blush apologies if they had known… Jim skips off to another well-set-up young couple of declared admirers, James and Greta Cousins poets in Sandymount, leafy with sea breeze and a baby grand piano in the sittingroom.

Jim is writing stories yeah for George Russell yeah for *The Irish Homestead*, the Pigs' Paper – imagine, Joyce, did you ever think you'd see the day, he's using a nom de plume, Dedalus the puzzle-maker good name for the Mad Hatter but it's a guinea a go so needs must is the dominant philosophy. And some of his poems are published yeah in various places he says, he's making a faint but discernible mark, a fella was telling me Yeats has him filed under gifted troublesome.

The 10th of June is Friday. The bulging wall and railings tall of Trinity. Turner the Botanics glasshouses ironworks man designed them the tops – Bumps – excuse me – into a girl. Gab-gab chitanchat. Galway. Her name is Nora.
No-ra.
(N) She takes in his tennis shoes, his yachting cap, his –
(J) the no glasses a try-out he's been told it works wonders for the lazy eye.
(N) Blue eyes she sees.
(J) Auburn hair he sees.
(N) a chambermaid in Finn's the sign she says is visible away down there.
(J) but just a blur around her. Nora. They make a date for the 14th – Tuesday.
(N) to meet at Wilde's house look you can see it.
(J) I can't but I know it's there. Ha-ha.

Tuesday railings leaning, no No-ra! He drops a letter to Finn's Hotel. Aw I may be blind etcetera. Tenacity Jim.
They meet on Thursday. The 16th of June.
Sunny walk the Dodder-babble
Sally Gardens singa-swing the rushes-oh
Light on his feet, my God the heat, I'm boiling up
She has a lazy gait I like haunchy-raunchy haughty she lets me
bodice-stroke a lovely sensoft slips her handy-pandy finngers
naughtinessinoramadonnamemadonnameinnominedomine
Aujee, he signs himself, aujeesea, Icarus Odyssey, ABCDEFG, an epistle
poesemenpoem scriptawrit on the slabs.
Now, she says, cymballing her – dextrosities.

Drunken Summer

Frenzy: Jimanora Jimanora Jimanora Jimanora
she calls him Jim the cronies call him Joyce
Jim Joyce Jim Joyce pulled akimbo think he liked it
being sacrificed on the rack of nomenclature
delighted I'm sure the treatment IS the cure
stretched he's running around with his pants on fire,
scribblinggeniusluteandlyreandtruthandgyreinthelabyrinthinemetropolollipopolis
oh bliss is this
one of her gloves he takes to keep soft leather night finngers what are you like Jim go
on before I change my –
mind yourself now in case you go blind
you're near enough already, take it nice and steady
like a good man.

The hots he's got
he hits the tots of sack and porter-potties in the smelly beer cellar Nora?
Through the labyrinth careering, artfully veneering, seeking a what am I looking for
how will I know somebody give me a –
Sign: Synge's *Riders to the Sea* rehearsals ripe for his
interruption – well hello the rabblement –
and his articulate eruption of buff-hoonery buff-hoonery
Oh throw him out!
A pair of strapping peasant islandmen with Trinity accents deposit him foul-smelly
prone in the entrance-corridor
the departing actresses lift their petticoats
lest they dip in the limp slorry mess
as they step over the not quite comatose
writer takes in the vertical view partout
Riders to the Sea… Shadow of the Glen
Riders to the thank you John Millington –
Sing the drunkenoraness of the drunkenoraness
the drunkenoraness of – Love is it?

Drunken summer Stephen's Green night spots a brazen lady propositions from the
bottom of his sack-filled poet-belly
to be punched with welly by her Falstaff felly who had gone behind a nearby tree to
pee
wet cobblestone puck-in-the-gob cap-in-puddle
next day mortified by a black crippled eye and wounded ego Nora remorse Nora
remorse I am not worz and worz and worz and worz I feel I am not worz fail me for
wunze I want for worz ah Nora Nora Nora love in a glove nod enuv too ruv

Mat Kane's Funeral

Then comes the news one day that Mat Kane has drowned out in Kingstown. Mat
Kane who has always been good. Mat Kane one of the father's well-off palaroundies
but one of the better ones who always gave May the light of day. Poor Mat Kane.
Kingstown to Glasnevin cemetery long bloody trip in the funeral trap, and the father
and son are riding in one,
John Stanislaus and Jim, John Stanislaus and Jim,
silent eyes averted, for the others very odd,
but funerals are always – damn unusual by God
they pass an organ-grinder grinding out a tune –
(Sings) Has anybody here seen Kelly
K – E – double L – Y,
Has anybody here seen Kelly,
Tell me if you can,
He's as bad as old Antonio,
Left me on my own-i-o,
Has anybody here seen Kelly,
Kelly from the Isle of Man.

Glasnevin Cemetery dusty hot
the caring angels sweat
stone monumentals ignore the passers-by
burn-crackle smoke-swirl pine-pins dry
shoe-prints pebble-scatter canopy sky
Mat Kane is laid to rest, R – I
People gathered in a dribbling fan
try not to soleprint the holy mounds,
feet to the side, Egyptian stone-stance,
among the back-markers the Joyce line, male,
heads cocked, tiff-stiff in hostilence,
duty bound to mourn together Mat Kane's end.

Enter Alfred Hunter soft-eyed man Alfred Hunter
deep toned bowler hat hand-held low Alfred Hunter
feeling the dinge, rubbing the band, Alfred Hunter
stands dividing Jim and John son and dad Alfred
tries to rectify but no no the separation fine, sniff
Alfred Hunter low-voices don't I know you both – Joyces yes? fine singers according
to Mat many's the time he
John Stanislaus moustache tip taut remind me, oh yes inquires about the wife yes
how long now?
Alfred Hunter low-voices married first day of Spring in '98, yes Saint Brigid's Day in
Rathmines.
Rathmines?

Alfred Hunter prods gently conversation rolls yes he's an advertising agent don't you know the *Freeman's* the *Times*

John Stanislaus tickled by the Rathmines Church where he himself and May God rest he flicks his eye and Jim can't help but smell the musty love letters he read from the secret box my darling May when she finally over there beneath now with George and Freddie and the first-born and John Stanislaus blinks as he sees again the softness the Mayness in his son Jim's gaze

Alfred Hunter little smile he makes and tied the knot indeed he did

go away Rathmines the 1st of Feb astounding coinci – Jim's birthday the second oh at 6 am in eighty-two the bawl and then the bells and the two blue eyes I remember as if it was yes yes yes...

suffice to say, Alfred Hunter, nice man, facilitated a peace, after months of none, that held the hope of the opposite of hate, between the Joyces, father and son. In *nomine patrii, et filii, et spiritu...*

Martello

Go-gar-tee... Go-gar-tee...

Medical student gregarious hilarious philosopher-repartee

Joyce he swagger-raggers in the national library

Iconoclast accomplices firing longwinded bullseye-shots

at targets of central Irish poweralysis...

So anyway Gogarty gets the lease to the Martello tower beside the Forty Foot, come out, Joyce, you must come out and join me blather about secular monks of a new civilibandon anarcho-ridiculosis...

Finally Joyce says yes, I will yes – because he Has No Money – grand all goes swimmingly every day in the Forty Foot Gogarty not Joyce wouldn't be bothered getting wet

Gogarty mentions another fella staying in the tower called Trench Gaeilgeoir poety-actory-scribe of sorts but in a rough patch at the mo demented whatever next thing middle of the night he ups and roars picks up a gun and tries to take potshots at a panther – a panther diving on him in the middle of the Martello – Aw the panther, the panther. Gogarty grabs the gun, shut up he says, I'll get him for you, and he shoots over Joyce's bed the pots and pans, pots and pans clattera-ping down around him orchestra cacophonapanic and pain he flees down the steps away into town from Kingstown dead of night near lost his wits nobody knows least of all HIM where he got to or how he ended up first in line at the National Library dim dawn porter opens up, hello, white as a washed sheet, one thing for sure, Gogarty is forever – Joyced!

The day ringa-dinga ringa-dingas dull,

until at last teatime chambermaiding break Nora,

strong soft arms around him, soothe, soothe a stór,

the Joyce put popped: –

Is there one who *understands* me?

Yes.
Is there one who understands me?
Yes.
Is there *one* who understands me?
Yes.
Is there one who understands *me*?
Yes. For better.
Or worz and worz and worz and worz.
Ring. Ing in my ears.
I due, at work in Finns.

Leavetaking

Nowhere to stay. A foundling, fay.
Can anyone help me, a genius, I pray?
On the couch in the North Strand with Auntie Jo.
Astray Mad Sweeney-like, where can he go?
With Cosgrave a-battering, the Kips-akimbo.
Monto Monto out-you-go pronto.
Biff and Bam came up the street
and left poor Joyce a lump of meat.
Cosgrave skidaddled, backbone of butter,
little did he know he was Joyced from the gutter.
Alfred Hunter chases them away,
picks up Jim, gentle sway.
Where do you live, young Jim, he moons,
Joyce says the universe, gags and swoons.
Arms around each other, veering east,
Hunter and Joyce head home for the feast
of tea and a plate of figs in Alfred's house in Ballybough,
where they muddle-talk ring-puddle sotto-voce schlok.

(J) They talk about flight, the Orvilles –
(A) you mean the Wright brothers Wilbur the other Kitty Hawk yes magnificent expansion on –
(J) Leonardo you know sketched a similar –
(A) men always fascinated wings we adore the feeling of elevation –
(J) more ways than the phallic it has become a cliché –
(A) the freedom of the birds since we first lay on our backs – fagged out from tough toil peering at the zenith – they go closer you see to –
(J) don't give me the God stuff!
(A) ...closer to the galaxy extremity which fading into infinity is per se we have to say an abstract metaphysical concept beyond our hitherto... fig?
(J) fly... wings...
(A) Icarus the son, Dedalus his father made them for him, Dedalus who also made

the most complicated labyrinth of all –
(J) a puzzle to keep us occupied through the longest winter night we give due thanks –
(A) if thanks the appropriate, indeed oh fathers and sons and the carried on and rebelled against…
(J) the last fig filched, white plate a moon on the velvet universe of tablecloth and a splash of the Milky Way tapers a feathery arrow to – Nora…!
(A) Blue-eyes, fly!

Stands, picks up hat to leave

What the Hell has this kind man been doing all day? Must put him in a story and see. Have to change his name though. He is not a hunter. Something more – Excuse me, Alfred, where's the door? I seem to be facing a mop for the floor. I won't forget you Albert. I – must – fly.

Picks up wings and straps them on.

He put it to Nora the very next day.
Come away with me, Nora, come away with me.
That night he sings, in the Ancient Concert Rooms,
on a bill with McCormack, tenor high B,
hello backstage tense bonhomie,
Nora in the audience is filled with
admiration for her sweetheart Jim,
when the nervous pianist balks and consigns him
to stand and sing alone, by himself,
Jim thrones himself at the keys
paddles the pedals, fingers the chords, and plays
the glorious Sinbad sail-songing out the Gulf
of ArabyDubbelin east with the hurrays
of his father ringing in his ears,
I Told Ye So, He Got It From Me,
Nora his forever whatever-if-any-faith-fully,
his Icarus wings he flaps,
his father for money he taps,
acquaintances pass his caps around,
a Berlitz job is seemingly found
in some far-flung one-or-the-othery,
Nora sneaks aboard the ferryboat Hurroo,
father and son do the quayside do,
Auntie Jo and the rest give him their best,
up the gangplank zithery zest awave,
into Nora's arms my love perhaps he said it thunk,
she to him my darling love they arch across their tied-up trunk,
the big ropes flung, the bow out to sea
away at last in flight we're free…

tap-tap hello remember me?

Tom Devin who saved John Stanislaus' tongue

less than a blessing, but they're – half hung caught in the act may as well throw themselves at his feet: –

we're eloping... he smiles, Love's Old Sweet...

Off flee-fly Jimanora ferry flurry ferry Holyhead

chuffa chuffa overnight to London where he gets her to wait in a park minding the trunk while he does a bit of crucially important contact work... Nora... Nora... Newhaven ferry ferry cross the channel to Dieppe the coast of France chuffa chuffa to Paris where he gets her to wait in a park minding the trunk while he does another bit of crucially important contact work... Nora... Nora... chuffa chuffa Gare de l'Est to Zurich Switzerland dawn the Gausthaus Hofnung where at last jiggle jiggle bedstead huffa-puffa just like... just like...

NO not just like because Nora not just like!

Jimanora not just like John Stanislaus and May.

Nora has come on a flight of her own, she has flown the nest not to be just like a Nother

but that's a story for a nother night a nother day

Rathmines market? Forget it! It's just a figment.

Like what Alfred Hunter gave a plate of to Jimmy Joyce in Ballybough, one sore drunk bawdiful night a hundred years ago. And he walked out and flewlysses a storylysses that shooklysses the featherparalysses off the birdiebeJaylysses of the dubbleuniversylles.

JJ Staines falls prone on trunk as found in the beginning.

THE END

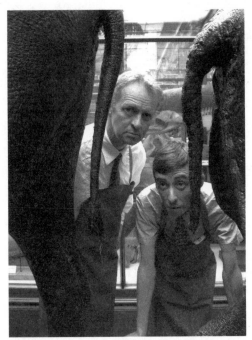

PHOTO BY KELLY CAMPBELL

Buridan's Ass
By S. R. Plant

BURIDAN'S ASS WAS FIRST PRODUCED IN SEPTEMBER 2004.

DIRECTOR: MICHAEL JAMES FORD
CAST: FRANK BURKE AND ARTHUR RIORDAN
DESIGN: S. R. PLANT
LIGHTING: MOYRA D'ARCY

Author's Note:

Good theatre is like good taxidermy: both transform the supine, whether the written word or the prostrate corpse, into something spectacular. In 2004, this delicate ritual was performed in the intimacy of Bewley's Oriental Room when alchemists (one directing, two in rubber aprons) breathed life into Buridan's Ass and, all too briefly, taxidermy took centre stage.

—S. R. Plant

Dublin. Present day. Interior of Mahone's Taxidermy Emporium. MAHONE, a man in his forties, lies on a counter uncomfortably close to a stuffed pelican. BLADES, MAHONE's young assistant, sits at a small table to one side struggling with an inside-out badger skin. Under the counter is a freezer chest. In a back room is an oven.

MAHONE: It strikes me that our little universe, Ernest, the one this side of that threshold, is congealing. Energy is being lost, it's seeping away like… like a generator running down. Do you know what happens at minus 273 degrees centigrade?

BLADES: *(Tentatively)* They salt the roads?

MAHONE: Nothing! Nothing moves except for helium, and no one knows how, or why… Why does it keep going through the motions?… A miracle of perseverance and yet it's known as an inert gas! Injustice is to be found at even the molecular level. When the Cosmos has run out of steam, when the celestial curtain finally falls, helium will be there as a reminder of the bathos of it all. One atom with two electrons slowly pulsating in a dead universe; you and me, Ernest, you and me.

MAHONE draws his coat around him and appears to drift off.

BLADES: Two electrons are better than one, Mr Mahone. Besides, we're not dead yet.

MAHONE: For you, Ernest, the glass is always half full… Despite its having no bottom. You should get away from here.

BLADES: Where would I go?

MAHONE: *(Mildly exasperated)* Out there! Into the real world. Make some money. I haven't paid you in weeks. How do you survive?

BLADES: My mother.

MAHONE sits up.

MAHONE: Doesn't she tell you to leave here?

BLADES: She says this job keeps me out of trouble.

MAHONE: Job? A loose use of the term. You must have noticed how business isn't exactly… business these days… in fact, take away that badger and our role as taxidermists would be in question. It's always advisable to have a Plan B, Ernest…

BLADES: I think we've got a problem.

MAHONE: Think of it as an opportunity for a new beginning….

BLADES: *(He taps the skin.)* This is the problem. I think we put too much alum in the mix.

MAHONE: I've been making that alum compound for twenty years. The last batch is fresh, I did it yesterday afternoon.

BLADES: It was after a lunchtime session at Conway's—

MAHONE: That was a business meeting.

BLADES: *(In disbelief)* With Big Mary from the poodle parlour?

MAHONE: A source of potential clients, Ernest.

BLADES: Oh.

They both become motionless, MAHONE apparently torpid and BLADES disheartened and baffled by the resistance of the badger skin.

BLADES: Something has gone wrong—

MAHONE: *(As if in a trance)* Indeed… but I wonder when? The first mistake was to leave the trees; we're obviously creatures of the canopy… close to the stars… and fruit.

BLADES: The skin is getting very stiff, Mr Mahone…

MAHONE: *(Looking across)* Keep rubbing in the compound, Ernest, it'll become supple.

BLADES: Funny how when it's inside out, it looks like an armadillo.

MAHONE: Yet another example of nature's celebrated symmetry. Now, while you get on with that, I'm going to leave you for a little while.

BLADES: Where are you going?

MAHONE: Deep into my subconscious. I need to find calm, Ernest, respite from vexations of the spirit.

BLADES: Your panic attacks are getting more regular, Mr Mahone, you should get help.

MAHONE: They're not panic attacks! They're psychic crises and I did get help, I paid a fortune to find out I was suffering from Buridan's Ass Syndrome, 'a fear of making decisions.' As if I didn't know that already; I just paid to have the problem christened.

BLADES: Why Buridan's Ass?

MAHONE: Clearly because I was sitting on the fence.

BLADES: Bit graphic, Mr Mahone.

MAHONE: I was divided, Ernest. Averroës would have understood… 'Tahafut al Tahafut'… 'The Incoherence of the Incoherence.' As you can imagine I felt lost.

BLADES: *(Puzzled)* I can imagine… But why his ass? Was it unusual, was it… big or something?

MAHONE: Ha! It certainly wasn't big; it was scrawny. He never talked about it. His detractors did, just to ridicule him, to ridicule his ideas. Buridan, the great nominalist philosopher who acknowledged no other authority than that of reason.

BLADES: Oh, that Buridan.

MAHONE: His enemies, his philosophical enemies, attributed to him the bizarre metaphor of the ass that starved to death because it couldn't decide which of two equal and equidistant bales of hay to eat. You see how no other image hits the spot?

BLADES: I do now, Mr Mahone. But how have you decided to do anything, become a taxidermist for instance?

MAHONE: I was born a taxidermist, Ernest. No choice there. Besides, Buridan's Ass only rears its head when the decision has emotional import. For me it first occurred during a traumatic experience with a turbot.

BLADES: A turbot… you mean the fish?

MAHONE: Yes, Ernest, *Rhombus maximus*, the warty titan of the deep.

BLADES: You were emotionally involved?

MAHONE: Yes… Though not directly. I was going out with a woman called Freda Moxley who bred Turbot.

BLADES: Freda the Turbot Breeder?

MAHONE: Freda wasn't just a Turbot breeder. She was also a very attractive woman; slinking among the breeding tanks in a snug fitting lab coat, her feline form refracted and multiplied ad infinitum. Fredas everywhere... and nothing but a rhythmic hydraulic hum to soothe one's pounding heart.

They both pause to savour the image.

MAHONE: No one before her had managed to breed Turbot in aquaria. I think that's what impressed me most of all.

BLADES: Quite a turn-on, Mr Mahone.

MAHONE: Mmm... do you realise, Ernest, that Turbot can only become sexually active when under pressure?

BLADES: Strange... cause that's normally the last thing you need.

MAHONE: Not for deep-sea creatures; Turbot need to be under a pressure of 8 atmospheres, that's 120 pounds a square inch, before the males can discharge their milt.

BLADES: Their what?

MAHONE: Their life-giving substance...

BLADES: Oh... 120 pounds a square inch... it must appear at quite a speed, Mr Mahone.

MAHONE: *(Ignoring BLADES' trivialising)* They're kept in specially reinforced tanks.

BLADES: Just as well.

MAHONE: One day I was helping out in Freda's lab, making minor adjustments to the water pressure, when her breeding tank exploded and a huge female Turbot came charging out, straight at me—

BLADES: You were Turbot-charged?

MAHONE: Ernest, it was a very distressing experience. I was lying on the ground, floundering, as it were, in spilt... milt, underneath one of the few Turbot ever made gravid in captivity. That's when it hit me.

BLADES: What did?

MAHONE: Buridan's Ass!

BLADES: Oh.

MAHONE: Covering me gasped the product of years of scientific research, whilst on the other side of the room sprawled the unconscious form of Freda.

Whom to save?

BLADES: You were going to ignore Freda and save the fish?

MAHONE: It was a fecund Turbot. A genuine dilemma.

BLADES: So what did you do?

MAHONE: Nothing, absolutely nothing.

BLADES: And Freda?

MAHONE: She eventually came to and staggered off. I was never to see her again. She disappeared into scientific oblivion, her career blighted by a morbid fear of pressure pumps.

BLADES: And the fish?

MAHONE: It suffocated, lying over me like a congealing shroud until help arrived. I had become completely catatonic. And there you have it: the birth of a syndrome. (*BLADES emits a low whistle.*) Since modern psychiatry was of no help, I have had to seek relief in other ways. Besides, I need to pave the way for romance.

BLADES: Romance? Who with?

MAHONE: Madame Faîtière, of course.

BLADES: This is her badger!

MAHONE: I'm glad to see things are slotting into place. Now, Madame arrives this afternoon to collect her precious pet, express gratitude for our taxidermic tour de force… and hopefully accept my invitation for an evening out. In the meantime I intend to put all thoughts of decision making out of my head by entering a state of torpor.

MAHONE lies down.

BLADES: A state of what?

MAHONE: Torpor. Similar to the meditative state achieved by certain Indian Gurus… except I'm not meditating.

BLADES: (*By way of encouragement*) There's no harm in having a kip.

MAHONE: Torpor is not 'kipping', Ernest, it's one of a range of survival tactics employed by fellow species, a state halfway between sleep and hibernation. Bats become torpid. It's tried and tested.

MAHONE draws his overcoat around himself.

BLADES: Like Dracula?

MAHONE: *(Affronted)* Nothing like Dracula. Dracula was a crazed misanthrope who was preoccupied with death.

BLADES: Oh, right. But what do I do after I've finished this? We can't both be tepid.

MAHONE sits up.

MAHONE: Torpid. Phone the zoo.

BLADES: I did that yesterday.

MAHONE: And?

BLADES: Everything's in perfect health.

MAHONE: Even the hyperactive sloth? That was bound to get injured.

BLADES: They put it on beta-blockers... Now it just hangs around with the others.

MAHONE: There must be something... What about the giant anteater? I heard that was in an awful state, staggering about, throwing up all over the place.

BLADES: It's pregnant.

MAHONE: They've only got the one!

BLADES: Something must have got to it.

MAHONE sits up on the edge of the counter.

MAHONE: *(Expressing distaste)* Presumably the zoo director; he'd do anything to spite me. Anyway keep phoning, something's got to die soon, hopefully before we do.

BLADES: They asked me not to. They said they found our enquiries to be in very poor taste.

MAHONE: Poor taste! Here we are on the verge of bankruptcy and they're worried about aesthetics. I've a good mind to go up there and—

BLADES: You're banned.

MAHONE gets off the bench and starts to pace around.

MAHONE: It's not legally binding, just the self-righteous posturing of a pompous zoo director.

BLADES: It was a bit of a coincidence that when you did visit—

MAHONE: It wasn't my fault there was a spate of heart attacks that day. Tennessee

Fainting Goats shouldn't be kept in zoos, they're too highly strung. In retrospect I shouldn't have taken my instrument case with me. They are also surprisingly perceptive… but for him to make a public statement… Remember, I won the slander case.

BLADES: Penny damages…

MAHONE: A biased judiciary influenced by anthropomorphic nature documentaries and simple-minded sub-editors.

BLADES picks up a newspaper clipping and reads from it.

BLADES: Yeah… 'Pet Hate: The very presence of Mahone, the Norman Bates of the animal kingdom, caused panic to spread through the petting zoo like a—'

MAHONE: Thank you, Mr Blades, I do remember! And it wasn't my presence, it was the smell of formaldehyde emanating from my bag. The goats associated it with trips to the zoo's incompetent vet. When those goats succumbed, they took this business with them.

BLADES: Natural justice, you could say.

MAHONE: Not at all! It was the unnatural intervention of the director.

BLADES: *(Quipping)*… like with the anteater.

MAHONE: Quite.

BLADES: This badger skin, I'm having a bit of trouble getting it the right side out again. I think it's the alum… it seems to be… set.

MAHONE, not listening, climbs awkwardly back onto the counter.

MAHONE: *(Resigned)* It's rigid, isn't it?

BLADES: Yes.

MAHONE: Set like concrete?

BLADES flicks the badger's unyielding skin with his finger.

BLADES: Yes.

MAHONE: That's it. Final proof that we really have reached absolute zero. Adrift on the Fermi Sea. Almost pleasant in a masochistic sort of way, assuming masochists enjoy the dolorous chill of the workhouse.

BLADES: Couldn't we just get her another one?

MAHONE: Unfortunately Mahone's luck has ensured that its colouration is unique. It's a partial albino, the result of a rare mutant gene. Besides, she'd had it for fifteen years, she knows it inside out… so to speak.

BLADES: People get very attached to their pets.

MAHONE: It wasn't just a pet... it once saved her life.

BLADES: How?

MAHONE: It was in Paris...

Impressed, BLADES takes renewed interest in the badger skin.

BLADES: It's French?

MAHONE: Yes... *un blaireau*. They're one of the commonest of the weasel family, they're found all over Europe. *Jazavac* to the Croat... *borsuk* to a Pole... *mäyrä* to the Finn...

BLADES: Did it drag her from a burning building or something?

MAHONE: No, she found it as a cub injured on the side of the road. It was at an extremely low period in her life, she had left her husband who had become impossible to live with—

BLADES: A violent man?

MAHONE: Oh, no, just a self-obsessed eccentric.

BLADES: Oh...

MAHONE: Nursing this animal back to life eased her depression. She resolved to start life afresh, and came here to Ireland. The badger was completely imprinted at this stage, it could never survive in the wild, so the authorities here seem to have turned a blind eye.

BLADES: What authorities?

MAHONE: *(Vaguely)* Societies... leagues.

BLADES: Like that crowd that picketed us. Standing outside for three weeks until they realised that no one came here anyway.

MAHONE: Exactly. She used to parade it on a lead in Stephen's Green. In fact that's where I first met the haughty and hirsute Madame. What a sight; fur coat, feather hat, crocodile shoes, an ambulant cabinet of curiosities! It's rare for a man to see a beautiful woman bedecked in the raw materials of his trade.

BLADES: *(Getting excited)* Like a mechanic seeing some young one wearing nothing but oily overalls—

MAHONE: Not exactly, no—

BLADES: *(Warming to the theme)* Or a fella who digs ditches seeing two lady mud-wrestlers—

MAHONE: No, not even remotely. You've been at that Internet again, haven't you? You should leave that alone, it's full of unsubstantiated nonsense. Where was I?

BLADES: A French lady taking her mutant badger for a walk in Stephen's Green.

MAHONE: Ah, yes. I intervened when her badger was attacked by a dachshund that had slipped its leash. Madame was apoplectic with rage but the Germans have selectively bred these dogs for generations for that express purpose—

BLADES: To attack pets?

MAHONE: To bait badgers! It had no choice, it was programmed. Except this particular dachshund was a miniature. It stood no chance against the snapping jaws of a full-grown badger. Almost by instinct I scooped up its headless corpse—

BLADES makes a 'cut throat' gesture.

BLADES: You mean the badger had…

MAHONE: Fraid so. I slipped it into a Ziplock bag and secreted the package into my overcoat. By the time the dachshund's owner arrived, all he found was a dog collar, still buckled… like some clue to a macabre riddle.

BLADES: So how did the badger die?

MAHONE: After the Stephen's Green incident it developed a taste for—

BLADES: Sausage dog?

MAHONE: An unfortunate sobriquet. There was a series of dachshund decapitations. It was only a matter of time before the Guards put together the missing pieces… as it were, and brought the badger in.

BLADES: *(Nodding knowingly.)* Ah… for questioning…

MAHONE: After the badger had been put down Madame brought the body here, I'd given her my card that day in the Green. You see, Ernest, I felt a little 'bonding' took place which I was keen to pursue… *(The phone rings, they are stunned.)* It's the telephone ringing, Ernest, an unfamiliar sound, I agree. I'm afraid you've got to answer it as I'm… I'm here.

BLADES: Oh, right. *(He picks up the receiver.)* Hello, Mahone's Taxidermy Emporium, how may I help you?…

MAHONE: If it's for Dermot, put the phone down immediately. Remember, we're taxidermists.

BLADES: *(Into phone)* I'm afraid I can't, Madam, but I would recommend Dermot Duffy, he specialises in that line of work… his number is right after ours in the phone book; Taxi, Dermot's… not at all, Madam, goodbye. *(Puts down the receiver.)*

MAHONE: Excellent telephone manner, Ernest. I'm sure Mr Duffy is delighted to have such a helpful receptionist. For God's sake! He's sabotaging our entry in the phone directory. 'TaxiDermot's'! Why can't he be 'Minicab, Dermot's.'

BLADES: He hasn't got a Minicab.

MAHONE: He's still taking business from us… It seems I'm not the only one to profit from nature's box of tricks. Dermot's strategy is called 'Batesian mimicry', imitating another species in order to profit from it in some way. Didn't you ask Dermot to change his name?

BLADES: I did, but he said he's always been known as Dermot. And he couldn't see how, as a taxi driver, he could possibly be taking business from us. In fact, he reminded me of how he actually brought us business in the shape of that dog he ran over.

MAHONE: *(In despair)* But no one had ordered a dog! People don't just come in off the street and ask how much is that unfamiliar dog in the window? The one without the waggly tail. *(Drained MAHONE slumps down onto the stool.)* Then again, people don't come in and order anything any more.

BLADES: There was that group yesterday.

MAHONE: They were looking for a plastic chicken… this is not a joke shop… This is not a joke shop… Why can't I say that with more conviction?

BLADES starts to get something out of his pocket.

BLADES: Maybe we should have a sideline in plastic animals.

MAHONE: Ernest, I would rather the business go under, to drown in my own bath water, rather than toy with rubber ducks.

BLADES stuffs what could be a rubber chicken back into his pocket.

BLADES: Clay pigeons?

MAHONE: Do you know what a clay pigeon looks like?

BLADES: A pigeon?

MAHONE: An ash tray! An ash tray in which to stub out three generations of Mahone taxidermy. *(Relenting)* The problem is, you're right. But it's too late to diversify. The money's gone and I don't know where.

BLADES: *(Trying to be helpful)* Over Conway's bar?

MAHONE: Networking is a legitimate business activity, Ernest, Conway's is where I keep my ear to the… ground. Besides, if I didn't have some social outlet I'd end up talking to this lot.

MAHONE gestures to the mounted specimens.

BLADES: Like Doctor Doolittle.

MAHONE: Unfortunately my animals are mute.

BLADES points to a bovine head on the wall.

BLADES: The yakety-yak, don't talk back.

MAHONE: *(After a pause)* Nobody talks back. When was the last time anyone phoned here that wasn't looking for a taxi?

BLADES: *(Suddenly remembering)* I nearly forgot, a woman phoned yesterday when you were out networking. She was looking for a 'zibby.'

MAHONE: A what?

BLADES: A 'zibby.' I said I'd look in the freezer but I knew we hadn't got one.

MAHONE: Well deduced.

BLADES: I thought you'd know what it was, so I told her to drop in later today.

MAHONE: Ernest, there is clearly no such word. Are you sure she didn't say zibeline, a type of Russian polecat?

BLADES: No, definitely 'zibby.' She had a foreign accent.

MAHONE: Gujarati… Welsh…

BLADES: I'm not sure… She had a lisp.

MAHONE: Were you able to decipher her name?

BLADES: Afraid not, Mr Mahone.

MAHONE: The undefined in search of the nonexistent. At least she's come to the right place. *(After a pause)* Torpor beckons, Ernest, although I don't know why I'm bothering. It's obvious that strategies for Madame's seduction are all irrelevant now… even if I was capable of choosing between them.

BLADES: Don't give up, Mr Mahone. There's got to be a way. The main thing is to take her mind off the badger.

MAHONE: But how?

BLADES: Take her for a fancy meal.

MAHONE: And I'd pay for it with what? Animal parts? The only collateral I've got is in this freezer.

BLADES: There you have it, eat that.

MAHONE sits up.

MAHONE: What?

BLADES opens the freezer and starts lifting out various animals.

BLADES: Look, turtle soup… frogs' legs…

MAHONE: We haven't got any frogs!

BLADES: There's these iguanas… and we've still got the body of that pelican for the main course.

MAHONE: Didn't you throw that out?

BLADES: There was no point, P.J. and Low Joe have stopped coming.

MAHONE: Who?

BLADES: The bin men. They said that that skunk was the last straw.

MAHONE: We mounted that last August.

BLADES: Exactly. The heat wave; Low Joe still has double vision – seeing how his nose was closest to the bin.

MAHONE: So what's happened to the, er, torsos since then?

BLADES: I take them home… For the dog.

MAHONE: Ernest, you haven't got a dog.

BLADES: I… I…

MAHONE: *(The truth dawns.)* And you've suffered no ill effects?

BLADES: My mother's a great cook.

MAHONE: *(In disbelief)* Mrs Plunkett's parrot?

BLADES: Pigeon pie. They all look the same underneath, Mr Mahone. My mother thought it was a wood pigeon that you'd shot.

MAHONE: Wood Pigeon? Shot? Ernest, that parrot started life amongst the forest giants of Senegal only to end it three decades later encrusted in puff pastry in a non-stick tin. How could you?

BLADES: Medium heat for forty-five minutes.

MAHONE: And no regrets?

BLADES: Should have left it in longer. The point is, Mr Mahone, you can eat all this stuff.

MAHONE: You've never heard of psittacosis?

BLADES: *(Looking blank)* Sitter…?

MAHONE: It's an avian disease. Have you ever had shortness of breath… hallucinations?

BLADES: They're what you get, Mr Mahone, not me.

MAHONE: Fair point. Maybe I should try the Parrot Diet.

BLADES: Budgie Burgers… *(Then, over-reaching)* Parakeet… meat?

MAHONE: You appear to be none the worse for it.

BLADES: A varied diet is important, Mr Mahone. Besides we ate all that stuff millions of years ago.

MAHONE: I suppose the Rift Valley was forested in those days. 'Lucy' would have tasted parrot.

BLADES: Is she an old flame, Mr Mahone?

MAHONE: … A very old one, Ernest.

BLADES: *(Referring to the freezer contents.)* You'll have to give everything fancy names…

MAHONE: *Gigot de je ne sais quoi*… 'Ragout de Road kill'… Do you think that'll swing it…

BLADES: Let's get it going. We can baste the pelican in seal fat. She'll be delighted you were making such an effort. And that way we can play for time, work on the badger.

MAHONE: This smacks of desperation, Ernest, but as usual there's absolutely nothing to lose. Now where's the turtle opener? *[MAHONE climbs down from the counter, picks up a meat cleaver and scrutinises the turtle. With the cleaver he points out first the upper shell (the carapace) then the lower (the plastron).]* Do you realise that the flesh nearest the carapace is called the calipash and that near the plastron the calipee?

BLADES: *(Looking hard at MAHONE.)* Maybe we haven't got time for this, Mr Mahone.

MAHONE: Scientific illumination? Or turtle soup?

BLADES: Both. Let's just roast the pelican.

MAHONE: *(Relieved)* Very good, Ernest, fire away.

BLADES: *(Enthusing)* A fine plump bird.

MAHONE: Do you realise, Ernest, that Jesus Christ himself was once known as *nostro Pellicano* – mankind's Pelican?

BLADES: I hadn't heard that one.

MAHONE: 'I am like the pelican of the wilderness.'

BLADES: Pardon?

MAHONE: Psalms. Just as Christ sacrificed himself for our sins, the ancients thought that the pelican died as a result of feeding its nestlings with its own blood. For them the pelican symbolised Christ himself.

BLADES: That's beautiful, Mr Mahone.

MAHONE: Of course, that could be why there are powerful cultural taboos against eating it… although that's probably more to do with the attendant liver parasites.

BLADES: Parasites?

MAHONE: Nematodes.

BLADES: What are they?

MAHONE: Worms.

BLADES: *(Reconciling himself to the fact.)* Worms… Better cook it on high. No point in taking any chances.

MAHONE: The whole thing's a chance, Ernest, this is a chance within a chance. We're entering the multidimensional domain of theoretical mathematics… uncharted territory.

BLADES: *(Demystifying)* It's an accumulator.

MAHONE: A what?

BLADES: At the bookies. An investment on four or more selections for one stake. An accumulator.

MAHONE: Oh.

BLADES: The odds are stacked against you but you can wind up on the pig's back.

MAHONE: A wonderful place to be. I suppose nematodes are as valid a life-form as any other... although it won't be easy convincing Madame of that if she feels a scrabbling in the rib cage.

BLADES: I think we should keep it to ourselves about the wriggly fellas, Mr Mahone, and while we're on the subject of keeping mum, don't mention how you ignored your bleeding girlfriend because of a fecund fish.

MAHONE: Sometimes scientific progress necessitates sacrifice, Ernest.

BLADES: Would you sacrifice me?

MAHONE is still holding the cleaver.

MAHONE: I wanted to talk to you about that.

BLADES: What!

MAHONE: Not killing you... I'm not a homicidal maniac.

BLADES: What then?

MAHONE: Sacrificing you on the altar of capitalism. Letting you go.

BLADES: I was waiting for you to sack me. I've been sacked from every job I've ever had.

MAHONE: Why are you sacked all the time?

BLADES: I don't know. Somebody once told me I just look like someone you sack.

MAHONE: Really... who?

BLADES: Up at the job centre.

MAHONE: The job centre?

BLADES: That's how I ended up here.

MAHONE: The job centre? Remarkable. To think that someone somewhere thinks this is a career worth pursuing.

BLADES: Well, actually they sent me to Taxi Dermot's but I got the address wrong.

MAHONE: When did you realise I wasn't a taxi driver?

BLADES: When I asked if you had a rank... and you said you were plain Mr Mahone, the taxidermist.

MAHONE: Oh… Well, despite that, you seemed to pick up the bones – the basics of taxidermy instinctively… skills I'd spent years perfecting.

BLADES: Well, it's not exactly… *(He corrects himself, aware of MAHONE'S concerned expression.)* It is quite complicated, especially mixing the chemicals.

MAHONE: Mmm… So the bold Dermot has supplied me with more than a mangled mongrel… *(Suddenly magnanimous)* Next time you see him, tell him he can keep his name. Of course, you could still become a taxi driver… or you could work in a bookmaker's, you seem very familiar with the terminology.

BLADES: A bit too familiar for my own good as far as my mother's concerned. That's why she likes me working for you. I've got no money to gamble away.

MAHONE: Logic of a sort. But it results in your being trapped in a doomed business.

BLADES: But I don't feel trapped, and anyway, things will pick up.

MAHONE: I wouldn't bet on it.

BLADES: They've got to, this is the only trade I know. And taxidermy is special. Nobody else gets accused of the things we get accused of.

MAHONE: That's not necessarily a source of pride.

BLADES: But without taxidermy I've got nothing.

MAHONE: Don't despair. What about that girlfriend of yours? Josephine… Dolores…

BLADES: Mary.

MAHONE: Big Mary?

BLADES: No! A different Mary. She ditched me.

MAHONE: Ah, hence your familiarity with mud-sports.

BLADES: Women just don't seem keen on taxidermists.

MAHONE: That's true, it must be the astringent odours, the association with death… it certainly isn't the long hours. It's difficult to see what we have to offer the modern woman.

BLADES: It's a pity fur coats went out of fashion. *(Suddenly inspired)* A poncho would be a doddle; just a hide with a hole…

MAHONE: I wouldn't like to rely on the passing gaucho trade, Ernest… although that seems exactly what we are doing.

BLADES: We shouldn't be waiting for trade anyway. We should be out there touting for business. Weren't you once in Saudi Arabia? Those sheiks would give us work. You must have some contacts from the last time.

MAHONE: Probably not the kind of contacts one would want to have. I don't think you appreciate the full import of what happened out there in the desert, Ernest; I've always spared you the details. They wanted to subject me to lapidation, a latinate term meaning murder by mediaeval mob; stoning to death.

BLADES: You're joking me. Why?

MAHONE: The result of a simple misunderstanding. You see, my father used to mount stags' heads for a certain government official who was particularly fond of the sauce. It was an unremarkable relationship until someone decided to send this man to booze-free Saudi in an attempt to curb his drinking. They found him a position as some kind of ambassador.

BLADES: And did he stay on the dry?

MAHONE: Yes, but as a result his aim improved and he became a veritable killing machine. The old boy started laying waste to the local wildlife and then sent for my father to mount the casualties. I never told you before, Ernest, as I didn't want to blunt your enthusiasm for the trade, but my father succumbed to arsenic poisoning. It was just before he was due to go, so Mahone junior was obliged to take his place.

BLADES: Your father was poisoned?

MAHONE: Arsenic, scourge of the taxidermist. It's the best preservative you can get. Unfortunately it's absorbed by the taxidermist's skin as well as the skin he's tanning, so you could say my father gave his life for his work. Don't worry, we don't use it any more, we make do with borax and saltpetre.

BLADES: That's a relief.

MAHONE: Although they're not completely without risk; Saltpetre is, after all, the main constituent of gunpowder.

BLADES: You mean… *(BLADES gestures to the mounted specimens with alarm.)* These could go off?

MAHONE: If detonated.

BLADES: Shouldn't they have warning signs?

MAHONE: *(With mild sarcasm)* We wouldn't want to cause the customers to stampede, Ernest.

BLADES: Ah… right. So you went in your Dad's place?

MAHONE : Yes, a poor replacement. He was steeped in the arcane lore of taxidermy – it was my father that developed the alum mixture that we use. That's why I know its effects are irreversible, he would use it to stiffen the skins of the trophy fish that he'd stretched for unscrupulous fishermen.

BLADES: Isn't that cheating?

MAHONE: Call it taxidermic license. A minor ethical breach compared with what occurred in Saudi. Out there in the desert I found a moral quagmire.

BLADES: Harems, eunuchs?

MAHONE: No. Corruption and intrigue.

BLADES: Oh.

MAHONE: I mounted a few rare Arabian oryx heads for the ambassador who was keen to bag the last of the species in order to get his name in the record books. As a result he was spending more and more time in the desert as the oryx became scarcer, until one day he never came back. They found his desiccated body weeks later. *(MAHONE brandishes the long, narrow horn of the oryx.)* Apparently he had been crouching in his makeshift hide when he was taken by surprise from behind by the endangered antelope, the horn ran him through, leaving the ambassador in an ignominious 'barbecue' position. It was all hushed up in the press, of course, the embassy didn't want the habits of the ambassador known. But at his funeral he had an open casket and if one looked carefully one could see that his toupée was raised, ever so slightly, by the tip of the horn.

BLADES: They couldn't get it out?

MAHONE: No one was keen to try… Besides, he was easier to carry that way…

BLADES: So an oryx killed him…

MAHONE: Yes.

BLADES: But how come you got into trouble?

MAHONE: Jealousy… Revenge… Who knows? Somehow, I became implicated in the ambassador's death. If it wasn't for the intervention of a certain exotic dancer, I would have been taken to a quarry and all hopes for a rosy future dashed.

BLADES: Pebble-dashed.

MAHONE: Exactly.

BLADES: What exotic dancer?

MAHONE: Pearl Kite and her Performing Civet.

BLADES: Performing what?

MAHONE: Civet. A sort of giant weasel that she'd trained to do tricks. She used it in one of her routines. She was one of the many acts that were employed by the Sheik's family. Unfortunately his family also controlled the local judiciary.

BLADES: But why did the dancer risk her life for you?

MAHONE: She was an exemplary human being. The type that steps up to the mark when injustice looms... We'd also had a bit of a dalliance a few nights previously.

BLADES: Oh!

MAHONE: I wasn't always like this, Ernest.

BLADES: But how did you manage?

MAHONE: What do you mean, how did I manage! Like anybody else manages.

BLADES: Yeah, but drinking's not allowed in Saudi Arabia.

MAHONE: Alcohol isn't the only trigger for mating behaviour, Ernest. Sometimes it can be aural.

BLADES: *(Wide eyed)* You mean...

MAHONE: The song of the nightingale, the cooing of a dove.

BLADES: *(Realising his mistake)* Oh, right.

MAHONE: My brief courtship of Pearl Kite was uniquely ornithological. I had been invited to one of the family's soirées held in an immense salon where elaborate spectacles took place.

BLADES: Belly dancers and giant weasels... And more belly dancers.

MAHONE: What I saw there took my breath away. A dancer transformed into a bird: *Archboldia papuensis*. Archibold's Bowerbird was leaping from table to table! The feather pattern was unmistakable, the costume replicated it exactly and the display dance was step perfect, just as the Bowerbird would have behaved to attract a mate deep in the New Guinea rainforest.

BLADES: And the weasel?

MAHONE: In its box. That kind of show would have got him way too excited.

BLADES: Yeah.

MAHONE: The other guests were amused by the eccentric behaviour but I was transfixed. I was, of course, obliged to make the appropriate response call *(he whistles a succession of plaintive notes)*. She was amazed! We continued to mimic the bowerbirds' display behaviour *(he adds an extra whistle)* following it to its inevitable conclusion lit by the naked light bulbs of her dressing room mirror. I still have their distinctive pattern scorched upon my back.

BLADES: I've seen it – like a giant horseshoe. I thought you'd had an operation and they'd opened you up like a clam.

MAHONE: Ernest, these marks are the stigmata of carnal bliss. It was a mating frenzy in there.

BLADES: Deadly.

MAHONE: An attendant of the Sheik overheard the screams…

BLADES: Screams?

MAHONE: Difficult to keep quiet when you're being branded, Ernest. Our steamy tryst was reported. The Sheik had serious designs upon my bird of paradise. He was a man used to getting his own way.

BLADES: That's why he wanted you dead.

MAHONE: I would have been if it weren't for Pearl Kite. She hid me in her dressing room, diverting the attention of the guards while I disguised myself in her clothing and practiced female comportment.

BLADES: What?

MAHONE: Ernest, the female pelvic girdle is proportionally wider than the male resulting in a significantly different gait. I was obliged to adopt this style of perambulation as best I could.

BLADES: Perambu…?

MAHONE: Walking… with short steps…

BLADES nods knowingly.

BLADES: Mincing. They call that mincing. I once worked at a holiday camp, they taught me how to mince when I had to dress up as Snow White.

MAHONE: *(Indignant)* The context is entirely different.

BLADES: *(Ploughing on)* It's funny though. I wonder if we were both mincing about at the same time?

MAHONE: Ernest, it's one thing to parade around as a Disney character for the amusement of five year olds, quite another to endure a forced march through one of the most inhospitable regions on earth.

BLADES: I suppose we did have access to a tap.

MAHONE: Had you escaped from your holiday camp and crossed a desert, you would have realised that mincing in sandy conditions is no easy matter.

BLADES: But if there is no one around, why bother?

MAHONE: You never know what's around the next dune.

BLADES: That's true. Did the Sheik's men come after you?

MAHONE: Of course. They searched for us with tracker dogs. Those dogs would have found us if it wasn't for that civet and its potent anal gland. The nauseous musk that it secreted destroyed the olfactory capabilities of the hounds. That malodorous mammal saved my life.

BLADES: Hadn't Pearl a car?

MAHONE: There were road blocks – we had no choice but to head out into the wilderness on foot.

BLADES: Without a compass?

MAHONE: Once again it was down to that civet. It just bounded ahead and we followed. It was in its element, forever scanning the horizon for the threat of predators. It once even saw off a marauding fennec fox…

BLADES: I saw them on the telly… Aren't they tiny?

MAHONE: They can give you a nasty nip if you're sleeping in the open. Remember, they're nocturnal… and carnivorous.

BLADES: But don't they live on insects?

MAHONE: And small rodents. Anyway, the point is that those three days in the desert, despite the blistering heat, tight dress and obscene taunts from passing Bedouins, were the most enjoyable three days of my life.

BLADES: Sounds great, so why didn't you stay together?

MAHONE: The palace posse. They caught up with us at Jiddah. We were about to board a tramp steamer bound for Cairo. Pearl was already on the gangplank but it was too late for me, they had cut off my path to the ship so, clutching the civet, I attempted to lose myself in the crowd. I could hear above the hubbub Pearl shouting 'Save Civvey! Save Civvey!' as I sprinted down the nearest alley.

BLADES: So you'd stopped mincing?

MAHONE: Life-threatening conditions impose a bounding gait on both sexes, Ernest. Several times my pursuers drew near and would have overcome me had I not fought like a dervish, striking out left and right. After dodging through a maze of side streets I shook them off and made it back to the quay in time to see the ship set sail and the face of Pearl recede into the Red Sea mists.

BLADES: That's romantic.

MAHONE: Anything but. It was a face stricken with horror, for what she saw hanging from my hand, like a painter's rag, was the lifeless body of that faithful civet. In my frenzied desire to escape I'd used it as a cosh, smiting the heads of a dozen palace thugs… once again that selfless weasel had saved my life. When I held that bloodied pelt aloft and waved goodbye, a little voice told me it would be for the last time.

BLADES: It spoke?

MAHONE: For God's sake, Ernest, I'd battered it to death. It was awful – in a vain attempt to atone I called to her and swore that I would mount Civvey and that it would always be here, waiting for her.

BLADES: So where is it?

MAHONE: Reduced to dust.

BLADES: How?

MAHONE: Mites – curse of the taxidermist.

BLADES: Another one?

MAHONE: The ultimate enemy, Ernest. Psocids can destroy a pelt in… months.

BLADES: So how did you escape?

MAHONE: I managed to stow away on a later sailing to Marseille, then hitchhiked home.

BLADES: You hitchhiked all the way back dressed like that?

MAHONE: Yes.

BLADES: Why didn't you buy new clothes in Marseille?

MAHONE: I was flat broke.

BLADES: How did you pay your way?

MAHONE: Adapt or perish, first law of the natural world. Use whatever means at your disposal – my clothing gave me a certain allure.

BLADES: You mean you…

MAHONE: The past is another country, Ernest.

BLADES: I think I would have phoned home.

MAHONE: You forget, I had no family, I'm a genetic cul-de-sac… and taxidermists have few friends.

BLADES: What about your one, the dancer? Did you ever see her again?

MAHONE: No, it was impossible. I had no address. She was completely nomadic. She sounded Spanish, which narrowed it down to one ninth of the world's population… As for her name, it turned out the Pearl Kite, *gampsonyx swainsonii*, is a South American bird of prey that was originally thought to be a falcon. Later investigations of its moult pattern and tarsal scutellations revealed it to be a kite masquerading as a falcon. You see the parallels?

BLADES doesn't see at all.

MAHONE: So, as usual, I found plenty of metaphysical irony and precious little else. Anyway, it's clearly a nom de plume… as it were.

BLADES: Some people have strange names. Mahone, for instance.

MAHONE: *(Mildly affronted)* What do you mean?

BLADES: Well, it's not exactly normal.

MAHONE: Ernest, unusual does not imply abnormal. When my grandfather, Vladimir Mahonovich Miarskov, fled from Russia and its murderous Bolshevik hordes, he came to Ireland and, in an effort to assimilate, he hibernicised his name to Mahone… unaware at the time of the unfortunate anatomical connotations.

BLADES: Couldn't he have changed it to Mahon or Mahoney?

MAHONE: At that stage the sign was painted. He was notoriously tight-fisted. Besides, it won't be an embarrassment on the Irish streetscape for too much longer, I am the last of the Mahones.

BLADES: You could still be Miars… kov.

MAHONE: No thank you, Ernest. *(Sniffs air.)* How is that pelican coming on?

BLADES: I'll just take a look.

MAHONE: Smells delicious.

BLADES: It's browning nicely. Madame will be delighted.

MAHONE: It's extraordinary, Ernest, a man would be lucky to meet that kind of a woman once in a lifetime, but twice. Mme Faîtière is of the same stock, it's eerie. The powerful haunches, the proud eyebrow. The civet, the badger... both members of the weasel family.

BLADES: It's a bit weird all right. I mean how many women are keen on weasels?

MAHONE: You talk about it as if it were a bad thing. These women are extraordinary individuals, Ernest.

BLADES: Still a bit odd all the same. Mind you, I used to have a ferret, and that's a weasel.

MAHONE: *(Keen to defend the social cachet of certain weasels)* There you go. It depends on what type of weasel you have... and for what purpose.

BLADES: We used ours for going after rats.

MAHONE: These women didn't do that kind of thing. Theirs weren't attack weasels.

BLADES taps the badger.

BLADES: This one ate a dog.

MAHONE: In self defence. And only partially.

There is a brief, awkward silence as MAHONE has lost the argument that BLADES didn't know was taking place.

BLADES: I've been thinking... you know how on the boat Pearl was shouting 'Save Civvey... Save Civvey'...?

MAHONE: Yes.

BLADES: It's a bit like the woman on the phone, the one with the lisp and the foreign accent who was looking for a zibby. 'Save Civvey, save Zibby.'

MAHONE: *(In a Spanish accent)* 'Save Cibby! Save Thibby!'

BLADES: That's what the woman on the phone said!

MAHONE: *(With dawning horror)* Good God, Ernest! Do you realise what this means? She's found me!

BLADES: Pearl Kite!

MAHONE: Yes, Pearl Kite! She's on her way here!

BLADES: And so is Madame Faîtière!

MAHONE: They're both on their way... Are you thinking what I'm thinking?

BLADES: We're a weasel short!

MAHONE: *(Standing stock still, staring into the abyss)* It's the ultimate choice! Once again Buridan's Ass is back to paralyse my mind.

BLADES is not listening. He has a hair-dryer thrust into the rear incision of the badger.

(Back from the abyss.) What are you doing?

BLADES: Drying the fur.

MAHONE: What's the point?

BLADES: You've got to try, Mr Mahone, this is no time to turn into a donkey.

MAHONE: It's too late, Ernest, the situation is hopeless.

BLADES: It's nearly done.

MAHONE: Ernest, it's inside out... and to think she used to stroke it so tenderly.

BLADES: She still can.

MAHONE: How?

BLADES removes the dryer and introduces his hand into the badger's rear incision and moves it in a rhythmic motion.

BLADES: Like that.

MAHONE: Oh, my God.

BLADES: It's warm.

MAHONE: You're taking its temperature?

BLADES hastily removes his hand.

BLADES: I'm just saying it's warm... in there...

MAHONE: It's a fine line between taxidermy and taxsodomy, Ernest, just a matter of stress, although... you're right, no one is accused of the things we're accused of. You, Ernest, are without doubt the world's first taxsodomist. *(BLADES senses a reason to be proud.)*... We're pioneers, Renaissance men. A scientist could stuff a badger but only an artist would reverse it. You're right, two electrons are better than one. I could never have done this without you, Ernest. Here's to helium!

MAHONE holds the badger aloft as if it's a balloon.

BLADES: That still leaves Pearl's civet.

Deflated, MAHONE puts the badger under his arm.

MAHONE: We're not out of the woods yet. What do we do?

BLADES: Have you still got the civet dust?

MAHONE: Of course not... That is, yes ... It's around us. Along with yak dust, bat dust... and dust.

BLADES: We'll put it in a jar – they do that with people.

BLADES starts a frenzied sweeping of a shelf.

MAHONE: Which people?

BLADES: Protestants.

MAHONE: For God's sake, Ernest! What are we to do?

BLADES: The sausage dog – have we still got it?

MAHONE: Of course, in the freezer... Provided you didn't... *(Mimes eating.)*

BLADES: No, no. *(BLADES holds up the dachshund torso.)* This could be a big weasel.

MAHONE: But it hasn't got a tail.

BLADES grabs a fox's brush.

BLADES: It has now.

MAHONE: What about the head?

BLADES: We'll use a cat.

MAHONE: Good idea. Women like cats. Where's my suture gun? *(MAHONE pulls a cat's head off a plaque and starts stapling it onto the dog.)* I'm getting the hang of this!

The doorbell clangs, MAHONE crouches in fright. BLADES squints through the letter box.

BLADES: It's a woman!

MAHONE: Which one?

BLADES: I can't tell, she's too close; all I can see is... dress!

MAHONE puts down the badger.

MAHONE: Any clues? Feathers... Pronounced eyebrows... Weapons?

BLADES: Hold on. There are two of them!

MAHONE: *(Clutching at straws)* Maybe it's the bin men.

BLADES: It's two women; and they're talking!

MAHONE sinks to his knees, his moaning strangely asinine, his head in his hands which are positioned to look a little like donkey ears.

MAHONE: Argh... Argh... Argh!

BLADES: Pull yourself together, Mr Mahone. What are you going to do? Be an ass... or be a taxidermist? *(Surprisingly strident)* You must decide!

MAHONE responds to BLADES' tone and rises to his feet, chest thrust out.

MAHONE : You're right, Ernest, it's time to kiss Buridan's Ass goodbye... to take control of my destiny. *(MAHONE staples the civet.)* From now on I'm going to call the shots.

BLADES: That's the way.

MAHONE picks up the badger and civet and strides downstage.

MAHONE: I smell romance...

BLADES sniffs the air and rushes to the oven.

BLADES: I smell burning!

MAHONE: ... the smouldering coals of desire.

BLADES: *(Straightening up)* The pelican's on fire!

MAHONE: *(Exhilarated)* Perfectly put, Ernest, perfectly put. *(He holds the civet aloft.)* Now show the ladies in!

THE END

SKIPALONG TH.CO. PRESENTS

TWO FOR A GIRL
AT BEWLEYS CAFE THEATRE

esb
dublin
fringe
festival

4TH - 10TH OCT
MON -SAT 6.30PM
MATINEES SAT&SUN 4PM
TICKETS 10 EURO
CONC&PREVIEWS 8 EURO

BOOKING INFO
1850 FRINGE (1850 374 643)
BOOK ONLINE AT
WWW.FRINGEFEST.COM

ESB DUBLIN FRINGE FESTIVAL 2004

PHOTO FOR FLYER BY FUTOSHI SAKAUCHI

TWO FOR A GIRL
BY MARY KELLY AND NONI STAPLETON

TWO FOR A GIRL WAS FIRST PRODUCED IN OCTOBER 2004.

DIRECTOR: MAUREEN WHITE
CAST: MARY KELLY AND NONI STAPLETON
DESIGN: BIANCA MOORE
LIGHTING: MOYRA D'ARCY

Authors' Note:

We wrote *Two For A Girl* shortly after we graduated from The Gaiety School of Acting. We wrote it because we wanted to put something on in The Fringe Festival and we thought it would be easier to write a two-hander for women than to find one.
We had no idea what we were talking about.
Within a year and a half we had written and toured two new plays, both of which Bewley's launched. Bewley's Café Theatre, which was run by Michael James Ford at the time, was instrumental in building our confidence and careers as writers and performers. It took risks on us and supported us financially, technically and artistically. We continue to be inspired by the space itself and the work produced there.

—Mary Kelly and Noni Stapleton

for Tom Stapleton

Scene 1

JOSIE: Travellers tell tales round campfires late into the night when nathin else is stirrin. When a traveller tells a tale they're listened to, their own people know to listen. It's differ to settled folk stories, there's a magic in it. Maybe tis the weight of the listeners, the quiet of the dark or that we go back to the day, the time, the minute and the age of when it happened. Not sure what it is but I know something – ye can't tell a tale without the listeners, they make half the magic.

Scene 2

FRANCES: Last week a young traveller boy came to my door and handed me this, (*Frances holds a scarf*) 'Josie Connors died in August and she asked me to give you this mam. 'Twas a gift from yer father to her in 1946.'

I nearly fell out of my standing.

She said if you're ever looking for her, she's everywhere, in every blade of grass and trunk of a tree and she wants you to know she never really left you. I've been in a twist for the week tossing and turning, strange dreams you know, and then, after he ran off down the road, I just stood outside my door for hours thinking of Josie. And I don't have time for this, I don't, I'm getting married next week. (*FRANCES picks up wedding invitation and reads.*)

'Michael and Emma Ryan cordially invite you to the wedding of their daughter Frances to Jim Nolan in St. Mary's Church, Cahir at 2 pm October 12th 1974.

'I'm moving down home today, and I'm definitely moving today. I was supposed to go last week but I got stuck. Jim's been on the phone every day wondering what's going on and he sent me up these

(*FRANCES indicates white lace glove*).

His grandmother's, something borrowed. He thinks I've changed my mind again but he is too afraid to say it. And I haven't at all. Thirteen proposals in as many years and half of them from him. When I finally said yes, I meant it. He knows something's wrong though. He'll come and abduct me if I am not down tonight… and I will be… it's just I think I have something to do first.

Scene 3

JOSIE: It all started three weeks ago when we stopped here alongside Ryan's farm. I have me tent – a cover, six wattles and a riggin pole to hould it. Me mother left it to me last year when she passed on, she were afraid for her unmarried orphan chile. I were twenty when she left us and passed the normal age for marryin. Even me father, God rest his soul, couldn't make me marry and belave me ye didn't say no to Mickey Connors easy. Me sisters think I'm cursed and John Jo, me brother-in-law, says I'm like a wild mare that can't be tamed.

Anyways the day we stopped John Jo came down from the farmer and said he's a good man and has harvest work for the feens. Within the week Mr Ryan were stopping at the gate and bein filled with tay on his way to or from somewhere. Within two week he were bringin tay and sugar and bread and not long after that he axed me to clain for him – that's not the way of it. Some travellers clain chimneys but never have I heard of a traveller clainin the house. He said he'd give me money – I said mate would do. Mrs Ryan is colder. She salutes when passin but her eyes are far away. She watches me clain, either she doesn't trust me not to rob off of her or she doesn't think a traveller can do a good job, and in a ways I don't blame her, she weren't even Catlic before she met Mr Ryan. She must think she's better than him, let alone me.

The first day Mr Ryan stopped to say hello, I had the most hands with no childer so I'd made him tay. The childer were climbin all over him and his pony and car, tearin out of him. 'Tis not normal to see a buffer who is able for twelve traveller childer pullin and draggin them. I handed him up the tay and spoke of the weather and where we'd been and where we were goin to. Then the men came over and talked timber and tin and horses with him and I came away draggin the childer with me. I heard him axin John Jo that day to call him Ryan, be his name ye know. Ryan, I says to meself, A Tipperary name.

Soon he was stopping every day and the childer got tired of leppin on him and the feens wouldn't always be there, so just me and himself were talkin, twas one o these days he axed me to clain for him. When I was leavin him that day I says,

Good luck, Sir.

And he says, Call me Michael.

I couldn't believe me ears, he didn't say Ryan nor Mr Ryan, he said Michael. I had me back to him at the time and I were afeared to turn around in case he'd see the smile I couldn't get off me face. So I didn't turn round, I just kept walkin and said, And you may call me Josie.

MICHAEL: She stopped by the well at the foot of the passage leading up to me farm in 1946 – Cahir, County Tipperary. She was joined by her three sisters – Lizzy the youngest, Mary and Kathleen and their two husbands – one a Joyce the other a Wall and their twelve children between them. And couldn't take my eyes off her.

Scene 4

JOSIE: I went into the wagon, me throat closed, me hands wet and me head knockin. Every time I'd picture his big circles of blue eyes lookin at me sideways and his kind smile and his big shovel hands on the reins, I'd feel sick. I do know this faylin from before or at least something like it. When I were fourteen year there was a traveller who stopped along side us in Letterkenny, he only stayed a night but I couldn't take meself away from him and I swear to all the saints if I'd been able to manage the horses at the time I'd have follied him. I've looked out for him ever since. And even though I never says it to anyone – I know I didn't marry coz of that faylin – I had a differ kind of sick faylin when me mother tried to get me to marry others. I threw me insides up in a ditch when she brought John Jo Wall over, so Kathleen got him instead. The traveller in Letterkenny's name was MacDonagh, Johnny MacDonagh… and Michael Ryan. Call me Michael.

KATHLEEN: Josie, I think ye have yer eye on Mr Ryan. *(Silence)* Josie Connors, don't even think about him again… Do you want that for your family? Do you want to have a show med of us?

JOSIE: No.

KATHLEEN: Do you want your baby sister never to be married?

JOSIE: No.

KATHLEEN: We'd carry it always Josie.

JOSIE: I know that, Kathleen… I have taken a liken to him though.

KATHLEEN: What are you tinkin? Tha he's goin te travel wit you? He's goin to stay stuck between them four walls up there the rest of his years… he's a married man! We have to leave here… I'm telling John Jo.

JOSIE: No, Kathleen, don't, let me clain for him another week and I'll axe him for money to help us along the way.

KATHLEEN: I'll be watchin you.

Scene 5

FRANCES: She would talk about Kathleen a lot… what it was like growing up in such a big family… there was always someone looking out for you. I can't imagine what that must be like. When you're an only child it's normal to be by yourself. The need to move I understand though, that restlessness, it's exciting. I can hop in the car and drive the length and breadth of the country if I fancy. But the thoughts of cartin ten children and a husband with me? It's not in me.

How on earth did that young lad even find me?

Scene 6

JOSIE: Mrs Ryan is in Dublin visitin her sister, Michael told me when I went in to clain for him this morning. Thank the Lord, I thought, not only do I get to tell Michael more stories when he comes in but she won't be makin me do the clainin agin and agin. Her stoney eyes follie me around the house and the only words she ever speaks are, Do it agin. When she's pleased 'tis done she says nathin. I read her face one day when she wasn't looking, a lady's face, lost in something. But that was all I could tell – she'd closed the road long ago. I wanted to tell him about Daddy bein the best bare fisted fighter in Ireland before he died, I told him nearly everything about me but not that. He'd like that – he'd laugh when I told him that and make a joke about me bein the same. I wanted to find out more about him too and how he'd saved his farm from his father who'd tried to drink it. He's a warm cup of tay on a frozen night. He put one of his shovel hands on the side of me face yesterday and it was so big his fingers lay on me head. He looked into my eyes and said, Thanks Josie.

It kept me up all night and I wanted him to do it agin. When Michael told me she'd gone to Dublin, I said nothing but started me work. I liked to get it done quick so I could make him tay when he was finished a job. But he follied me and took me by the wrists with his big shovel hands. I hate to say it but John Jo's ugly red face came into me mind for a second and then I looked up into Michael's face and that was all I could see.

He spoke slowly and as if he were afraid. I have a gift for you, he said, No need for cleaning today.

How was it that a traveller girl and a big farm owner could be standin there with the excitement of childer between them? Then he let go of my wrists and took me by the hand into the room where he slept and across the bed were the most beautiful scarf you'd ever seen – hand embroidered with silver bits in it. It was lyin on pink silky paper and me eyes nearly rolled outa me head. Michael picked it up and put it around me shoulders. Then I started roarin and I couldn't stop meself. He kept on axin me what were wrong, but I didn't know how to say, I'm destroyed you can't be my husband. So instead, I said it was because nobody had ever got me such a fancy gift before and he laughed and said he wouldn't have gotten it if he knew I'd cry as hard.

Then I laughed and we wrapped it up gently and made tay.

I knew Kathleen would be waitin te see if I stayed on past the time it takes te clain – so I was delighted there was no clainin and me and Michael could talk and maybe he'd touch me agin.

Scene 7

FRANCES: (*Takes red umbrella from its gift wrapping*). Imagine giving someone an umbrella as a wedding present. Strange, isn't it? I got it from an elderly gentleman I used to work with called Mr Fitz. Now, he wouldn't talk to anyone – anyone – only myself, but even then he only ever called me Miss Ryan. We kept in touch for a while after I left to join the Post Office, but sure I haven't heard from him in years. I thought he was dead. He used to eat toothpaste. Strange the ones that come out of the woodwork. I've been teasing Jim about all the oddballs that might turn up to our wedding;

You'd want to watch out, I said to him, Or I'll run off with Mr Fitz.

And the look on his face when I said it, I shouldn't tease him really.

He's just after ringing me again to tell me he loves me. I know what he's at so I reminded him of the time I drove into the back of a tractor cause I was daydreaming about him.

Yeah! I drove right into the back of a tractor and made shite of me lovely Morris Minor.

Now, doesn't that prove I've always been cracked over you?

I think it made him feel better.

Scene 8

JOSIE: After I finished telling him about Daddy bare-fisted fightin, I told him about Johnny MacDonagh in Letterkenny and soon he knew everything, the wet hands, the knockin head and how happy I was to be near him. It all came out. He looked so happy I bowed my head. Here I was a traveller girl telling a married farm-owner buffer I had a campfire in me body ever since I laid eyes on him. That's when he lifted my chin and kissed me. The single girl bein kissed at twenty-one years of age. Maybe twas unusual but I knew for sure on this day, in that moment, I weren't cursed. We went back to the bed where the scarf had been and I did what no traveller girl in history has done as far as I know. It might have been for one afternoon, but for that time Michael Ryan was mine.

Scene 9

KATHLEEN: We're leavin Josie, we've left your tent below, don't even dream of follyin us.

JOSIE: No, Kathleen, wait on… Did you spake to John Jo?

KATHLEEN: I told ye I'd be watchin ye… stay away up here now and don't come down till we've gone.

JOSIE: No, Kathleen, wait and we won't tell a soul and I'll go with you and nobody will…

KATHLEEN: Unless your mind blew away one windy night you knew what you were doin to us… yer too dangerous to hold on to.

JOSIE: Kathleen, Mammy wouldn't want you to leave me.

KATHLEEN: You've some neck, Josie Connors. I'm glad me mother's dead 'cause if she weren't this would kill her.

JOSIE: Kathleen, you have to let me come down and see Lizzy and the childer.

KATHLEEN: Lizzy won't marry now and the childer will carry the shame along with the rest of us… John Jo's ready to bate you, Josie… don't come down till we've gone.

JOSIE: What'll I do on me own? You have to let me see Lizzy and the childer… Come back and see me.

Scene 10

JOSIE: There was nothing too strange, ye know about me layin down with Michael when it were happenin, but with me family gone and then seein this rich lady who were smart and dressed so pretty with her motor car comin back te Michael; I felt more stupid than anythin. Here I were alone on the grass, a traveller who'd strayed so far twere shameful. What were I thinking not stickin te me own? I were so mad this morning I tore down me tent and ran into the woods and roared. I roared and cried for me mother and father to come back and get me, to take me with them. I prayed to Jesus Christ for all the help he had.

Oh, I'm a cursed traveller girl alright whose mind musta been blown away one windy night.

Scene 11

FRANCES: Josie! Josie was wild and free and always up for a bit of divilment. And Mammy, Mammy is soft and kind, very stylish but a bit rigid, you know? I had two mothers you see, doesn't sound like a bad thing and 'twasnt really… not exactly normal though is it? God, Mammy could cut you with a look. We had murder when I was a teenager. I certainly didn't have her wrapped around my little finger, not like Daddy.

Daddy, can I leave the convent school and go to the tech?

Whatever you want.

Brilliant! No nuns, loads of fellas.

Run it by your mother first.

Ah no! Sure I knew what she'd say: Frances Ryan, you will not go there after all your good education and learn to be a hussy and a drunk.

Back then I thought she didn't want me to be happy and she was just mean and sad. When I was small, I thought it was because she used to be a Protestant. I thought that's what a Protestant meant. I never spared a thought for her then. She must have felt so bad so often and so scared for me at times. I gave her hell! And what did she do? Fed and clothed me, kept me in pocket money and dances. Stayed up daubing my eyes at night when they would be burning and streaming red from the smoke of Josie's fire.

I must give her a call and let her and Daddy know about Josie's passing.

Scene 12

JOSIE: Twas only two week ago I started showin and that's when I realised there were a child inside me and nathin feels wrong about it. I have an old wagon now and I'm getting by on the bit o clanin I'm doin for Michael. I know the lady will never think Michael and I lay down together cause I am so below them in her eyes that even if she'd seen it she probably wouldn't have believed it. But we've had nothing but longin eyes for each other since that afternoon and even though I love this lump inside me, I've been afeared to say anything to anyone. Tis now it's true I'm sorry I'm not with me own. I'd have the help of ten hands and the safety of my people. I've been prayin for me sisters to come back and get me. Twas only this morning when Michael saw me bump that another person knew. I saw so many tales in his eyes twould take me a lifetime to explain them. We were stood at the end of the passage and I knew one thing, neither of us knew what to do. There were a hundred questions in both our eyes but the only one that mattered to me was would he come travellin with me and the chile?

Scene 13

MICHAEL: Josie, let me and Emma have the baby and you can always see it. We'll tell Emma a traveller got you in trouble and you can't manage.

JOSIE: No.

MICHAEL: I don't want to see you going into a home, Josie, what else is there to do?

JOSIE: I don't know.

MICHAEL: The baby will be well looked after... what other choice do you have with your family gone?

JOSIE: I thought that maybe we'd... I don't know.

I want to see the sea, me mother and father's graves, I want the wind on my face and a new story in my heart every day, Michael. I want to read new faces, I want to dance with ten other travellers round a camp-fire till the sun shows itself, I want too many childer axin me when the food will be made, I want the home that me sisters are and me mother and father were I was roarin and cryin for thirteen hours straight and then there she was.

Scene 14

EMMA: Josie the traveller woman had her baby today. Well tis an ill wind that doesn't blow somebody some good. She's beautiful. She's a beautiful little girl. Michael said to call her Emma after me, but I said no. No, we'll call her Frances, after my mother. When I held her for the first time today, wrapped up in a soft while shawl all wriggling and warm and tiny, Michael looked down at us with a light in his eyes I haven't seen for a long time. Things will come right between Michael and I now. I just… I have a feeling. Michael and Josie have come to some sort of an agreement. They seem to have an understanding. She couldn't raise the child alone. I'm glad we were able to help her like this really and tis for the best that the town thinks she's mine. I made sure of that, it wouldn't be fair on Frances not to. Twas easy enough really to stay away from Cahir the whole time Josie was pregnant, and worth it. She's a gift. I love her so much. And I'll mind her always. I must put my beads by her cradle to keep her safe.

JOSIE: I took her from the lady and prayed over her. I read her eyes and we both knew. You see, buffers need to own things – land and people and belongings, so if she were at their end of the passage or mine, it didn't matter… her little traveller soul and mine were joined. After that I went down to the wagon to rest.

Scene 15

MICHAEL: Are you alright, Josie?

JOSIE: I am, I just need to rest a while.

MICHAEL: She's grand, isn't she?

JOSIE: She is.

MICHAEL: Thank you, Josie.

JOSIE: She's still mine, Michael.

MICHAEL: I know, and you can stay here all of her life if you want to.

JOSIE: No, I can't, I'm a traveller, I'll be coming and going all of her life. I sometimes think you understand nathin… you'll never stop me seein her.

MICHAEL: Never… and… if things were different.

JOSIE: We're differ, Michael.

MICHAEL: *(Pause)* We are.

JOSIE: I've been comin and goin since Frances was born, when I go, travellers move away when they see me comin and I can't hurt me family any more by follyin them. And all the time I'm pulled back here to the same eyes and ways and whispers. If it weren't for Fran, I'd lay down and not get up again… Tis hard to think yer wrong though when yer chile is trippin over herself to lay eyes on you.

Scene 16

FRANCES: Tell me the one about when you were a girl like me in Cavan.

JOSIE: You've heard that one ten times, Frances.

FRANCES: But tell me again.

JOSIE: I were ten year old and me mother and father took me and me sisters and brothers up to the burnin of me uncle's wagon.

FRANCES: Why?

JOSIE: When a traveller dies the family burns their wagon.

FRANCES: Why?

JOSIE: A traveller can never be stuck to the one spot and when they burned me uncle's wagon, the spirit of him could travel forever on the wind… with the smoke.

FRANCES: Could ye see his spirit in the smoke?

JOSIE: No, but he was all around us then when we remembered him in stories and songs around the camp. I was only small like you and the noise and cracklin of the fire was so loud, I started to cry. I ran away and hid in a ditch, but me father came after me and told me about respectin the dead and traditions and that when he died I'd help burn his wagon and when I die my family will burn mine.

FRANCES: But then where will I play?

JOSIE: Sure, maybe you'll have your own wagon by then.

FRANCES: Could I?

JOSIE: Why wouldn't ya?

FRANCES: I'd paint it red like yours.

I used to love it when Josie would come back. The excitement was nearly too much for me. And it was the same feeling every time I heard the horse clip-cloppin round the bend or saw the smoke from her fire at the gate. Josie was back. I would fly down to the gate with my mother calling after me to be home by teatime and I wasn't to go into the woods or fall into the fire. All *Don'ts* and *Nos* and *Be carefuls*. But Josie was back and she never said no.

FRANCES: Josie! I can't believe it! You're early this year, Johnny and Clicks said they saw you on your way back when they were in Nenagh last week but sure, I didn't believe them.

JOSIE: Well you may believe them! And what sort of a name is Clicks?

FRANCES: It's cause he never leaves the dance without pairin off with someone.

I loved talking about the dances with her. She was great for chat about love and men and being in your lover's arms.
Josie, nobody says lover nowadays.

JOSIE: Well I says it don't I! And I seen you sneakin out so you may go up and tell your mother where you are before she catches you and I'm blamed.

FRANCES: I don't care about her. I hate her. We're not talking.

JOSIE: What happened?

FRANCES: At the dance last night.

JOSIE: Yes?

FRANCES: You know how she always drives up before it's finished and shines her headlights onto the dance floor and watches till it's over? So I have to leave as soon as I see the car comin no matter who I'm dancing with?

JOSIE: I do.

FRANCES: Well, Tommy Flynn wouldn't let me go and he's the best dancer I know. He's brown as mud and tall like Daddy. He's the best lookin fella in Cahir and with all the chat and dancing I didn't notice the lights shinin on us. And… well, when he kissed me… she beeped the horn!

JOSIE: Ah, she never did!

FRANCES: She did! I hate her. I'm so embarrassed. She wouldn't even speak to me on the way home she was so cross and then when we got in, she shouted somethin about me frightenin her and she's not cut out for me and I came from nothing good.

JOSIE: From nathin good?

FRANCES: I know she means Daddy. Why is she so horrible? She's married to the kindest man in the world and she barely even speaks to him.

JOSIE: So what happened then?

FRANCES: I roared back at her and that shut her up and now we're not talkin.

JOSIE: What did ye say?

FRANCES: I told her she had a dead animal rotting inside her.

JOSIE: God above, Fran.

FRANCES: So it went on like that year after year till the next time she would take up her tent and bundle it into the back of the wagon sayin...

JOSIE: Tis in me blood chile, God bless you till I'm back.

FRANCES: And I don't think I ever asked her to stay, despite all the chat and the fun. No. But I understand now why every bit of me wanted to bundle myself into the wagon like the tent and go with her. I never did stow away, though. I think that was an awful hard feeling for a child, young woman, to understand. It felt like I was being pulled out of myself and stretched out all over the whole of Ireland.

I just spoke to Mammy. I think she got a shock when I told her about Josie. When she asked how I found out, I told her about the young lad coming to the door but I left out the bit about the scarf. I didn't tell Daddy about it either. No point there being more secrets between them at this stage. He was very quiet though and he asked me if I was okay. Sure what do you say? The whole thing was a holy mess from start to finish.

JOSIE: God bless you till I'm back. In a way I could never say no to Fran and why should I? I gave up that job when she were born but even though they had my chile I always felt like I had her friendship... till it all went wrong. Things would have been differ for sure if I hadn't been snorin that night.

Scene 17

FRANCES: I wasn't let out for weeks for kissin Tommy Flynn. Driven to and from school, thanks be to God Josie came back, she was the only other soul I was allowed to spend any time with, until one day Mammy came in and said I'd fail my exams if I stayed down with her any more. Jesus, I was ragin. So I climbed out my bedroom window and ran down to

Josie's but she wasn't there… out in the woods probably. Now normally I would have waited for her but I took a mad mind that night and I kept walking. Half a mile to Cahir, then a short cut through the fields towards the lights of the dance. Stopped for a smoke in the ditch by the bandstand before goin in and shared the one stick of red lipstick with all the girls, Biddy Curtin's mother's.

We'd pool our pennies before goin in so Johnny Keane didn't bother countin them. Jesus the poor fella was never paid what he charged I'm only in the door, hardly enough time to get a mouthful of whiskey from the Slug Morrissey's hip flask, when I turn round and see Tommy Flynn in a clinch with Grace-Ann O'Brien. He catches my eye.

Did your Mammy let you out then?

Everyone laughs. I'm mortified. Feck him! I look round but the girls don't know what to say so I grab the first man I see and dance the legs off Jim Nolan for the night. He doesn't know what's after hittin him and at the end of each tune I hold onto him and we dance the next. He's not the greatest dancer but he's gettin some practice in tonight. I feel like everyone's watchin me and whispering so for divilment I say, out loud:

If we sold your farm, Jim, would it keep us long in dances in Dublin?

About a month, he says, but if we kept me farm twould keep us fed and healthy for years.

I'm smilin right up into his face now and I definitely like that he's able for me and we dance and drink the rest of the night away, and I forget about the whispers.

On the way home I've a knot in my stomach and my palms are wet. I'm nervous! Over a small farm owner from Banra? What's happenin to me?

Outside the wagon by the gate, there's no sign of Josie but then I hear her snores comin from the tent and Jim goes to leave but I take his hand. We kiss for a second but then he stands back.

There's no need to be a gentleman, I whisper.

Can't help what I am, he says.

And I'm embarrassed now for sayin it. I don't want him to think I'm brazen.

There's a long silence between us. I'll go, he says.

No wait, stay and talk. Sit into the wagon with me for a little while longer and… and we'll talk.

And he does. We talk for hours, another kiss and we fall asleep, side by side.

In the morning I wake up to the sound of Josie singin and my heart stops… till I hear her reach for the bucket and head for the well.

Jim, Jim wake up… get up will you for God's sake. It's bright. I'll be murdered if we're seen.

Then from outside the wagon I hear the sound of Daddy's voice.

Josie.

Oh Jesus!

Josie, I can't find Fran. Is she here?

Jesus, it's Daddy!

The door opens and the look on his face when he sees the two of us.

What's goin on? What's goin on here?

Wait, Daddy, it's nothing

But he cuts me off. Get up to the house Frances. Then he roars at me. Get up!

Jim tries to say something but Daddy goes for him and wrestles him out of the wagon and I'm cryin and screamin at them to stop. Daddy lands a punch on Jim that knocks him down. He turns to me, where's Josie he wants to know.

Daddy, don't be cross.

Where is she?

Out at the well. Will you let me explain?

May she pray I don't find her. Get up to the house, Frances. Get up!

Scene 18

EMMA: Michael, I'm not cut out for her. I'm not able for her any more. Staying out all night with some young fella. She'll end up in the same condition as Josie and then what will happen to her? Then where will we be? God forgive me but when she turned to me this morning and that wild look in her eye, trying to tell me twas all innocent and Josie wasn't to blame. I can't hear that woman's name in this house again, Michael. I let it slip, Michael, I think, I think I let it slip. The words were out of my mouth before I knew what I was saying,

You're a Tinker's daughter. You're a Tinker's daughter through and through.

Scene 19

JOSIE: Look at me, Frances… hand of God show me your face chile. So you know the truth of it now.

FRANCES: Yes.

JOSIE: You were cryin.

FRANCES: Was I… no I stuck my head in the stream. It was poundin.

JOSIE: What was said to you, Frances?

FRANCES: Oh… that I came from nothing good. I'm a tinker's daughter through and through.

JOSIE: What ye came from was nothing shameful.

FRANCES: Then why would you leave me?

JOSIE: I had no choice.

FRANCES: You always have a choice.

JOSIE: No I didn't, we didn't know what to do and when Michael said he'd take you, well then I knew you'd always be safe.

FRANCES: So, you and Daddy?

JOSIE: Tis a natural thing to be angry. Your blood isn't suited to hidin the truth.

FRANCES: I'm not angry, I just want to go away… wake up somewhere far away from all of this. I want to leave Cahir, I want to be rid of the three of you and your secrets, I want to see new faces and places and stories and not be stuck in the middle of their mess. I want to run away to Dublin with Jim Nolan. I want him to sell his farm and keep us in dances there forever. I want to sell Mammy's motor car and go shopping in Cork. I want to rob a horse from Daddy and just keep going. I want to tell Mammy about Daddy. I want to throw your tent in the river for lying to me.

JOSIE: I have to leave, Frances. Will you come with me?

FRANCES: No I can't. I won't. When are you going?

JOSIE: At first light, Michael's bringing me a horse down.

FRANCES: Penance for the bruise on your face? Did he hit you?

JOSIE: I fell in the woods.

FRANCES: I thought travellers didn't like lies.

JOSIE: I fell in the woods, leave it at that. I'll always be with you, Fran.

Scene 20

JOSIE: He tried to pull me up to sittin that day. I still don't know if I were sleepin with the dead or drownin in me madness, but it took the force of his two shovel arms to pull me up to sittin, me head dropping and me soul sinkin. He held me face still so I'd look at him but I shut me eyes tight. So he gave up and spoke.

I was told to go and if I had my people with me I may have took her in the night. And it may sound funny but I knew be his eyes that he weren't a bad man, just a man that were filled with a sadness he didn't know he could be freed of. It were an old wagon but a fine strong pony and the rhythm of his trot let me mind rest. He tore me out of Cahir and twas a whole day and a night before I stopped again proper, to rest.
They'd ruin me chile with their hard sadness but I'd no care for any of it any more. For all I knew I'd ruin her myself. The cursed traveller slept that night without torture, she were movin agin. I think that was the night me own sadness turned frozen.

Scene 21

FRANCES: The house is full of deafening silences, nobody seems able to mend it, I have to go.

JOSIE: Bantry! Stop leaving sods of grass at every crossroads… I have to leave her make her own way.

FRANCES: Dublin! New digs in Molesworth Street. The style up here is something else… and the dances!

JOSIE: Portarlington! Travellers moved off when they saw me comin to their camp today… left some warm clothes behind.

FRANCES: Athlone! Much prefer the post office though Mr Fitz was sad to see me go. Savin like mad for a car.

JOSIE: Kildare! Sold flowers today… cooked mate for dinner.

FRANCES: Home for Christmas, Cahir seems like another world to me now. Met Jim Nolan at midnight Mass. Lovely to see him again.

JOSIE: Lahinch, County Clare! Watched the sea watchin me… Fran's at dances breakin hearts no doubt.

FRANCES: Navan! Passed by a camp this morning, I miss the smell of an open fire.

JOSIE: Leitrim! The winter is bitin. Stuck between two worlds.

FRANCES: Mallow. Crashed the Morris Monor, Jim's looking awful shifty these days, must be gearing up for another proposal.

JOSIE: Monaghan! Found me sisters. The childer are all grown. Lizzy wouldn't look at me. Kathleen axed me to leave before John Jo came back… Lizzy never married.

FRANCES: Wexford! Wondered about trying to find Josie after all these years, sure maybe our paths will cross.

JOSIE: County Waterford! Me knees are givin out. The seagulls are telling me to rest… Dreamt Fran was wanderin.

FRANCES: Carlow! Could have sworn I saw Josie, just me eyes playin tricks though, she was far too old.

JOSIE: Carlow! Spoke to me parents' graves, they're not speakin back.

FRANCES: Cork! Rang in the new decade with Jim on McCurtain Street… Should old acquaintance be forgot?

JOSIE: Letterkenny! Johnny Mac Donagh and Michael Ryan… me head is not the same… need to go back for Fran.

FRANCES: Dublin! Shopping for a wedding dress. If Mammy stops at one more church to light a candle, I'll scream.

JOSIE: Spiddal! Getting weak… tired… watchin the stars watchin me.

FRANCES: August! Indian Summer, I wonder does she ever think about me?

JOSIE: Kilkenny! Tis getting warmer… still tired.

FRANCES: September! Blazing row with Mammy about icing, up to me eyes in wrapping paper and ribbon. Made up my mind to find Josie after the wedding when things have calmed down again.

JOSIE: Thurles! The birds told me to back to Fran... hurt me back getting water... have been layin down all day, have had nathin to ate...

FRANCES: October! Got the land of my life this morning, I can't believe she'll never meet Jim. Took my keys and drove to Galway Bay, no purse, keys, nothing. No phone call to Jim even, I'll be the death of him.

Scene 22

FRANCES: I walk up to the camp just outside Galway Bay.

Evenin Mam, one of the men says to me. My name is Frances Ryan, I am looking for Josie Connor's Wagon. Suddenly every eye in the camp on me is suspicious. I'm Josie Connors daughter.

Everything stops. I want to run, but I stand still. A big woman calls from the far side of a trailer—

John Jo, will ye look close at her face— She says more but its in cant so I don't understand. Now everyone's talking fast, all in cant, and I don't understand anything any more and my legs are shaking and all I can think is all the yearning in my blood that's kept me moving all these years, it doesn't make me a traveller. I am as out of place here as I can be. My head's reeling and I think I am going to faint, when she says: Come in, biore, you've your mother's blood in you.

And my legs give way and I put my head in my hands and sob my heart out. The woman's name is Kathleen Wall, Josie's sister. We sit and talk and she gives me cups of tea... about twenty cups of tea and we have lonely, lonely talk of Josie. They've hardly seen her since 1946 and she speaks of the hurt and the shame that Josie brought down on herself and her whole family, all the while saying that twas no fault of mine and they'd never put the blame on the child. I ask again about the wagon and Kathleen is quiet for a long time. It's to burn it, Kathleen, begging her through my tears.

Josie's wagon is in a field a few miles outside Thurles. Farmer by the name of Cleary. I wonder was she on her way back to see me?

As I'm leaving, Kathleen takes my hand and presses a button from her cardigan into my palm. You're welcome any time. Two big tears roll down her cheeks and she says, There were no badness in your mother, she just made up her own ways.

I know.

Josie Connors, you're breaking hearts all over the land.

Scene 23

FRANCES: *(Takes scarf out of case and puts it on.)* Lahinch, County Clare! Rained every day of the honeymoon. Mr Fitz's umbrella came in handy in the end. By the last day we couldn't brave the weather any more so we stayed in the caravan underneath the blankets eating cheese sandwiches and drinking wine till it got dark. Just before we fell asleep, I turned to Jim,

I've something to tell you…Travellers tell tales around campfires late into the night, when nothing else is stirrin…

JOSIE: When a traveller tells a tale, they're listened to. *(FRANCES fades out.)* Their own people know to listen, it's differ to settled folks stories, there is a magic in it. Maybe tis the weight of the listeners, the quiet of the dark or that we go back to the day, the time, the minute and the age of when it happened. Not sure what it is but I know something, you can't tell a tale without the listeners, they make half the magic.

THE END

PHOTO BY SARAH FITZGERALD

Is There Balm in Gilead?
By Michael Harding

IS THERE BALM IN GILEAD? WAS FIRST PRODUCED IN NOVEMBER 2007.

DIRECTOR: CAROLINE FITZGERALD
CAST: MARY MCEVOY AND SEÁN MURPHY
DESIGN: CAROLINE FITZGERALD
LIGHTING: MOYRA D'ARCY

Author's Note:

Mary McEvoy phoned me one day and asked me did I have a short play that would suit the intimate stage of Bewley's. I said I had a short piece inspired by the life and work of Edgar Allen Poe and that I would be delighted to offer it to her.
I was absolutely delighted with the result.
I have a strange relationship with Poe. I think there is a long shadow of obscure and bleak comedy that reaches from the dark drumlins of Cavan, through his seed and breed, and surfaces sometimes in his work. Caroline FitzGerald, Seán Murphy and Mary McEvoy brought a wonderful energy and fun to the piece, which fitted splendidly into the intimate and charming old world of Bewely's Café.

—Michael Harding

A note on the play:

The woman might be a person in the life of Edgar Allen Poe, or might be a character from his fiction. The man might be a person in from Poe's fiction, or indeed, Poe himself. Or perhaps they are neither of these. It's not certain. The play should be costumed in the darkest gothic, and be played in the most intimate manner possible. There should always be a shimmer of the erotic between the two persons on stage, even in the long periods when the man is saying nothing, but is merely present. The actors should be encouraged to find extraordinary choreography where they can, but all movement should be formal, and slow, and perhaps at times pause, and present the audience with still images, like old photographs. Lighting, too, should sometimes offer sepia still poses, where nothing is said for a long time and then the woman continues. The play should be played to the backdrop of continuous sound. A single door creaking, in a rhythm, should be looped so that a pattern of sound repeats ever so gently in the background.

THE WOMAN: *(She is dressed in evening clothes of a wealthy lady of the eighteen-forties.)*

    Hello, Moon.
    I'm going to talk about the bed.
    Being in his particular bed.
    A good bed. There is no flaw.
    No embroidery.
    Mother would have agreed.
    She gave me the pillow cases.
    Those pillows. Handed them over in the bedroom she did.

    You're being very cruel, she said. I didn't know what she meant.

    I meant to lie down and sleep.
    That's all I wanted.
    She had this thing, in the left eye, so it closed a bit. But she smiled.
    Yes.
    She smiled.

Mother was perfect.

Marry him if you want, she said. No bother. If that's your wish.
And she smiled.

A light around her grey head.
Rain on the window pane.
Clouds from Michigan.
And then I'm lying on the bed. Awake.
Enduring.
The sound of bugles.
Marching feet.
And bells.
Ding dong.
Afterwards I can feel a sort of tightness in the chest. The
whispering wind.
The silence of the house.

One hundred breakfasts.

I'm sweeping the floor of the earth. Forever.
And he's at the front door saying, isn't it a pity we don't have a tap
for the water.

But dare I move my legs under the sheets?
Find the cold spot.
Thank God, I say, for mother's linen.

And he sleeps.
And he's awake.
One minute he's staggering around the streets in joyful
astonishment. The next, he's staring at the wall.

Let me put it this way. It's not what I expected.

*She rings her bell. A man appears. Stands in the shadows. He is still. Clothes of the same
period.*

Is it cold tonight?
Have you seen the cat ?

What are you doing ?
And let me know if you see a cat. Or a purse. Or a fiddle or a
spoon. Or the man in the moon. Yes.

It's not what I expected. Let me put it that way. This way. Not what

I expected at all.
And if you are to insist on being here, then the least you could do is stay quiet.
I don't wish to frighten anybody, but there is a shadow on the floor. And it's moving.

Finding sanctuary in her story to the moon.

But dare I move my legs under the sheets?
Find the cold spot.
Thank God, I say, for mother's linen.
And he sleeps.
And he's awake.

Oh yes, thank God, I say, for mother's linen.
Yes. I knew what was coming. I knew that would be part of it.
Like big stars. And alligators. And insects.
The alligators were an eye opener. Especially in the drawing room.
And they put different spices in their cooking pots here.
May I say…
There's just so long you can endure someone staring at you. Just so long you can remain exposed. Before you're inclined to ask. Is this the same person you went to bed with?
Who did you go to bed with?
How many of him are there?

Why don't you touch me? Come here. Touch me.
Hold me.

Oh, it's so easy for people to say just stop thinking about him!
But I don't have a choice.

And the most awful part was that I dreamed of him.
No matter that he made my skin crawl.
His white arse.
His waking arse.
His sleeping arse.
His dreaming twitching rump.
No matter. I'd turn over, fall asleep and dream that I was limp, and shiftless, in his strong arms, and he carrying me to the boat, on the river. And he oiled his moustache sometimes. I did enjoy that.
But I'd keep dreaming… I'm limp. In his arms.
I'm dead in his arms.
And that's a terrible fright. So I wake. But I'm waking in a strange room. Of course, it's still a dream. You see. I'm dreaming that I'm

dreaming, so I wake from the first dream, wake up in a room. And he's not there. But it's still a dream.
Or is it?
What's that noise he said to me once. I was playing the piano. What's that noise.
I said it's the sound of someone being dragged to an unwanted destiny.
Oh, he smiled all right. But you could see he was slightly uncertain about what to do next.

Speak!

Sir, I need you.
So, if I were a woman, would you love me?
If I were the dog, would you beat me?
If I were dead, would you kiss me?
Would you love me, sir? Would you love me?
Would you wait for me?

If I were a corpse, would you kiss me?
Kissie kissie kissie, sir!

Is wince the correct word. I can master the algebra, but I'm not entirely at home with... speaking.
Anyway. I think it's wince. He winced.
I'm not saying that right. His smile froze. Yes. That's it. The expression was dead and sour.

Pretend to be asleep. That's what I did.

So I pretended to be asleep. I was always doing that. While he took off the braces.
His boot straps.
Pretend to be asleep.
Where else can you go at a moment like that?
And the first thing I thought odd was when he opened the razor. Because he only and ever shaves in the morning. On the porch. With a swing mirror.
He opens the razor, but he doesn't shave, because I know the sound. The grating sound of the blade on the bristle. So I know he's opened it. But he's not using it.
Pretending to be asleep feels like the wrong room to be in now, but how do you get out of a room like that?

I banish him by walking naked round the room, singing a little song to myself, *Sweet Divine Jesus*, let it be the cat, let it be the cat that he is after with his bayonet, his open ended razor.

He leaves the room. Goes downstairs.
And I'm up, naked, walking around the room, trying to inhabit it.
Trying to dispel his presence. Does that sound like love?
To be cornered.
To have no wonder left.
To feel that warm and soft are not words but traps.
To feel pity for a dry dead wasp on the porch. And all about me…
nothing… but his breath, his chocolate breath, filling the
darkness… his breath like an envelope of fog, binding me in his
tight and perverted grip. How precious it is, I thought, to be a
human being, and not an insect. Or the cat.

THE VISITOR: Is it because I love you that I stay?
Or because I stay that I think I love you?
That I have to say I love you?
Or do I say it?
No, you never say that.
Why do I think I say it?

THE WOMAN: Because you think about it. You think about saying it. And not
saying it and whether it's true or not.
And in the meantime you say nothing and love nobody.
Do you want to stay?

THE VISITOR: Would you forgive yourself? Tomorrow. If I did?

THE WOMAN: Don't sit there.

THE VISITOR: Why not?

THE WOMAN: The cat sits there.

THE VISITOR: Right.

THE WOMAN: Well?

THE VISITOR: Well, what?

THE WOMAN: I said, don't sit there.

THE VISITOR: I heard you.

THE WOMAN: So get up.

THE VISITOR: No.

THE WOMAN: No?

THE VISITOR: *(Shouts)* No!
Sorry.
I have a wretched headache.
Does that mean something to you?
A headache.

THE WOMAN: Something to eat?

THE VISITOR: No.

THE WOMAN: No?

THE VISITOR: I said no.
Well I was thinking more of something like a sandwich. Glass of milk perhaps. That sort of thing.
I can get it myself.
Thank you.

Trite as it may seem I have a headache.
And not that it matters, but it was my house too, you know. I mean, there were two of us. It was mine as much as yours. In fact it belonged to neither of us. But in so far as you say… mine… then I also may say… mine.
(THE WOMAN laughs.)
What are you laughing at?

THE WOMAN: What am I laughing at? You arrive out of the blue. You have a headache. Sorry, but do I know you?

THE VISITOR: Of course, you know me.

THE WOMAN: Do I?

THE VISITOR: Yes.

THE WOMAN: Do I? Do I, Do I, Do I?

THE VISITOR: Yes! Yes! *(Shouting at THE WOMAN)* Yes… yes… yes!

THE WOMAN: Fuck off!
I said fuck off!
(Rings her bell with relish.)

THE VISITOR: I'd better go. You want me to go.

THE WOMAN: I think we're being watched.

THE VISITOR: You want me to go?

THE WOMAN: I know it's not an afternoon for love. Too many small rain showers. You need dry heat. Or snow. Either extreme is good for love. But when it's cold, and damp, and it's raining that steamy rain, it leaves you disappointed. Don't you think?

THE VISITOR: You want me to go?

THE WOMAN: Yes. No. I'm sorry for saying fuck off. I didn't mean it. You've been back. Haven't you? To the house where we lived.

THE VISITOR: Yes. And it rained all night. Battering the roof. You know, I sat at the window. Remembering our first night in that house. Remembering both of us at that window, staring out at the sheets of rain. Wondering. The house is still there. Where it always stood. Funny thing that about houses. They outlast us all. Last night I woke. Thought I saw you again. As you were.

THE WOMAN: Did I look well?

THE VISITOR: Oh, yes. You looked very well. The fire was on. Coal fire. Throwing out an extraordinary heat. And a foul odour in the room, I must admit. And your face as cold and empty as the grave.

THE WOMAN: You're lying.

THE VISITOR: I never lied.
We even cleaned the dishes away in silence.
And then you ask, is something wrong?
There's always something wrong, if you have to ask the question.
But I didn't say that. I said, no, of course not, there is nothing wrong, my darling. Her lips were like… frosted fruit.
We put the feast away in the cupboard, and then it was over.

THE WOMAN: Me! You are speaking of me! You saw me! You saw me. As I was.

THE VISITOR: Yes.

THE WOMAN: I was beautiful. You walked with me.

THE VISITOR: Yes.

THE WOMAN: Were you walking with me?

THE VISITOR: Yes, I was walking with…

THE WOMAN: Where were we?

THE VISITOR: On the stairs. Going down.

THE WOMAN: Where did you say we were?

THE VISITOR: On the stairs. Going down.

THE WOMAN: Walking with me?

THE VISITOR: Yes, I was walking with you.

THE WOMAN: Going down?

THE VISITOR: Walking.

THE WOMAN: You. Was it you?

THE VISITOR: That's all there was to it.

THE WOMAN: Yes. I hear it!

THE VISITOR: It's probably a cat! Must surely be a cat!
Well, you see, I fancied the cat was avoiding me. I did. Caught him.
And he scraped me.
That's what happened. I had the razor in my hand. Grabbed the
cat by the throat and cut out his eye. Right eye. Out of the socket.
The cat looked awful. And then I slipped a noose round its neck
and hung it from the limb of an apple tree.
So where was she? In the cellar?
I descended. I was looking for the cat, and instead, I found her
there, on the stairs, blocking my way.
Is that you? Is that you?

THE WOMAN: Stop it! Please! Stop it!

THE VISITOR: Damn it, you are blocking my way!
But why? Why interfere like that? I'm here on the stairs to the
cellar, a razor blade in my hand, full flight to make sausages out of
the cat and you stop me.
She stopped me.

THE WOMAN: I said stop it! Stop it! I've had enough.

THE VISITOR: No. No. I have no brakes. No brakes. What are you looking at? It's my business. My face. My razor. My business. Will that do. Ha. Ha. Ha. Will that do?

THE WOMAN: Now, what do we do?

THE VISITOR: I would have thought that was obvious.

THE WOMAN: There's something behind the wall.

THE VISITOR: I believe it's the cat. Simple as that. When you hear a noise. It's invariably… the cat. Where's the door?

THE WOMAN: He tried to kill me. In a way, I suppose he succeeded.

THE VISITOR is trying to get out.

THE VISITOR: I have tea in the evenings. Cold salad. It's always left in the fridge. With a plate of meat. Oh, sometimes beef, I mean if there was a roast, earlier in the evening, for dinner. But even without the beef, there's always ham, or corned beef, that sort of thing. I have tea. In the evenings. I have a life. Going on somewhere else. At this precise time. Christ look at the time. Ha. Ha. I'm not meant to be here.

THE VISITOR fails to find a way out. He is exhausted.

THE WOMAN: I feel much better. Whatever it was. I don't know. But I feel much better. (*She looks at him. Disappointed.*) I wouldn't give the skin of a dried turd for him now.
But that solves nothing. We're still in here.
We still have to rub our big white arses up against each other.

Oh, you were very funny alright.

I wish mother was still with us. I could talk to her.
She'd understand.
Go back to the beginning, she would say.
But she knew we can never go back.

He almost killed me. Or perhaps he did.

Anyway. Question – How to get home on a dark night?
Answer – Follow the moon.
Question two – How to get out of the forest?

Answer – Imagine which way mother is pointing, and then walk in the opposite direction.

I was standing at the window. In this night shift.
And he was behind me.
Was that it? Was It? Him? Behind me?
Get away from me!
Just look at him…? You can see that under the clothes, he's completely naked. *(She scrutinises him.)*
And he seems old. In his flesh. And white.
How would you describe him… a derelict building? Bones of straw? Jelly for flesh? Toxic blood? Would you describe him as bloated?
Bloated, yes. I wonder is it really him?

Excuse me. Hello. Hello.

THE VISITOR: What?

THE WOMAN: You were shaving. You had that thing… the razor… in your hand. Yes? And you went downstairs. And I followed you. You were in a temper. It was you, wasn't it? Wasn't it? *(He makes no reply.)* It was you. It was just a room. Your room. Your bed. And then you returned. Walked back into the room. Was it you?

THE VISITOR: Of course, it was me.

THE WOMAN: But *was* it?

THE VISITOR: It was always me. It was me when we met for the very first time…

THE WOMAN: …by the river, where we camped, and lit the fire, and you had that boat?

THE VISITOR: What boat?… It was me in that room before I rushed downstairs, and then you came after me…

THE WOMAN: And then?

THE VISITOR: It was me. It is me. It will always be… me?

THE WOMAN: That is… unless you're someone else.

THE VISITOR: Pardon?

THE WOMAN: Unless you're someone else.

THE VISITOR: Are you a plank of wood, or am I a plank of wood? How could I be anybody but me?

THE WOMAN: I'm simply asking who is… me.

THE VISITOR: Me is the me we are now beholding, in this wretched state of unhappiness.

THE WOMAN: Is it?

THE VISITOR: I get up in the morning and look at myself in the mirror. And I know it's me. I don't have the slightest doubt on the matter.

THE WOMAN: How.

THE VISITOR: *Pardon?*

THE WOMAN: How do you know it's you when you look in the mirror?

THE VISITOR: Because it looks like me. Jesus, what kind of fog are you wandering around in?

THE WOMAN: You think you know *me*. But you don't.

THE VISITOR: Perhaps that thesis has some merit.

THE WOMAN: You agree?

THE VISITOR: Yes.

THE WOMAN: Yes?

THE VISITOR: Yes.

THE WOMAN: *(Wary of him now.)* Yes is always a metaphysical version of jumping off a cliff. Blindfolded. I hope you're aware of that.

THE VISITOR: Yes is always a mistake.

THE WOMAN: Look. *(She points at props on the stage.)* His jug of water. His basin and towel.
The loyalty of crockery.

His piss. His saliva. His faeces looking at me in the bowl.

And his bed. His room. That's all I know. His things. So I presume it is him.

Do *you* understand my point?
Even when the one you're most familiar with looks you in the eye, you really don't know what you're dealing with. You know those moments when he's staring at you? And you know he's not really seeing you. He's seeing someone else, while he stares at you. Well, those are the moments when you begin to understand.

THE VISITOR: Do you really think that life is just about eating, and shitting and having good bowel motions?

THE WOMAN: And I ran away with him. I think. I eloped. I waited by the river. With the boat. The boat would take us far away. And I waited, there, by the bank of the river. Waiting.
I will know you coming by the sound of your horse. By the crack of your whip. By the crack of your whip, I said. I was running away with him.
Who was he? I don't know. But I will know you, by the sound of your whip.

We can discuss everything tomorrow. That's what he used to say. Limp in his arms. Smoke from the fire. The smell of fish on the river bank. I looked into his eyes and asked… just who are you? And his brown eyes sparkled. We can discuss everything tomorrow, he said.
Shame. That's what I felt, when he kissed me. I think shame is the purest of all sensations. You can get other things behind love. Or sorrow. But behind shame there is only more shame.
That's who I am, I thought. I am ashamed.

THE VISITOR: I am a shark. I never sleep.

THE WOMAN: What? What is it?

THE VISITOR: I don't belong here.

THE WOMAN: That's not him.
That is not my man. My man is beautiful. He is wonderful. And he is camped somewhere, far away, beside a river. I know he gathers. Water in a bucket. Smoke from his fire dissolves into the air. And I know I will meet him. Sometime.

Are you ill? Here. Sit on the bed.

She places him on the bed beside her and nurses him on her breast.

Drink.

Relax. Try to relax. Here. From here. The bellybutton. Relax from there. That's the spot. As far as I remember, I whispered. I love it when you are still. Very still. I whispered it. And was gone. *(Whispers)* Now, be still.

It's simple really. You're just not... the person you think you are. And that knocks you off the horse. And then you must face the juices of an unlived life swirling around in your tummy.

Nobody loves anybody. Now be still.

He is still in her arms.

Hello, Moon. I'm going to talk about the bed.
Being in his particular bed.
A good bed. There is no flaw.
None.

THE END

BEWLEY'S CAFÉ THEATRE
LIST OF PRODUCTIONS 1999-2008

1999

Her Big Chance by Alan Bennett
Director: Michael James Ford
Cast: Karen Ardiff
Design: Halina Froudist

Too Much of Nothing by Mark O'Halloran
& David Wilmot
Director: Michael James Ford
Cast: Mark O'Halloran & David Wilmot

Whatever Happened to Joe Magill by Lorcan
Roche
Director: Caroline FitzGerald
Cast: Paul Roe

The Humours of Breffni by Jack Lynch
Performed by Jack Lynch

2000

A Fishpond All on Fire by Tif Eccles
Director: Michael James Ford
Cast: Stella Madden & Gerry Walsh
Design: Sinead Cuthbert & Nicola Hughes

How He Lied to Her Husband by George
Bernard Shaw
Director: Kelly Campbell
Cast: Rory Keenan, Tara Quirke &
Arthur Riordan
Design: Sinead Cuthbert & Nicola Hughes

Excitement by Gerard Stembridge, from
the story by Maeve Binchy
Director: Gerard Stembridge
Cast: Kathy Downes
Design: Sinead Cuthbert & Nicola Hughes

Oscar and the Sphinx by Glynis Casson
& Michael James Ford
Director: Michael James Ford
Cast: Glynis Casson
Design: Bronwen Casson

Couch by Siofra Campbell
Director: David Wilmot
Cast: Gertrude Montgomery, David
Wilmot & Eithne Woodcock
Design: Siobhan Barron

2001

Bad Sunday by Mark Wale
Director: John Delaney
Cast: Martina Austin, Jessica Freed,
Brendan McDonald, Aoife O'Beirne &
Eoin Shanley

Conversation with a Cupboard Man by Ian
McEwan
Director: Karl Shiels
Cast: David Pearse

The World's Wife by Carol Anne Duffy
Director: David Horan
Cast: Iseult Golden & Carmel Stephens
Design: Melanie Rodgers

As Married as We Get by Kevin McGhee
Director: Mark O'Halloran
Cast: John Delaney & Susannah de Wrixon
Design: Sinead Cuthbert & Nicola Hughes

This Property is Condemned by Tennessee
 Williams
Director: Bairbre Ní Chaoimh
Cast: Sarah Jane Drummey & Owen
 McDonnell
Design: Sabine D'Argent

Private View by Vaclav Havel
Director: Caroline FitzGerald
Cast: Michael James Ford, Mark
 O'Halloran & Sighle Toibín
Design: Sabine D'Argent

The Head of Red O'Brien by Mark
 O'Halloran
Director: Mark O'Halloran
Cast: Ciaran McIntyre
Design: Kelly Campbell

2002

Lovely Betty by Kelly Campbell, Karen
 Egan, Tom Murphy & Mark
 O'Halloran
Director: Karen Egan
Cast: Kelly Campbell, Tom Murphy &
 Mark O'Halloran
Design: Nicola Hughes

The Belle of Amherst by William Luce
Director: Noelle Browne
Cast: Geraldine Plunkett
Design: Bronwen Casson

The Way Of All Fish by Elaine May
Director: Sighle Toibín
Cast: Liz Bracken & Justine Mitchell
Design: Nicola Hughes & Sarah King

I Can't Remember Anything by Arthur
 Miller
Director: Robert O'Mahoney
Cast: Des Cave & Susan Slott
Design: Emma Cullen

The Star Trap by Michael James Ford
Director: Michael James Ford
Cast: Amelia Crowley & Alan Smyth
Design: Emma Cullen

Fred and Jane by Sebastian Barry
Director: Caroline FitzGerald
Cast: Mary McEvoy & Colette Proctor
Design: Emma Cullen

One Too Many Mornings by Mark
 O'Halloran & David Wilmot
Director: Michael James Ford
Cast: Sean McDonagh & Mark
 O'Halloran

Dickens in Dublin adapted by Laurence
 Foster
Performed by Laurence Foster

2003

The Lily Lally Show by Hugh Leonard
Director: Mark O'Halloran
Cast: Barbara Brennan
Design: Emelia Simcox

Crabbed Youth and Age by Lennox
 Robinson
Director: Michael James Ford
Cast: Frank Burke, Catharine Fullam,
 Richie Hayes, Susie Lamb, Dermot
 Magennis, Geraldine Plunkett &
 Gene Rooney
Design: Emelia Simcox

Do Not Adjust Yourself by Kate Perry
Director: Morna Regan
Cast: Karen Egan, Larry Lowry, Dermot
 Magennis, Kate Perry & Gene Rooney
Design: Morna Regan

Election Night by Donal Courtney
Director: Joan Sheehy
Cast: Edward Coughlan, Emmet Kirwan
 & Micheál O'Gruagáin
Design: Caitriona Ní Mhurchú

Missing Football by Peter McKenna
Director: Rachael Dowling
Cast: Stephen Kelly

The Happy Prince by Oscar Wilde
Director: Bairbre Ní Chaoimh
Cast: Michael James Ford
Design: Emelia Simcox

The Nightingale and the Rose by Oscar
  Wilde
Director: Michael James Ford
Cast: Liz Bracken
Design: Emelia Simcox

The Dock Brief by John Mortimer
Director: Bairbre Ní Chaoimh
Cast: Philip O'Sullivan & Mal White
Design: Bianca Moore

So Long, Sleeping Beauty by Isobel Mahon
Director: Michael James Ford
Cast: Philip Judge & Bernadette McKenna
Design: Bianca Moore

One for Sorrow by Mary Kelly & Noni
  Stapleton
Director: Maureen White
Cast: Mary Kelly & Noni Stapleton
Design: Bianca Moore

2004

Paint it White by Dubravko Mihanovic
Director: Laurence Foster
Cast: Tom Murphy & Micheál O'Gruagáin

Just a Little One by Dorothy Parker
Director: Trevor Knight
Cast: Karen Egan & Susannah de Wrixon
Design: Bianca Moore

Lost Letters of a Victorian Lady by Michelle
  Read
Director: Jo Mangan
Cast: Damian Devaney, Michelle Read
  & Neil Watkins
Design: Orla Bass

Jimmy Joyced! by Donal O'Kelly
Director: Sorcha Fox
Cast: Donal O'Kelly
Design: Paula Martin

The Remarkable Rocket by Oscar Wilde
Director: Trevor Knight
Cast: Michael James Ford
Design: Emelia Simcox

Buridan's Ass by S. R. Plant
Director: Michael James Ford
Cast: Frank Bourke & Arthur Riordan
Design: S. R. Plant

Two for a Girl by Mary Kelly & Noni
  Stapleton
Director: Maureen White
Cast: Mary Kelly & Noni Stapleton
Design: Bianca Moore

2005

Coming Up Roses by Juha Siltanen
Director: Juha Siltanen
Cast: Miia Lindstrom, Pat McGrath,
  Angelika Meusel & Kai Tanner
Design: Tuomas Lampinen

Casanova's Limp by S. R. Plant
Director: Michael James Ford
Cast: Michael Andrews, Amelia Crowley
  & Marion O'Dwyer
Design: S. R. Plant

Full Blown Rose by Roz Hammond
Director: Matt Cameron
Cast: Roz Hammond

The Twelve Pound Look by JM Barrie
Director: Noelle Brown
Cast: Elizabeth Moynihan, Fionnuala
  Murphy & Robert O'Mahoney
Design: Bianca Moore

The Race of the Ark Tatoo by David Hancock
Director: David Horan
Cast: David Heap
Design: Sonya Haccius

2006

Hughie by Eugene O'Neill
Director: Kelly Campbell
Cast: Des Cave & Michael Judd
Design: Martin Cahill

The End of the Beginning by Sean O'Casey
Director: Alan King
Cast: Brendan Conroy, John Olohan &
   Dairne Ní Dhonnchu
Design: Martin Cahill

Dreaming of Mr H by Anto Howard
Director: Anto Howard
Cast: Emma McIvor & Gary Murphy
Design: Niamh Redmond

Bacon by Pip Utton
Director: Geoff Bullen
Cast: Pip Utton

Horst Bucholz and Other Stories by
   Matthew Wilke
Director: Noelle Browne
Cast: Philip Judge, Alan King, Brendan
   Morrissey, Mary O'Driscoll &
   Stephen O'Rourke
Design: Martin Cahill

Melody by Deirdre Kinahan
Director: Veronica Coburn
Cast: Steve Blount & Maureen Collender
Design: Marie Tierney

Submarine by Ulick O'Connor
Director: Caroline FitzGerald
Cast: Steve Blount, Sean Murphy, Sean
   O'Neill, Geraldine Plunkett & Mal Whyte
Design: Chisato Yoshimi

Allergic to Beckett by Gary Jermyn
Director: Michael James Ford
Cast: Gary Jermyn

Hedy Lamarr and the Easter Rising by
   Michael James Ford
Director: Trevor Knight
Cast: Michael James Ford
Design: Jack Kerwin

And They Used To Star In Movies by
   Campbell Black
Director: Alan King
Cast: Ciarán Black, Feidlim Cannon,
   Amelia Crowley, Alan Howley, Alan
   King & Neill Watkins
Design: Caelan Bristow

Don't Forget to Breath by Norma Sheehan
Director: Audrey Deveraux
Cast: Judith Roddy

Moonlight Mickeys by Colin Thornton
Director: Darren Thornton
Cast: Peter Daly & Colin O'Donoghue
Design: Kieron McNulty

Rebecca's Robin by Deirdre Kinahan
Director: Alan King
Cast: Georgina McKevitt
Design: Caelan Bristow

2007

Life Shop Till You Drop by Alice Coughlan
Director: Alice Coughlan
Cast: Clodagh Reid

Requiem of Love by Patricia Burke Brogan
Director: Caroline FitzGerald
Cast: Donnacha Crowley
Design: Patricia Burke Brogan &
   Caroline FitzGerald

Living With Johnny Depp by Joanne
   Mitchell
Director: Micaela Miranda
Cast: Joanne Mitchell

Bear Hug by Robin French
Director: Donal Courtney
Cast: Jessica Freed, Philip Judge & José
   Montero

This is a Play by Daniel MacIvor
Director: Simon Managhan
Cast: Marcus Lamb, Geraldine Plunkett
   & Judith Ryan

Hue and Cry by Deirdre Kinahan
Director: David Horan
Cast: Will O'Connell & Karl Shiels
Design: Steve Neale

Fireworks by Iseult Golden
Director: Alan King
Cast: Dorothy Cotter, John Cronin &
   Neil Watkins
Design: Steve Neale

Tic by Elizabeth Moynihan
Director: Geoff Gould
Cast: Aoife Duffin, Dennis Foley, Alison
   McKenna & Russell Smith
Design: Steve Neale

The Remarkable Rocket by Oscar Wilde
Director: Trevor Knight
Cast: Michael James Ford
Design: Emelia Simcox

Maladjusted by Derek O'Connor
Director: Joe Whelan
Cast: Jim Nolan

The Shawl by David Mamet
Director: Paul Meade
Cast: Matthew Keenan, Gerry McCann
   & Jennifer O'Dea
Design: Laura Howe

Is There Balm In Gilead? by Michael Harding
Director: Caroline FitzGerald
Cast: Mary McEvoy & Seán Murphy

Dickens in Dublin
Written and performed by Laurence Foster

2008

Bad Sunday by Mark Wale
Director: John Delaney
Cast: Ian Lloyd Anderson, Lisa Bisset, John
Delaney, Liz Fitzgibbon & Caroline Power

The Art of Swimming by Linda Radley
Director/Design: Tom Creed
Cast: Linda Radley

Pagliacci, the Opera by R. Leoncavallo
Director: Alice Coughlan
Cast: Rhys Jenkins, Colm Lalor, Simon
   Morgan, Joan O'Malley, Wojciech
   Smarkala & Ralph Stehle
Design: Alice Butler

Ruby Tuesday by Rose Henderson
Director: Deirdre Molloy
Cast: Rose Henderson & Helen Norton
Design: Deirdre Molloy

Roman Fever adapted by Hugh Leonard
Director: Michael James Ford
Cast: Alberto Albertino, Helen Norton
   & Maria Tecce
Design: Jack Kerwin

Setanta Murphy by Garrett Keogh
Director: Garrett Keogh
Cast: Luke Griffin & Garrett Keogh
Design: Garett Keogh

The Tower by Joe Joyce
Director: Caroline FitzGerald
Cast: Tom Hickey & Bosco Hogan
Design: Alice Butler & Caroline FitzGerald

In High Germany by Dermot Bolger
Director: Donal Courtney
Cast: John Delaney
Design: Donal Courtney

Rum and Vodka by Conor McPherson
Director: John Delaney
Cast: Chris Gallagher

Raccoon by Tom Hall
Director: Johnny Hanrahan
Cast: Julie Sharkie
Design: Johnny Hanrahan

All Around My Head by Daniel Reardon
Director: Trevor Knight
Cast: Neili Conroy & Daniel Reardon
Design: Moyra D'Arcy & Miriam Duffy

The Friends of Jack Kairo
Written and Performed by Simon Toal

Notes on the Contributors

Sebastian Barry was born in Dublin in 1955. His plays include *Boss Grady's Boys*, *The Steward of Christendom*, and *Our Lady of Sligo*. Barry's most recent plays are *The Pride of Parnell Street*, Fishamble Theatre Company, and *Dallas Sweetman*, Paines Plough/Canterbury Festival 2008. His plays are published by Faber. His last two novels, *A Long Long Way* and *The Secret Scripture,* have been short-listed for the Man Booker Prize.

Donal Courtney is originally from Killarney, County Kerry. He trained as an actor at the Gaiety School of Acting, Dublin, graduating in 1991. Since then he has worked as an actor, director and drama tutor throughout Ireland, Europe and Australia. He has written two other plays, *Closing Time* and *Rumplestiltskin*, a play for children. He lives in Dublin with his wife Adeline and son Jonah.

Christopher Fitz-Simon was raised in Eleven Houses – the title of his recent much – acclaimed memoir of the 1940s. Among his other books are *The Boys*, a biography of Micheál MacLíammóir and Hilton Edwards, and *The Abbey Theatre: The First 100 Years*. A former drama director in RTÉ, he was Literary Manager and Artistic Director of the Abbey Theatre.

Michael James Ford is a Dublin based actor, writer and director. He was Artistic Director of Bewley's Café Theatre from 1999 - 2005 and directed many plays for the company including *Too Much of Nothing*, *One Too Many Mornings* and *So Long, Sleeping Beauty*. His own plays and adaptations include *Dinner in Mulberry Street*, *Mr Vasek*, *The Star Trap* and *Hedy Lamarr and the Easter Rising*.

Michael Harding (1953) has received both the Stewart Parker Award and an RTÉ Arts Show/Bank of Ireland Award for his theatre work. The Abbey Theatre has staged many of his plays, including the acclaimed comedy *Una Pooka*. His most recent play, *The Tinkers Curse*, was nominated for Best New Play at the Irish Times Irish Theatre Awards 2007, and his new novel, *Bird in the Snow*, was published by Lilliput in October 2008.

Mary Kelly is a writer and an actor. She graduated from the Gaiety School of Acting in 2002. Since then she has written, produced and performed her own work. Mary has also worked as a freelance actor on stage, television and radio. Her most recent work is *Unravelling the Ribbon* (Nick Hern Books) which she co-wrote and performed in and which has had two nationwide tours.

Isobel Mahon is a writer and actress. For radio she has written *The Bureau of Investigation* and *Preservation of the Species. So Long, Sleeping Beauty* has also been produced in America, Scotland, BBC Radio Four and the Gay Pride Festival, Canterbury. Her recent writing for theatre includes *The Life and Times of Selma Mae* and *The Born Again Virgin* for the Mill Theatre, Dundrum. She has also been a regular writer for the RTÉ series *Fair City*.

Mark O'Halloran is a writer and actor and is from Ennis, County Clare. He has written the screenplays for the films *Adam & Paul* and *Garage* and the television series *Prosperity*. He is currently working on a new television series called *4Storeys*, a screenplay called *Us,* as well as a number of stage plays.

Donal O'Kelly is a writer and actor. His solo plays include the award-winning *Catalpa* and *Bat the Father, Rabbit the Son*, as well as *Jimmy Joyced!* Other recent works are *The Cambria, Vive La* and the music-theatre piece *Running Beast*. Other plays he has written include *The Dogs, Hughie On The Wires, Trickledown Town, The Business Of Blood* (with Kenny Glenaan), *Farawayan, Asylum! Asylum!, Judas Of The Gallarus, The Hand*, and *Operation Easter*.

S. R. Plant worked for many years as production manager for Druid Theatre Company. During this time he developed an obsessive interest in taxidermy and eventually moved to an isolated farmhouse in rural France where he wrote *Buridan's Ass* and the historical comedy, *Casanova's Limp*. He now devotes much of his time to his online journal, 'Musings of a Failed Taxidermist'.

Noni Stapleton is an actor and writer and has performed extensively in theatre, film and television since graduating from the Gaiety School of Acting in 2002. She is a founding member of Skipalong Theatre Company, co-writing and performing in *One for Sorrow* and *Two for a Girl*.

Mark Wale studied mime with Étienne Decroux in Paris, and film at CECC in Barcelona. *Bad Sunday* was written for The Little Sisters of Tragedy, with whom he had spent the previous six years making and touring improvised clown shows. He now writes film and television scripts and lives in Dublin's North Strand with his partner and daughter.

David Wilmot was born in Dublin in 1971. *Too Much of Nothing* is his first published work. He has directed *Couch* by Siofra Campbell at Bewley's Café Theatre. He is also an actor, and was last on stage in Martin McDonagh's *The Lieutenant of Inishmore*.

ACKNOWLEDGEMENTS

It was Mark O'Halloran who first approached me during the summer of 2007 with the idea of doing this book. Having been to see a few plays in Bewley's Café Theatre over the course of the past ten years, the idea of publishing this anthology was one that appealed to me and it seemed to be an ideal project for the Stinging Fly Press to take on.

Since that first meeting, Mark and Michael James Ford and Kelly Campbell have all played a role in helping to source playscripts, contact authors and gather together the production photographs. Help was always there when it was needed, but otherwise we were free to just get on with it.

This book would not have been possible without the input of Emily Firetog, my co-editor. She has done the lion's share of the work, keeping everything and everyone moving along.

Thanks are due to all the writers of the plays for their involvement in preparing their scripts for publication. Thanks also to Christopher Fitz-Simon for taking on the introduction and bringing all his knowledge and experience to bear on it.

I also want to thank Sarah O'Connor for proofreading the final manuscript, Fergal Condon for his work on the book's layout and cover design, and Ros Kavanagh for his photographs of the Oriental Room.

Finally, thanks go to Veronica Campbell, Iseult Golden and David Horan at Bewley's Café Theatre who continue to work to keep the space alive and the plays rolling.